The Civilization of the American Indian Series

PUEBLO ANIMALS and MYTHS

PUEBLO ANIMAL

nd MYTHS

by Hamilton A. Tyler

UNIVERSITY OF OKLAHOMA PRESS : Norman

By Hamilton A. Tyler

Pueblo Gods and Myths (Norman, 1964)

Library of Congress Cataloging in Publication Data
Tyler, Hamilton A.

    Pueblo animals and myths.
    (The Civilization of the American indian series; v. 134)
    Bibliography: p.
    Includes index.
    1. Pueblo Indians—Religion and mythology.
2. Animal lore. I. Title. II. Series.
E99.P9T89   299'.7   74–15902
ISBN 0–8061–1245–X

To Savoie Lottinville

PREFACE

THE following work began in a study of animal gods planned for *Pueblo Gods and Myths*. At that time I found the position of animal deities difficult to fix. Nevertheless, a number of animals appeared as supernatural spirits, while others were developed gods—in that they had shrines, altars, images, and rites. Since these "Beast Gods" often shaped the affairs and destinies of mankind, they could have been included in the pantheon along with anthropomorphic and abstract deities.

Pueblo animal gods are intermixed with lesser animal spirits, sometimes as familiars or "pets" of other deities, or they may be the forms taken by gods in epiphanies, and often they work as spirit messengers between gods and men. On the other hand are the visible animals that provide food, clothing, and symbols for man to use. Everyone recognizes that man is only a single part of the natural world and that the whole must somehow be tied together. For us this means the scientific system of classification. We relate to animals as distant kin whose remoteness is charted in tables at the end of zoology texts.

The Pueblo Indian uses different premises, but he too is trying to make the world around him meaningful, and for that a system in which each creature has its place is a necessity. The Pueblo system is religiously based, but religion is primarily an attempt to order the world and to establish man's place in it. When these Indians left their isolated pueblos either for work or travel, they met first of all not other men, but a horizon of animal life. It was natural to order the cosmos by analogy with the immediate vision: the earth, the sky, the plants, and the animals.

These are obviously bound together around man. A Hopi of

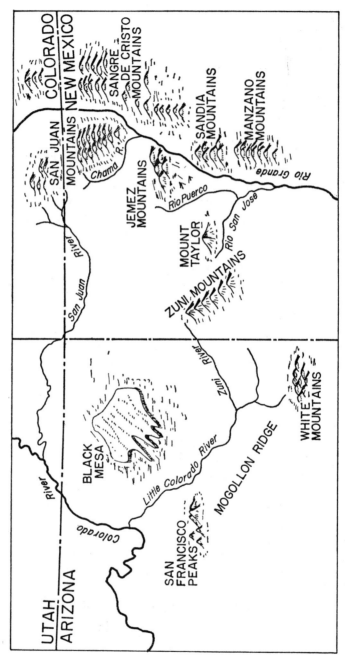

Map of Pueblo Territory

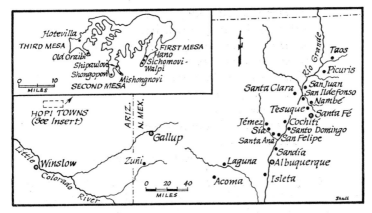

The Pueblo World

the past century told Alexander Stephen that "the whole universe is endowed with the same breath, rocks, trees, grass, earth, all animals, and men." To link these parts together there must be rites, ceremonies, and myths. These are repeated regularly, since the important tie is always in the present, even though warrants are handed down from the past.

For most ceremonies a rather exact knowledge of wildlife is required. Birds, for example, are separated into more than two hundred named species and about half that number are important in ceremonialism. A subsequent volume will be devoted entirely to Pueblo ornithology. In the Pueblo system of nature even the least of animals is included, but for reasons of space the mice, squirrels, porcupine, and other lesser beasts were excluded from this book. As a result only the major animals find a place here, but the reader should keep in mind that behind these greater ones there is a continuum of both spirit and lore which extends to all who breathe.

This inclusive view is expressed in a Pueblo prayer of quiet tone. No terror is felt before the mountain lion or grizzly bear, nor is there a distinction between great and small. All animal kinds are addressed:

Yonder on all sides our fathers,
Priests of the mossy mountains,
All those whose sacred places are round about,
Creatures of the open spaces
You of the wooded places. . . .
You of the forest
You of the brush,
All of you who in divine wisdom
Stand here quietly. . . .
—Ruth Bunzel, *Zuñi Ritual Poetry*

For all of these cornmeal, shell, and pollen are offered, so that they may stand about quietly for the sake of a general harmony.

Man also helps with an annual cycle of ceremonies in which the same animals play an important part. Dances and dance-dramas are held in an amphitheater surrounded by the mountains of the six directions. Four of these are the visible horizon points, while the Zenith and Nadir join to enclose man in a landscape that is at once real and divine and one that is populated by both gods and animals.

Hamilton A. Tyler

Healdsburg, California

CONTENTS

PUEBLO ANIMALS and MYTHS

 *Chapter I*

BADGER

BADGER is placed first in this account in order to make the simple but important point that economic values and use are not necessarily the determiners of the role an animal plays in the symbolism of a culture. The high place of the badger in Pueblo thought and rite is not due to the value of his flesh or pelt, although it is true badgers might be eaten on occasion. A Hopi wrote in his journal: "We liked meat and ate almost any kind that we could get. The old people showed us how to make deadfalls to catch kangaroo rats, prairie dogs, porcupines, badgers, chipmunks, squirrels and turtle doves."[1] Most of this list of small animals trapped by Hopi children is on the edible side, but no other reference to eating badgers appears in Pueblo literature.

The importance of badgers in the Pueblo view rests not on occasional use as food, but rather on their role in ritual, with its attendant mythology, and on their use as a clan animal, which brings together associations related to certain ceremonial duties of that clan. There are popular theories of totemism which hold that clan members think of themselves as descended from the animal for which the clan is named, but this view does not apply to the Pueblo Indians even though most of their clans do bear the name of some animal, plant, or aspect of nature.

For the moment it is only necessary to note that there is a special tie between the clan members and the animal for which they are named, and that the role of the clan itself varies among the different Pueblo groups. With the Hopi and Zuñi the clans are strong and are closely integrated with ceremonial activity, while among the western Keres of Acoma and Laguna only a few clans have important roles to play. In the Río Grande

3

pueblos clans are sometimes nominal, being relegated to the role of mutual aid societies, and these differences in clan status are reflected in differing modes of integrating animal symbolism into ceremonialism. In the western Pueblos it is often the clan that is the vehicle for introducing the symbolic role, while the Río Grande Pueblos must find other means, such as the ritual of societies, for incorporating animals into their world view.

Where there is a relationship between badger and Badger clan people, it is one of special partnership in both the natural and the social order. Each has special and related functions, the animal in nature and the clansman in sociey, and all are tied together by associated ideas. While animals and men are very close to one another, men are not descended from the former, and in fact the sequence trends in the opposite direction. Animals are often said to have formerly been men, or again we will find that they are still basically human beings, but with the special ability to put on or take off their coats of fur as the occasion demands.

One Hopi story begins, "Long ago the Badger and the Small Gray Mice were Hopi, but they were very bad and hence became these two animals." The idea of a "fall" as an explanation for the origin of animals is never a central thought, but it appears in this particular story to make a cautionary point, warning children and sick people that it is very bad not to eat when ill and that one of the best cures is simply to eat and get well.

Before continuing with the place of Badger in the Pueblo scheme of evolution, it may be well to introduce the pugnacious beast himself. Badgers, the most engaging members of the mustelids, are placed by biologists midway between the bears and cats, having as their closest relatives the skunks, an arrangement which is seconded by popular opinion as to their personality. Badgers have always impressed observers both with their tenacity in a fight and with their phenomenal ability in digging, should they choose to escape an encounter. Badger has not the overwhelming power of a bear or a lion, of whom he is the "little brother" to the Pueblos' way of thinking, but he does have great spirit. He will face up to a dog several times his size, or a pack of dogs, and generally give a good account of himself.

The badger's self-confidence is backed up by a thick skull, a tough and loose hide which makes him difficult to grasp, long dense fur, and perhaps also by the knowledge that he is unpalatable to the larger carnivores, and usually to man as well. Our verb "to badger" is based on the fact that he will respond to harassment in a combative manner. A Pueblo Indian of the Río Grande told, "with great glee, of the fighting qualities of this animal and its great energy in digging. They told also of how a badger caught one of them by the trousers and held on until it was dragged a long distance to the river and into the water."[2]

The badger has a more honest face than the raccoon, since his black mask is interrupted by a white stripe running vertically over the top of his head. The hair of his wide, flat body is of a yellowish grey, his tail is short, as are his legs, but the claws on his forefeet are exceedingly sharp and long. The badger is most careful of these claws, which are an inch or more in length and warrant the careful manicuring he gives them frequently. The Southwest badgers, which weigh from twenty to thirty pounds, do not hibernate and unlike the European species they are locally migratory, foraging up into the Transition zone or even higher during the summer when the ground is soft enough to dig. Year around they are most abundant in the Sonoran zones.

The Pueblo badger lives by digging out ground squirrels, gophers, prairie dogs, and woodrats, or by catching whatever is available in the way of insects and lizards. Sometimes in the course of his digging he comes across rabbits or skunks that have holed up in old burrows, but in the open a badger is seldom so lucky as to catch a rabbit unless the circumstances are unusual, such as hunting in partnership with a coyote. In digging the badger is both tireless and most skillful, which stands him in good stead when either food gathering or in a fight, for in the latter case he can dig himself into the ground faster than a man can shovel. During the course of his searches for food, he tunnels, enlarges holes, and throws up earthworks that are readily observable in open country, where one may sometimes approach close enough to watch this contentious fellow at work.

It is this incessant digging that has given Badger his special place in one of the Pueblo accounts concerning the sequence of life. While the orgin of various animals is by no means fixed in mythical accounts, most beasts are thought to have been brought to life only after mankind passed through the fourfold underworld and emerged onto the surface of the earth. Badger, on the other hand, not only shared the experience of the Emergence with humankind, but aided them in the process. According to the Acoma origin myth the ascent of the human species into the daylight world was a slow and tedious event, but in time the Two Sisters, twin mothers of mankind, came out into the light, followed by Badger and Locust. "Badger was very strong and skillful and helped them." The two sisters, or mothers, had planted the seeds of four kinds of pine trees in the underworld. One kind grew to the top of each level, until the fourth pushed a small opening into the upper world, letting a little light shine down below.

"The hole that the tree *lanye* made was not large enough for them to pass through, so Tsichtinako advised them to look again in their baskets where they would find the image of an animal called dyup (badger) and tell it to become alive. They told it to live, and it did so as they spoke, exclaiming, 'A'uha! Why have you given me life?' They told it not to be afraid nor to worry about coming to life. 'We have brought you to life because you are to be useful.' Tsichtinako spoke to them again, instructing them to tell Badger to climb the pine tree, to bore a hole large enough for them to crawl through, cautioning him not to go out into the light, but to return when the hole was finished. Badger climbed the tree and after he had enlarged the opening, returned saying that he had done his work. They thanked him and said, 'As a reward you will come up with us to the light and thereafter you will live happily. You will always know how to dig and your home will be in the ground where you will be neither too hot nor too cold.' "[3]

Thus the grunting badger has had one kind of usefulness dating from the time of his creation, but it has been in the mythological rather than the economic realm. The fact that he was brought to life before the other animals has in turn had an effect on Acoma Indian society, at least in theory, for the same sequence is reflected in the order of the creation of Acoma clans. The first clan mothers there, in the order of their birth, were of the Sky clan, Water clan, Badger clan, and Fire clan, while a second group included Antelope, Deer and Bear clans.[4] The arrangement is most curious, since this is the only mention of a Badger clan at Acoma, forcing one to conclude that this order is either a logical fiction designed to correspond with the myth, an ancient circumstance, or an account borrowed from other Pueblos.

In any case we will hear much of the sky-water and badger-fire associations which are basic patterns among several linguistic groups. At Acoma's neighboring Keresan pueblo of Laguna, there actually was a Badger clan which had control of the kachina dances, and the last surviving kiva there was called "badger house," and there is a tradition that the Badger clan was descended from a Zuñi woman who migrated to Laguna some four generations ago.[5]

With that clue we may turn to Zuñi to begin the account of Badger's role in community life. The Badger clan is important numerically at Zuñi, comprising about ten per cent of the population, but numbers tell little as clans with important duties may shrink rapidly or disappear altogether, due to circumstances that have nothing to do with their roles. It is the role of clans in ceremonies and the mythico-religious theories surrounding such activity that is of primary interest. To begin with, it is a Badger clansman who impersonates Shulawitsi, or Fire-brand Youth, in the winter solstice ceremony.

The logic of such associations is often more like the "free-associations" that are pertinent in psychiatry, in which one thought leads to another and that to a third, than it is like conscious logical theory. With respect to the badger, his digging

7

is the basic idea, but this can be rapidly expanded by association with grubbing out the kind of roots that the Indians use as a base for the fire-drill in kindling fires, especially those used on sacred occasions. From there the idea may jump to another thought, that of fires in ovens and of cleaning the burnt coals and refuse out of these, a ritual that accompanies the solstice ceremonies at stated intervals. At this point it is a very short series of steps from fire, to solstice, to sun.

Perhaps, again, the thought of digging will turn the mind to quarrying, which is necessary when one wants to make a new grinding stone, which is once more related to ovens by the mediating thought of bread. If the associations take off in a different direction, as they do at Hopi, the digging may remind one of roots, although not those used in fire making. Some roots have medicinal value, and in that case we are led into the subject of curing.

The name of the Zuñi fire-spirit, Shulawitsi, is said to mean "spotted," and dappled he certainly is. His impersonator is a youth, naked except for a fawn-skin breech cloth, whose body is painted black with discs of red, yellow, blue, and white over-laid. When a fire is to be kindled, and this is true even now if this fire has a ritual purpose, a hardened stick such as an arrow shaft which has been heat-treated is used for the drill, which is turned in a soft dry piece of root. "To the Badger people was given the knowledge of fire, for in the roots of all trees, great and little, which the badger best knows how to find, dwells the essence of fire."[6] Thus it is that the impersonator of this spirit of fire must be selected from members of the Badger clan.

The same idea has secular as well as sacred extensions: "Fire making is always the prerogative of the Badger clan. Anyone who builds fires easily and quickly is dubbed tonashi-kwe (Badger person)."[7] In the sacred context the priests, on the day preceding the winter sun or solstice observances, select a man of the Badger clan who will tend a fire that is kept burning in one of the kivas throughout the ten days of the observances. This man is called tsupal'ilona, or the "one who keeps the blood pudding," since the sacred fire is thought of as a pudding—blood, like fire, being at the sources of life. The fire tender selects the impersonator of Shulawitsi from among the younger boys of his family. The youth must be of the Badger clan one year, and child of the Badger clan the next, which in practice amounts to appointing one of his sister's young sons for one year and one of his own for the following season.

Bunzel says, "There is some association between fire, the office of pekwin, and the Badger clan."[8] Actually there are several associations and all of them are interrelated. Firebrand Youth is called "little pekwin," because of his role in this new-fire ceremony. The big pekwin is the sun watcher, whose name in fact indicates his office, pekwin meaning "deputy" to the Sun-father. This officer is charged with keeping the date for and announcing all ceremonies. Since the dates for all other following ceremonies are based on the timing of the winter solstice, the Pekwin is above all responsible for determining that date, which is accomplished by sighting the rising sun from behind a petrified stump to the east of town, until he determines that the sun has risen at a certain point on Corn Mountain, indicating the southern limit of the sun's journey.

The new-fire is but an urgent replica of the new sun whose strength will be rekindled through man's imitative fire. Badger's function here gives him something of a controlling role in the winter part of the ceremonial year, with the Hopis too, where the new-fire is also in the hands of a Badger clansman. The Zuñi name for the ceremony is Itiwana, which means middle. It is also the name of the pueblo which is thought to be the middle point of the cosmos, and Itiwana is likewise the middle point of both the natural and the ceremonial year, in the sense that then all the cults and their attendant powers come together in a concentrated focus on the pueblo, before springing toward a new cycle of life.

During this coming together and at the time the new-fire is to be lighted, there is a procession of notables including, besides the Pekwin and the War Chiefs, the Keeper of the Big Shell who arrives carrying this very sacred object. The Big Shell seems to have been an actual conch shell which was blown as a trumpet in times of dire threat, with the expectation of magically dispelling the enemy. It was probably this or a similar Big Shell that appeared, according to accounts, in the resistance to Coronado's attack on Zuñi in 1540. When the Spaniards arrived before the pueblo, the Indians were in formation. "Armed with bows, arrows, and war clubs, and protected by leather shields, they were blowing a horn, making hostile gestures, and ordering the Spaniards to go back in the direction from which they had come."[9]

On the previous night one group of Spaniards had heard the "trumpet" sounded by a scouting party of the Zuñi and had interpreted it as a call for retreat by the Indians. Doubtless it was not this, but the first attempt to drive off the invaders by means of Big Shell's magic. Those distant events might seem to be at some remove from the topic of Badger, but they are not. Cushing tells us of the group of priests who were "Master keepers of sacred things . . . each according to his nature of kinship." One of these sacred things was the Big Shell. "It was thus that the warmth-wanting Badger-people were given the great shell, the heart or navel of which is potent or sensitive to fire, as the earthquake and the inner fire is the coiled navel of the Earth-mother. On the sunny sides of hills burrow the badgers, finding and dwelling amongst the dry roots whence is fire. Thus the 'Two Badgers' were made keepers of the sacred heart-shell, makers and wardens of fire."[10]

Cushing's poetic language may or may not be an accurate reflection of native thought, but the content of what he says can often be verified. He is repeating here what he was doubtless told by the Zuñi—that Badger clansmen were the keepers of the sacred conch whose power came from its inner fire. This fire was in turn thought to be related to the subterranean fires that cause volcanoes to erupt, sometimes with thunderous earthquakes. The mythology of both Acoma and Zuñi makes frequent reference to the great fires that attended the eruption and lava flow at the eastern foot of the Zuñi Mountains, where lava beds are much in evidence.

Since the badger plays a prominent role in the winter solstice, he has a special connection with the winter sun. "The badger, who digs his hole on the sunny side of hills and in winter appears only when the sun shines warm above them, who excavates among the roots of the juniper and cedar from which fire is kindled with the fire drill." A contradiction of sorts arises in native thinking at this point. Badger is the Zuñi beast of prey representing the South direction, which fits well with the fact that the sun in winter is in the south, and he stands for season and direction. However, from another point of view summer reigns permanently in the tropical lands to the south; when speaking of the colors in the directional system it is said that, "The south is designated as red, it being the region of summer and fire, which is red."[11] Thus we see one of the inherent difficulties in fitting together with tight logic all the changing parts of an elaborate construct.

Badger is not associated with this fire of summer, but he does have a place in the development of agriculture, which came from the south, his direction. Husbandry is associated with the south direction,[12] and Badger has a specific connection with the multi-colored seeds of corn. In beginning times, after the people had emerged from the underworld, there was a time of migration in search of the middle place, and it was during this period that the Zuñi were given their ceremonies and the all important corn plant on which they were to subsist.

The first corn plants were encouraged in their growth by the Corn Maidens, who grasped the stalks and pulled them upwards so that they would be as tall as the maids themselves. Where their hands grasped the stalks, joints were formed on the plant, such as the ones we see there today. Indian corn is not all yellow or white, as ours is, but has ears which are red, yellow, white, black, and multicolored, each of whch is fitted symbolically into one of the cardinal directions. How they came to have these bright colors again has to do with Badger and fire.

"And now, in the night, the keepers of the great shells (of the Badger kin), brought forth fire with their hands from roots, and kindled it in front of the bower toward the east, that its heat might take the place of the Sun and its light shine brightly on the dancers, making their acts verily alive; and as the dawn approached, the youth and first maiden were led apart as before by the mother making matron, and together embraced the first of the full grown plants.

"And as they embraced the first plant, the fire flamed brightly with the first catching flush of the wood, and yellow was its light; and as they embraced the second plant, the flames were burning smokily with the fuller grasping of the wood, and blue was the light; and as they were embracing the third plant, the fire reached its fullness of mastery over the wood, and red was its light; and as they were embracing the fourth plant, the fire was fumeless and triumphant over the wood, and white was its light; and as they were embracing the fifth plant, the fire gave up its breath in clouds of sparks, and streaked, of many colors, was its light; and as they were embracing the sixth plant, the fire swooned and slept, giving more heat, as it were, than light, thus somber was the light, yet, as they were embracing the seventh plant, its wakened afresh, did the fire, in the wind of the morning, and glowed as does the late fire of the wanderer, with a light of all colors."[13]

While these elaborations that stem from the badger's digging and its subsequent relation to fire have been worked out on the level of mythology, the same set of associations, with different intent, appears in ritual. One instance occurs in the coming of the Chakwena Oka kachina, of whom we will hear in more detail in later chapters. "She" comes at the time of the solstice, "to bring women good luck in childbirth," where the analogy to digging out is obvious. The ritual involved is "owned" by a member of the Badger clan, a male who impersonates the Chakwena woman. She arrives in the village about nine o'clock at night, accompanied by the Salimobia, warrior and seed-bearing kachinas who carry yucca whips. These are used for the dual purpose of policing and inducing fertility, for which reason the crowd following this procession provokes its own flagellation.

The Chakwena Oka woman approaches the door of each house and, as she nears it, the feminine dweller opens the door and throws out a shovelful of live coals. "These have been waved around in every room of the house, as a rite of purification."[14] Later on the same Chakwena engages in a rite of lying in, for the increase of human offspring and livestock. The purification by live coals is an element that has not appeared until now in Badger's story, but it is a thought capable of further extension. Perhaps the whippings just mentioned have a purifying as well as a fertilizing intent, since both ideas seem to be present in the ceremony.

There is yet another Zuñi kachina who, according to Cushing, appears only once in every four or eight years, which is surprising considering the everyday nature of his function. This kachina is responsible for cleaning out the ovens which stand outside the houses around the village. Cleansing in this instance has the dual meaning of encouraging the removal of refuse from the ovens and of purifying these structures of bad influences— a point which anyone who bakes will understand. This kachina is black as soot, wears a domed mask in the shape of an oven, and is adorned with various brushes and tufts of hair. "A bunch of stiff hair surmounts his crown, out of which issues, like a flame, a red eagle-plume to symbolize fire. . . . On either cheek is painted, in glaring yellow, the paw of a badger or some other famous burrower."

This oven demon acts the part of a clown and indeed travels with a company of veritable clowns as he staggers about, taking every object for an oven, attempting to clean out even burros and ladders. When at last he comes to a true oven he leaps into this with a growl, and from its dark interior sweeps out bits of bread and things that have been purposely left there in expectation of his purificatory visit. He does not cease his frantic work until all the ovens in town have been swept clean of their last cinders and dust.[15]

A more remote association between badgers and digging appears in connection with quarrying a new mealing stone, on which corn for bread to be baked in the ovens is ground. In order to gain the best of influences for the future *metate*, the whole process is surrounded by ritual, in which Badger necessarily plays a part. "On the morning of the day succeeding the last night of their vigil, they repair in single file, headed by a particular clan-priest (usually a 'Badger,' who on no account touches one of them) to the quarry."[16] The proscription on the Badger clansman against touching the quarrymen is to assure that the stone will not crack when it is first put into a fire for ripening. The raw stone has an unhappy tendency to break at this time, despite all of the ritual care taken to ward off evil influences.

When turning from the Zuñi to Hopi usage, the significance of Badger is not so tightly bound up with the clan, and we get to see more of the animal himself in the symoblism. Hopi "Badger people" do have a myth that explains the origin of their clan, which is notably not one of linear descent from the clan animal. The minor event which gave rise to their name occurred shortly after the people had left the underworld. "After they came up they found a man at work digging. 'What are you doing, our uncle?' they said to him. 'My brothers and nephews and my sisters, where are you going?—'We are going to a place called Sitahkwi to make our home. . . . 'Is that where you are going?' —'Yes.'—'Well, you are my relatives.'—'What kind of man are you?'—'I am a Badger. Well, my nephews and brothers, I had better go with you.' "

The relationships mentioned are all at one remove, since in a matrilineal system of descent, which the Hopis have, the first mother and succeeding females carry the names, and it is plain that Badger-man is not such a source, but was merely somehow related to them as a fellow member of the clan. The myth goes on to tell of a child who was crying. To still this child they gave him a butterfly to play with, making the group to which he belonged the Butterfly clan. Next, "as they travelled on the child became sick. They asked Badger, 'What can we do to help the child? He gave medicine to the child to cure it. He said that he was a doctor and he called himself *duikya* (doctor). He cured the child."[17]

Badger and Butterfly people are linked together in a phratry because of a simple bit of logic. As a result of his digging ability, Badger controls all roots, thus becoming responsible for the early growth of wild plants and ultimately for their flowering. Since butterflies are attracted to these, they are related to him, joining the two clans together with ties so close that when one group of Badger people had nearly died out, the survivors joined the Butterfly clan. Not long thereafter, however, the entire group was again calling itself the Badgers, which indicates how strong a hold this animal has in native thinking.[18]

Of more importance for the present account, however, is the fact that Badger was able to cure the little child with his medicine. In the discussion of Zuñi, it was mentioned that Badger was the directional animal for the south, a position which he also holds in the cosmology of the Hopi and the Keres. This set of directional animals, made up of the beasts of prey, has an important role in curing ceremonies. While all the beasts of prey act as curers, in the non-Hopi pueblos it is the Bear who is the prime spirit of medicine. In the Hopi villages it is Badger, the younger brother of Bear, who fills this role.

Curing may be broadly separated into two divisions: one effecting its remedies by the use of herb concoctions, and the other by rites of incantation, singing, sucking, and the like. Actually, the problem is more complicated since the two types intergrade, and there are also bone doctors and others with special skills, such as treating snake bites and lightning shock. But herbal remedies tend to be set apart, and Badger is the patron of this kind of cure in particular. Badger, in his constant explorations of the soil, has a very great knowledge of the various roots which have medicinal value. "The Badger people understand medicines, hence they prepare the medicine—for instance, charm liquid—for the Flute, Snake, Marau, and other ceremonies."[19]

There is of course room for argument as to whether the Snake medicine is a pharmaceutical or purely a charm liquid, but there is a distinction made in the native mind, and it is expressed in two rather humorous stories about competition between Badger and the Small Grey Mice, who at that time were also doctors, of the non-herbal sort.

"The Badger doctor cured people mostly by herbs, of which he made decoctions and lotions. The mice effected their cures by singing, rattling, rubbing, kneading the bodies, scraping the skins, and by other means of sorcery." The story, which shows a considerable degree of irony if not downright skepticism, begins with a Badger doctor who lived in a kivalike house north of Old Oraibi. He charged fees for his services and was thus annoyed to hear that the mice had cured a hunter who had broken his leg and had not charged him for it.

Thinking to test the powers of these mice-doctors, he said, "I am going to feign sickness and shall call them over, and if they can tell me my ailment, I shall believe in them." In order to add a touch of realism, Badger took to his bed and ate little or nothing for several days, then he sent a messenger to the mice with the information that he was possibly dying. "The Badger was still very angry and had hidden a stick under his bed. The mice, however, had brought no medicines with them." A whole troop of the little mice filed in, led by their chief who observed the groaning doctor.

The mouse chief immediately began to sing: "Rabbit meat cook for us! . . . Four times he fasted." Having thus let Badger know that the had detected his fraud, the mice trooped back up the ladder. Meanwhile he began striking out at them with his stick. Being weakened because of his fast, he failed to hit any of them, but this attack accounts for the fact that field mice are now scattered all over the countryside where they eat the seeds that the Hopis plant. In return, however, "If any Hopi works in his field or travels anywhere, or is away from his village for any purpose, and becomes sick or gets hurt, these Mice in an unseen secret way take care of him so that he does not die."[20]

While this story would seem to represent a triumph of the psychiatrists over the internists, Badger's kind of doctoring is taken quite seriously, despite the inevitable doubts. At one time there was a Pobosh curing society at Hopi whose members had Badger as their patron. This was a society of the Keresan type whose members were supposed to practice celibacy, a circumstance which may have contributed to the dwindling away of the society. In 1893 the Scotch anthropoligist Alexander Stephen fell sick at Hopi, and in this strait one of the two remaining Pobosh members undertook to cure him.

"To begin with, he got one of my bowls and, filling it nearly full of water, placed it between me and the fire before which I was lying on a pallet, and then sat down beside me.

"Opening a small pouch that he constantly wears, he took out four small quartz and other pebbles, typical of the emblematic cardinal colors. . . . Beginning with the yellow pebble, he dropped them into the bowl, one at a time, with low muttered prayers to Bear, Badger and Porcupine who are called brothers. . . . He then crushed a small fragment of dry herb root between his fingers and sprinkled it upon the surface of the water in the bowl, and this he told me made the charm water."[21]

The pebbles associated with the directional colors have the function of orienting the cosmos around the sick person, of drawing in and concentrating the cosmic power there for the cure. Badger is of particular importance to the Pobosh society, a fact which is expressed in an altar set up by the curer. Four herms with crudely carved faces are set up in the form of a square, representing the horizon directions, while Badger here represents the sixth direction, or the Below.

"At the end of the songs Badger, *Honani*, came up in the centre of the square, from the Below, carrying a bundle on his back which contained all medicines, and in his left hand he carried downy wing feathers of the buzzard.

"He said, 'I know all medicinal charms, and I have the feather for *navo'chiwa*, to drive away all bodily ills. . . .' The kachina all said, 'now we shall change into Badger clan people and you shall be chief.' This chief and a great many of these kachina Badger stopped at Oraibi . . . the Badger who came up from Below was the first of the Po'boshtu."[22] Thus in myth an explanation and warrant is given for the proceedings of the Pobosh society doctor.

The Powamu ceremony of the Hopi is in the hands of the Badger clan and the ceremony itself is thought of as strong medicine for rheumatism,[23] in addition to its central purpose of cleansing and purifying the fields in late winter. The idea that Badger can cure aches and pains is by no means limited to the Hopi Indians, as the same thought has persisted in England until the present time. Neal, in his book on the English badger tells that , "Up to the time of the war, an old villager near Cheltenham regularly prepared badger grease and sold it without difficulty to people who would come long distances to get it. Several people I know," he continues, "are convinced of its usefulness in cases of strains and sprains and use it regularly on horses and other animals."[24]

The superb condition of the badger's musculature, as evinced by his rapid digging, is evoked to cure the pains in the same muscles of human beings or domestic stock. There is also a more abstract extension of badger's meaning in the Hopi Powamu ceremony, which has to do with the growth of crops. The Hopi ceremonial year is twice divided. From the Niman or farewell kachina ceremony in summer, until the winter sun or Soyal ceremony the masked kachina do not dance—with one exception. During this time the people are too busy with their crops to engage in long ceremonies, although there are numerous shorter ones.

The other, or ceremonial half of the year, is again divided. From the Soyal to the Powamu in late February, the Badger clan has control of the ceremonies, a fact which associates him with the winter season as at Zuñi. In the Powamu ceremony, the

Kachina clan chief joins with the Badger clan chief in this end-of-winter activity. Thereafter, throughout the spring and early summer the Kachina clan is in charge of ceremonial life.

The Powamu is a growth ceremony, not only for cleansing the fields, but also for testing the germination of beans and corn, which will serve as a sign for the coming season. The songs of the ceremony are not directed toward animals, but rather to the plants and to the birds of summer, but at one point a priest speaks: "You from Ki'shiwuu, come here; just here I want you." This place lies about sixty miles northeast of Oraibi and is either the real or the mythical home of the Hopi Badger clan. The Badgers are thus called into this ceremony where they are needed, since at the time the following summer's crops are all still in the underworld, and as Badger does his work in that realm his help can be useful in controlling their future growth.

There is an instance at Zuñi where Badger's connection with winter is joined with curing rites. The organization which unites these two ideas is the Sword Swallowers' society. Members of this group, who use canes rather than swords, of course, have the not unlikely function of curing sore throats, as well as stomach and headaches, at any of which they should be most expert. Their ceremonies, however, also have cold- and snow-bringing powers, and they take place in January and February. Snow is of great value as its moisture contributes to the sprouting of seeds in late Spring when rain is scarce. Badger, along with the other beasts of prey, has a place in their myth and rite.

The myth of this unusual society indicates that their members were first taught medicine and craft by a god or culture-hero named Poshaiyanne[25] who ruled at Shipapolima. The specific art of swallowing flint knives or wooden canes was taught them by Knife Wing, a half-anthropomorphic, half-eagle deity with wings and tail of flint knives. In the mythical age, the original medicine men were transformed into the beast gods of the directions, and were set the task of acting as warriors to accompany members of the Sword Swallowers on their journey to Zuñi. These beast gods were the Lion, Bear, Badger, Wolf, and

Shrew, to which are added the snakes of the six directions. No mention is made of the Eagle of the Zenith, as Knife Wing here takes his place. In the ceremonial chamber of the society, the latter deity is surrounded by figures of the four beasts, but the shrew is not represented.[26]

In ceremonies of the Sword Swallowers, various deities who figure in the myths of the group are impersonated. "The third warrior, who personates Badger, is of the Badger clan."[27] These four beast warriors accompany their director to a spring outside Zuñi, during which pilgrimage the director carries a white plume and his face has been dusted with white meal, both signs being symbolic of the snow that the mission is designed to promote.

The Pueblo world view often fits together as a series of concentric patterns, in several of which we have noted the position of Badger. He has yet another role. As beast of the South, he is associated with winter, fires, the sun, and with curing, which pertains to the beasts of prey of each direction. The beasts of prey have another important function, as predators, which relates them to the hunt. Sometimes the directional animals are varied for this role, the list changing to include only the most ferocious beasts, in which case the wildcat or even the jaguar may find a place. At Acoma, Badger loses out as animal of the South in relation to the Hunt society,[28] but not at Hopi.

On Hopi Second Mesa, rabbit hunts are under the control of the Badger clan. Anyone may call the hunt, but since it is Badger's prerogative he must first be consulted. Before the hunt is undertaken its leader makes prayer-sticks for the rabbits, for a Gray Fox deity, and for the Mother of All Animals. "He takes these to the house of the Badger clan hunt chief in the evening. Both smoke a corn husk cigarette, then the leader tells his plans for the hunt. The hunt announcer calls out from his housetop the next day's hunt."[29] This crier outlines the areas to be covered by the hunters, the time of gathering, and then he takes the prayer-sticks for the Fox deity and Mother of All Animals to a shrine and deposits them.

At Zuñi, Badger does not seem to have a role in relation to rabbit hunting, but members of the Badger clan take part in a special turtle hunt which is held every fourth year. Because of the time span involved, this activity cannot be considered hunting in the usual sense. It is a sacred pilgrimage to the home of the gods, which is beneath the waters of a lake at the junction of the Zuñi and Little Colorado rivers, some eighty miles southwest of the pueblo. "On the fourth day following the solstice the officers of the Kachina society and the impersonators of all the kachina priests, accompanied by the chief of the Hunters' society and men of the Deer and the Badger clan leave for the home of the gods. The lake is reached on the evening of the second day. Offerings of prayer-sticks are made at various shrines and turtles are hunted."[30]

While Badger does not have an official role in Acoma hunting, there is nonetheless a story from there in which he figures in rabbit hunting. In the tale, he is joined, by way of competition, with Coyote who is the more important hunter. This aspect of the story is based upon the fact that badgers and coyotes not uncommonly do hunt together to the mutual benefit of each.

In this Acoma hunt story Badger's cold-bringing powers and his association with winter are emphasized. The two animals are desirous of a Navaho Maiden who promises to accept them if they bring her rabbits on the following day. " 'Nephew,' said Coyote. 'Yes,' said Badger, 'Let us sing a song for success in hunting that there may be snow tomorrow,' said Coyote. 'Then if it snows let us go hunting rabbits,' said Coyote. 'Let us do so,' said Badger. Then they sang." After these two have begun to sing, it begins to snow, which of course makes it easy to track rabbits. Badger keeps reporting back on this snowfall until at last it is very deep, when the two start their hunt.

During this hunt Badger catches a great many rabbits, doubtless aided by the snow which impedes their flight, but Coyote catches only a few. The importance of numbers is that the hunter with more game will be the most welcome. Since rabbits would retreat underground when pursued, Badger has great luck in digging them out until Coyote, tiring of his own failure, fills in a plug of sand behind his hunting companion. Coyote then seizes all of the rabbits and returns with them to the maid, claiming that the sand fell in and killed Badger. Suspecting some treachery the girl insists that they wait for a time to see if Badger will return, which he does as soon as he digs himself out. The Navaho maiden then questions them. " 'How many rabbits did your nephew Coyote kill?'—'He killed five,' said Badger."[31] Unexpectedly, and probably outside of his true nature, this badger expresses no animosity toward his friend and insists that he be fed.

It was mentioned earlier that there is a contradiction between myth and reality with respect to the Acoma Badger clan, but that at neighboring Laguna this clan did exist and was in charge of certain ceremonies and animal fetishes, including that of Badger. At Laguna the clan head prayed to these fetishes and the Badger people controlled the kachina dances, whereas at Acoma it is the Antelope clan which has that function. There are several variant myths which explain how these two clans came to supervise these kachina ceremonies.

Shortly after the time of the emergence, the people became curious about the home of the kachinas whose door had been locked for many years, sealing up the kachinas in the same way that game was impounded in the beginning. When the people decided to look for this home of the kachinas, they consulted Paiyatemu, demi-god of the Sun, who told them the place they were seeking was in the middle of the West. To locate the place they took a journey in that direction, seeking advice from Spider Woman whom they met along the way.

"She told them that if they would not tell anyone who gave them the information, she would tell them all they wanted to know. They promised and she told them to go to old Badger Woman and she would open the door for them." Badger Woman agrees readily enough, but is angry that someone sent the people to her—the informants, she believes, are not Spider

Woman but some minor spirits whom she turns into the insects that live along the edges of ponds and streams.

"The old Badger Woman had a pet antelope fawn and she told the clowns that they could go into the Katsina Kutret by diving down in the crater in the center of the Zuñi salt lake, and that in four days she would open the door." The clowns, who are acting as scouts on this expedition, waited four years, which is the time really indicated by "four days." "In the meantime, the Badger Woman's antelope had attained its growth, and then she took the antelope with her and went to the door of Katsina Kutret. The antelope took a short run and struck the door with his head and raised a great dust. This he did four times. At the fourth time the door flew open and there was a great explosion and the Katsina people came out. They were all yellow and sickly. Because the people were brought forth this way, is the reason for the Badger and Antelope clans having first place in the Katsina dances."[32]

In another version, Badger and Antelope are intermediaries with the Sun, Badger Woman giving the kachinas paints which the Sun has given her, in order that they may paint themselves as they are now seen. Behind the first version is the historical fact of penning up herds of antelope by driving them into compounds, but however the myths are constructed, they always serve to link these two clans in their control over the kachinas. Some students have assumed that the priority of the Antelope clan once existed at Laguna as well as at Acoma, but recent evidence indicates that the Badgers had full charge at Laguna. There they tell yet another myth to justify this role, saying that the kachinas soon ran away from the people. The Antelopes tried to get them to return, but failed, whereupon the Badgers succeeded in bringing them back once more.[33]

In the foregoing accounts drawn from Zuñi, Hopi, and Acoma-Laguna, Badger's symbolism has been developed primarily in relation to the clans of the same name, but it would be wrong to assume that this is a necessary circumstance in the case of each animal. Bear is at very nearly the opposite pole with respect to clans, as his delineation stems primarily from the societies, although there are Bear clans of importance. Among the Keres of the Río Grande, who are of course closely related to Acoma and Laguna, there are Badger clans, but the clan is of no great importance in the scheme of social organization. In Santo Domingo, for example, there is a kiva-kachina organization which is not based on clan membership, and there are a number of societies, concerned with the hunt, war, curing, clown activities, and the like, none of which is directly based on clans.

Thus, although Bourke reported a Badger clan for Santo Domingo in 1881, called Dyupi hano—Badger people—it plays no specific role in ceremonies, and there is no development of badger symbolism through that channel. At Sia the Badger clan is called Tyupi hano and there the animal, but not the clan, has a role in mythology. At both Sia and Santa Ana, Badger has the same mythic role as at Acoma, in enlarging the entrance opening at the time of the emergence. This Sia badger was more industrious than his Acoma counterpart, since he made the opening so large that even elk and buffalo could walk out with ease, but then they could not have done so at Acoma in any case, since there these animals were not brought to life until after the mountains and grass were created.

The Tewa pueblos of Santa Clara and San Ildefonso also had Badger clans, called Kea-tdoa, but the Tewa clan is a most ephemeral entity. The Towa pueblo of Jemez and its extinct counterpart, Pecos, likewise had Badger People. Jemez does have clans with specific functions,[34] but the badger does not appear in existing accounts, nor among the animals on kiva wall decorations there. Perhaps this may in part be explained by the fact that, until well into the historical period, the Jemez Indians lived farther up into the mountains where badgers, except in their summer rambles, would not be a conspicuous feature of the environment. While there is no significant elaboration of Badger in these Río Grande pueblos, the mere fact that they felt impelled to identify a clan with him indicates the high standing he holds in the Pueblo world view.

There is one important quality of Badger which has been postponed in his account until now, although it might well have followed his role as a curer. There exist three important myths, two from Hopi and one from Acoma, in which Badger either raises people from the dead or enables the living to reach the land of the dead. The subject matter of these myths puts them directly into the Orpheus tradition, in which a journey is made to the land of the dead and one who is deceased is restored to life.[35]

Several points can be made before considering the narratives themselves. First of all, raising the dead is in a way the ultimate test of the power of a medicine man, as it is also an act contrary to the laws of nature. The Graeco-Roman god Asklepios became so powerful in his medical skill that he resurrected Hippolytos, the favorite of Artemis. Since this violated the natural order, even though instigated by a goddess, a thunderbolt from Zeus struck dead this father of both ancient and modern medicine. Badger is not dispatched for his efforts, but the Pueblos are firm believers in natural order and their doctors were not given to attempt this kind of miracle.

Insofar as infernal knowledge and ability are concerned, Badger is a good candidate for such work, both because of his underground explorations and his ability in curing. The latter qualification is limited, however, by the fact that he is an herb doctor and in raising the dead a bit of magic is also required. Perhaps one reason for his connection with the dead is that badgers frequently dig among bones in graveyards. Even in our non-Indian culture he is sometimes called "grave robber," apparently because he prefers to dig in sandy ridges, which are the places early settlers selected for burials.[36] Pueblo burial grounds were also located in such sandy places, and these were certain to be inhabited by a number of small rodents, who found themselves a living among the cycles of life there, and these were in turn pursued by the digging badgers.

There is a third medium through which Badger may be connected with the underworld and it derives from his association with winter. In this season the crops are thought to be growing underground, waiting for the time when they will be called up by means of seeds which are planted to indicate where a plant should emerge. The joining of the fertility myth with the underground journey does not seem to be worked out in these particular stories, but it will appear later on.

The first story concerns the son of a Hopi village chief from Second Mesa. This mournful youth spent his days on the edge of the village watching graveyards, wondering what became of the dead and whether or not they have an afterlife. His father, observing this preoccupation, consulted the other chiefs as to what could be done about it. He was told that Badger Old Man had the medicine and knew about it, so the elders spoke to him. " 'This young man is thinking about these dead, whether they live anywhere, and you know about it, you have medicine for that, and that is the reason why we called you.' 'Very well,' he said, 'so that is why you wanted me. I shall go and get my medicine.' "

Badger then went home and searched through his medicines until he located the right one, then he ordered the elders to bring him on the following day a white kilt called an owa—a ceremonial dress. Next the elders were instructed to blacken the youth's chin with shale and to tie an eagle feather to his forehead. "The next morning they dressed up the young man as they were instructed, preparing him as they prepare the dead. Hereupon the Badger Old Man spread the white owa on the floor and told the young man to lie down on it. He then placed some medicine into his mouth, which the young man ate. He also placed some medicine into his ears and some on his heart. Then he wrapped him up in a robe, whereupon the young man, after moving a little, 'died.' 'This is the medicine,' the Badger Old Man said, 'if he eats this he will go far away and then come back again. He wanted to see something and find out something, and with this medicine he will find out.' "

The trip that the youth then makes to the Underworld is out of the range of concern here.[37] After a difficult journey and converse with the dead in the Underworld the youth makes the return trip. "When he had just about arrived at his house his body, that was still lying under the covering in the room where he had fallen asleep, began to move, and as he entered his body he came to life again. They removed the covering, the Badger Old Man wiped his body, washed off the paint from his face, discharmed him, and then he sat up. They fed him and then asked him what he had found out."[38]

The second Hopi myth comes from the Third Mesa village of Oraibi and tells that a badger lived at Badger Gulch, while his friend Coyote lived nearby. One day when the two were hunting together with no success, Coyote remembered that he had some time before found the body of a Havasupai maiden who had died. He suggests to Badger: " 'Let us go and hunt the place where the Kohonino maiden has died, and let us revive her. You are a doctor and will certainly know how to do it.' So they went to the place and there sure enough were the bones." Here, surely, is expressed the fact that badgers as well as coyotes frequent graveyards.

"They gathered the bones and placed them on a pile. The Badger had on a black kilt. This he spread over the bones. . . . Then the Badger was thinking that the maiden would have to have some flesh and some color, so he sent the Coyote westward to Cohoh-toika to get some dry grass." This he placed with the bones, next ordering water from Hidden Spring with which he mixed red paint. Then, ordering Coyote away, he began to sing. "He poured some of the paint over the bones and grass. He then repeated the song several times, always pouring some of the paint over the material as he concluded the song. All at once the bones began to move under the cover. He waited a little and then removed the cover and, behold! the maiden was alive. She sat up and looked around. 'Why do you want me?' "

Badger tells her that it is not he who wanted her, but the coyote, and as the three went toward home Coyote began to covet the maiden. Badger objects to this turn of events: "That is not the purpose for which we brought her to life. She was to be our clan sister. We wanted her to build a fire for us." The whole proposition was, in any case, contrary to the natural order of things and doomed to early failure. Coyote, overcome with desire, rushed at the maiden, bit her on the leg, and she died again. Badger took her back to the place where they had found her and began to dig a grave, thinking at the same time how he might kill the evil Coyote. This he achieves by the familiar trick of persuading the dolt to disembowel himself.[39]

The Keresan myth from Laguna-Acoma is of even greater interest because of the importance of the woman here resurrected by Badger. She is the sister of Arrow-Youth, the friend of Great Star and a patron of hunters. His sister, Yellow Woman, is the mother of all kachinas in this myth and thus an agrarian fertility goddess, though in parallel myths she is the Mistress of Game. Yellow Woman has been killed by witches who have taken out her heart and hidden it under a water jar. Her brother buries the body under a ladder in their house, but two wolves are seen to carry it off. The Nawish kachinas observe them unwrapping the bundle and see there their "mother." The lifeless corpse of Yellow Woman is then carried by the Nawish kachinas to their home at Wenimats. Meanwhile, since the death of his sister, Arrow-Youth has been unable to kill any game, which is understandable since she is a patroness of game.

The kachinas cover the dead "woman" with a white mantle on which there is a black border, then they go in search of Badger, who is found in the west corner, meaning probably the southwest corner which represents the South. The mother of these specific kachinas, the Nawish, has found him. " 'Badger-Old-Man, here stretch out to me your hand,' thus she said to him. . . . Then on it she put pollen." Thus paid for his medical services, Badger goes to where Yellow Woman is lying dead. "Then he took out medicine. Then her entire body he rubbed with medicine. 'Enough,' said Badger." After warning those present not to cry, lest it might be difficult, he commences to sing: "Bones I put together; pa, pa, papapapa." He then seats himself in rotating positions and sings for each direction. When he finished Yellow Woman arose.

This resurrection proved to be only a partial success at first, however, "Thus spoke Badger, 'Enough,' said he, 'she cannot be alive yet today because her heart is hidden in White-House.' "[40] Badger is commenting here on the fact that her heart is still hidden in the Keres mythical home, so she may not appear during the day, for the fact is that Yellow Woman is closely associated with the moon, as befits a Mistress of Game. In another myth this is made more specific: "In the daytime slept their mother, but at night she walked about."

After further rites she put on her dress, and then she could walk about in the daylight, too. From this myth it is possible to conclude that Badger himself is a very powerful spirit who can bring to life a goddess, regulate the phases of the moon, and as was seen earlier, play the role of associate in charge of the winter ceremonies of the sun, which in turn control the whole ceremonial year. Likewise, as a fire spirit, he attends to the new-fire which brings the new sun. All in all, this is quite a cosmic role for a pugnacious little animal who has no economic value at all.

Chapter II

PRONGHORN ANTELOPE

A HERD of pronghorn antelope nearly always suggests to the observer something of unreality. Perhaps silence accounts in some degree for the seeming mystery, as the experience is so unlike that of a sudden encounter with a deer or a bear, who will start and crash off into the underbrush, or merely stand and stare in the same fashion as any human observer. Since one usually sees antelope at a range beyond hearing, only their swift movements prevail as the herd strives along the horizon, often on the borders of a vast arena. Once from a train window I watched a herd of startled, racing antelope, keeping pace nearby with ease for a short time. Groups of these graceful animals would leap high in the air in unison, some going in one direction, other groups in another, so that the effect, emphasized by the white on their necks and bellies, reminded one of breaking waves in a heavy sea. Nothing could be more unreal than the suggestion of such an image on the sagebrush flats of Nevada.

Charles Lummis, who observed the pronghorns in the time before their rapid decline, remarked on the mysterious nature of the sight. "Mid-ocean is not more lonesome than the plains, nor night so gloomy as that dumb sunlight. It is barren of sound. The brown grass is knee-deep—and even that trifle gives a shock in this hoof-obliterated land. The bands of antelope that drift, like cloud-shadows, across the dun landscape suggest less of life than of the super-natural."[1] The image of cloud shadows, which is most apt, is not one to have escaped the Pueblos who were constantly on the watch for the fleeting clouds of summer. The rain clouds in turn suggest the kachina dancers, those rain-bringing intermediaries between men and the world of spirits.

Even the scientists have to some extent fallen under the spell cast by the pronghorns, for the biologist Einarson writes: "Antelope are the phantoms of the prairie and much that has been said or written about them has a preternatural tinge."[2] However mysterious the behavior of antelope may appear, these effects are well grounded in the biological attributes of the animal. Some of these seem almost as though designed to create unusual effects. The hair of the antelope, for example, is so completely under the animal's control that it may be raised, lowered, or held to any angle at will. The animal is thus able to flash suddenly the longer white hairs on his rump, to express excitement or to signal danger.

Sometimes after a hard run the entire herd will come to a sudden stop and all of the animals will simultaneously quiver their hides, producing a visual effect that can be seen for two miles or more. Then, after this momentary flashing, the dun colors of the herd blend once again into the background and the elusive animals become invisible in the distance.

It is the speed that contributes most to the antelope's ability to create mirage-like effects. With a cruising speed of thirty to thirty-five miles an hour these animals can become true will o'the wisps, since they can be idling nearby one moment and yet vanish beyond the horizon in an incredibly short space of time. Antelope can put on short bursts of speed that achieve sixty miles an hour, which is impressive even to us and to an Indian on foot must have seemed little short of miraculous.

To gain this spirit-like speed, and for the body to stand up under the pounding that accompanies it, the antelope has developed a number of adaptations in legs, hooves, and respiratory system. While these arangements are exceedingly effective they do have limits, and once that point is reached the animal is stricken with sudden and complete exhaustion, a fact which was put to good use by Indian hunters.

Since the terrain they cover is often broken and rocky, the pronghorns' legs are adapted to covering difficult ground at high speed. This perfect set of adaptations for the use of speed as a defense is triggered by a nervous disposition. The buck is ever ready for signs of danger, real or supposed, which he communicates by flashing the white rump signal. If the animals are scattered in small groups an interlocking signal system is available, and they may choose whether to run or to hide. Since their coats consist of various buffy, sand shades with underparts of white to break up definite shadows, concealment can be most effective at times. However, even with these advantages antelope often fall victim to enemies. Their young are taken by all the predators of the plains, and in bad weather the adults lose their defenses.

A recent author notes that the antelope, being more adaptable than the bison, successfully made the shift to broken and less desirable areas, and to higher elevations, the herds no longer being found in the Lower Sonoran zone unless recently planted there. Changes in the numbers of antelope are of considerable interest, since this animal formerly served as the most important "big game" for the western Pueblos, and as a consequence it plays an important role in mythology and ceremony there.

Both the Pueblos and the antelope are so thoroughly adjustable to a sparse environment that, given somewhere near an even chance, they will make the most of it. This similarity of the animals and the Pueblos, the hunted and the hunters, and the unity of both in a common habitat is a central tenet in the Pueblo world view, accounting for the ritual displayed by the Indian in relationship to the animal. When an antelope, or other large game, is killed by an Indian it is treated to a variety of rituals by the hunter, his family, and friends.

When an Acoma hunter kills an antelope, he brings it back to the pueblo. There his mother comes out of his house with a handful of cornmeal, which is trickled along the ground, through the door, and even up a ladder if they live on the second story. This trail of meal is the "road" over which the spirit of the antelope travels. Then the body is brought in and laid out on the floor with its head toward the fireplace. Beads, preferably ones made of lignite, since hooves are supposed to be made of that material, are laid across the animal's neck where they remain until the spirit leaves the body, in perhaps an hour.

Relatives who come in rub their hands over the body, then across their own faces to impart the beauty and strength of the animal to themselves. Next there are words of welcome, such as, "We are glad you have come to our home and have not been ashamed of our people." The animal is fed a little meal by all visitors, because he will be reborn and this is to suggest that he should also come to their house. Before skinning, the beads, which have an attractive power as can be seen by the fact that women wear them, are removed and blown into the next room.

After skinning, the entire head, including horns, is boiled whole in a broth of corn, pinon nuts, and pumpkin seeds; these are said to be the earrings of the animal. At Acoma the clan of the hunter's father is called in to eat the head, while the mother of the hunter's father takes away the eyes and eats them. Doubtless the grandmother of a grown man needs this to assist her vision. Conversely the hunter may not eat them lest he become watery-eyed before his time. The skull is placed on top of the house to dry, after which it is taken down and painted with a black line along the length of the face, while the under-jaw is painted white. Balls of cotton with black centers are placed in the eye sockets.

A string is then tied from horn to horn and prayer feathers are attached to it. The hunter takes the head back to the mountains or the plain where he got it and prays that it will come alive again.[3] This short series of rituals is but a part of those that surround man's relation to game animals. Ritual begins with prayers before the hunt is called, taboos before and during the hunt, the placing of feathers, beads, shell, and other articles in game tracks, the building of hunt fires, culminating in the return of the animal's head to the place of its former life. "It is an ancient belief of the Zuñi," according to Cushing, "that the life of a deer or other 'game being' is restored, or elevated to a higher plane of existence, by means of incantations and rites of an initiated hunter."[4]

Two consequences follow from this view: the first being that the animal really wants to be taken, or to "come to the village," and secondly that it will thus allow itself to be taken easily—if the proper rites have been performed. Antelope have a rather peculiar habit which is likely to reinforce the latter belief. They are excessively curious animals, so much so that Dr. Kennerly reported in the mid-nineteenth century that to bring one into gun shot the hunter had merely to hide and shake his hat or hankerchief to arouse this curiosity. He added, however, that this was only in the less frequented regions.[5]

The Indians found further confirmation of the efficacy of their rites by contrasting the abundance of game where they hunted with the paucity of the same game soon after the arrival of the white hunter. Antelope and deer speedily disappear in the vicinity of white settlements, because once they have been killed by Americans they do not come to life again. This difference brings us to methods of hunting as practiced by the Pueblos and its seasonal limitations, which were in effect a conservation measure.

Antelope range in two different groupings. During most of the year they move about in small herds of perhaps a dozen or so individuals. Then, in winter after the rutting season is over, these smaller groups begin to come together into large herds that number in the hundreds. To some extent the type of hunting practiced was influenced by the seasonal habits of the animal, as great surrounds were only practical when large numbers of antelope could be found together. According to the Hopi, the best times to hunt were in the moons corresponding to August and October, when the animals were fattest, in December when snow might make tracking easy and perhaps impede the flight, and lastly in March and April when the animals have their young with them.

The spring period would scarcely appeal to a conservationist, but the young did anchor the animals to one area and at a time when the Indians were free from agricultural duties. The saving fact in relation to game was that the basic diet of Pueblos was corn, squash, and beans, whose tending required time, which meant that the pressure against game was not constant. The simplest method of hunting was lone stalking. Two men simply picked up an antelope trail and followed it for two days, during which time determined hunters can wear down either antelope or deer. When caught the animal was either slain with the bow and arrow, or captured by hand and smothered. Such individual hunting bypasses the whole Pueblo spirit of community endeavour and leaves little room for the ritualism which is essential for balanced relationships in the natural world.

The group hunt, or surround, is much more in the Pueblo spirit, since it necessitates all of the steps normally employed in any religious ceremony. The man who arranges the hunt, at Hopi, becomes the "hunt chief." He makes two prayer-sticks, one for the Mother of All Animals and one for the Grey Fox deity.* These he takes to the Badger clan chief,[6] because they "own" all animals. While they discuss the project over a smoke, the antelope is referred to as a "rat," the real name being taboo since the animal would run away if he heard his name mentioned.

A crier then announces the hunt and takes the two prayer-sticks and some cornmeal to the shrines of the two deities mentioned. These he deposits with prayers for success in the hunt and that no one may be injured. The hunt is also announced in other villages, as a goodly number of men and boys are a decided advantage. Four days are then taken for the preparations of food and weapons, during which time continence must be practiced by the hunters. Dreams occurring during this period are omens, and to dream of having intercourse—or to have no dreams at all—are bad omens. It is interesting to note that the sexual taboo here is the reverse of the situation during a deer hunt of the Santa Ana Indians of the Río Grande. There the hunters spend the first evening telling of their prowess. In

* The Grey Fox deity invoked earlier was called Kwe'wi'i. According to Stephen this is the Hopi name for Grey Wolf, Beast of Prey for the East. With the disappearance of wolves, fox seems to have taken that place.

both instances hunting power is equated with sexual power, but on Second Mesa a positive power is based on negation and transfer.

If the hunt took place before the modern relaxation of ceremonialism, the hunter's body was painted with yellow pigment, an eagle feather was tied in his hair, and he wore a ceremonial kilt. Hopi hunting of antelope was at this time to the southwest of the villages and on toward the Little Colorado River. During the hunt the men had to be serious-minded, neither laughing nor joking, and above all they must harbor no evil thoughts toward their fellow hunters. After they had camped near the herd, the hunters expelled the odor of women and babies, which antelope and deer very much dislike, by rubbing their hands over the body, then blowing on the hands.

The evening is spent in camp, singing special songs that are restricted to this occasion. While sitting each man makes six prayer-sticks: one for the Mother of All Animals, one for Hunting Man deity, Mak di'wi da'ka, one for Masau'u or Skeleton Man, one very long stick for antelope and deer that they may increase, one for the Sun, and one for Coyote. This last is made so that coyotes may chase the game and tire it out. With the rising of the sun in the morning, the hunt chief presents that deity with a final bundle of prayer-sticks and supplications for success, while each man passes his hand through the hunt fire, just as one would harden an arrow shaft. This fire represents the Sun god's strength-giving power on earth.

When the hunt itself begins, the men and boys spread out in two lines to form a loose circle several miles in diameter. A number of these hunters are mounted, if possible. Next, two men go into the circle to start the game, which may run in any direction. Naturally a number of the antelope escape through the loose circle, but as it is drawn tighter and tighter the remaining animals speed first in one direction and then another, only to be turned back each time. If necessary, arrows are used on larger or difficult animals, "But approved practice was to throw the exhausted animal to the ground, point its head towards the village that rain might go in that direction, and then grasping the nose and jaws with the hand, press the head into the sand until the animal was smothered."[7]

The thought was that, as the spirit is the breath, this method caused the antelope spirit to go directly to its home and so be born again. To slit the throat or to otherwise let blood might cause a whirlwind or sandstorm. The hunter making the kill then divided the game with the next three men to arrive. A fire was immediately built so that the liver could be cooked and eaten on the spot to nourish the exhausted hunters. The left foreleg and right hind leg were given to the first man to arrive, the opposite pair to the second, while the third man received the internal organs and the blood which was carefully drained into the paunch. This left the killer the horned head, body, and hide. The latter was not valued by most of the Indians, but the Pueblos treasured even a thin skin.

Since the dead, including dead game, have considerable power, there must be purification rites. Just as in the case of a human death, the odor of the dead antelope must be blown away, so each hunter takes a bowl of burning juniper leaves and bark with which he smokes himself thoroughly. This bowl with its ashy content is placed in a shrine below the village. At Hopi only the tongue may be eaten the first day by the hunter and his family, a complete reversal of the Acoma practice, where the hunter may not eat the tongue lest it make him thirsty. The following day there is a feast for relatives and friends, but most of the meat is dried and kept for later use.

Leslie White recorded the biography of an Acoma Indian who described an antelope hunt in which he took part in the year 1887. By that time there were no antelope left near Acoma, so the hunters had to travel far to the south, near the present town of Datil. For this expedition of seventy-four hunters, four cooks were required, and they took eight burros to bring back the dried meat. At that date the hunt involved a mixture of ritual and practicality. The hunters wore an antelope costume which consisted of an actual head of the animal worn over their own, while some kind of a shirt completed the disguise. As they encountered a large herd the kill was great, it being claimed that 744 animals were killed in one day, 34 being killed by one hunter.

The effects of this hunt could well have been disastrous to the antelope herd at a time when they were being assaulted on all sides. However this may be, ritualism was not forgotten in the haste. "When a man would start to skin an antelope he would take out its heart and dip his shaiyak [hunting fetish] in its blood to feed him; then he would put the fetish back in his pouch. If the antelope were female, the hunter would take out her stomach, cut it open, and then place her vulva in the stomach and sprinkle them with pollen. If the antelope were male, his penis and testicles were similarly placed in his stomach and sprinkled with pollen."[8]

There was yet another way in which antelope were hunted, the chute and pound method, around which much lore has accumulated since some of the pounds or corrals were built of stone and have survived. The effectiveness of this method is based upon the fact that antelope are very loath to jump over the slightest obstacle, even though they are capable of tremendous leaps. There seems to be some psychological block involved, since a running antelope who is suddenly faced with a fence will plunge beneath the wire with scarcely a pause in his pace. Caton mentions instances where antelope have been kept in captivity behind a four-foot fence.[9]

While some of the corrals were made of stone, the more common method and one that was shared with a number of other western Indians was to make these of poles and brush. An ancient Hopi named Ha'ni told Stephen that these were used in the old days before the Hopi had any horses for use in antelope hunting. The labor involved must have been tremendous, since the central pen alone would be an area 600 by 300 feet. This was built in elliptical shape in some suitable mesa nook. It was made of tree boles set close together, interlaced with smaller limbs, the whole wall sloping inward slightly. At one end an opening of some twenty feet was left in the corral and from this "wings" of brush were built out for as much as 800 to 1000 yards to form a vast funnel. The whole of this structure was called chubki, or antelope house, while the actual stockade was called sheep house.

Beyond the wings, piles of brush were set at frequent intervals, close enough together so that a man could guard the gap and the same arrangement was extended for several miles on both sides. An element of chance then had to intervene on the side of the Indians, since they waited until a band of antelope grazed into the neighborhood of the corral, whereupon a watchman warned the villagers of its approach. At that point eight active young boys were sent out to the animals while the villagers went to the trap. The youths would make the best possible use of arroyos to surround the band of antelope on three sides. "All were provided with cedar bark and the fire making board, and two at the far end of the antelope would start two smokes and imitate the cry of the wolf."

By a succession of such activities the boys would hopefully drive the band in the direction of the wings, where men stationed at intervals would keep the animals moving toward the corral. Then, "The antelope running through the stockade, two men who had been stationed at the gate with piles of heavy brush-wood, all ready, would instantly close the gate. The chief of the hunt and the other men were stationed outside the stockade and shot the antelope down."[10] Needless to say, the animals would often enough refuse to co-operate, which was attributed to men with bad hearts, or a ceremonial failure on the part of the hunt chief. The antelope might fail to go anywhere near their house or, "if they smelled those evil persons, they would break away."

Sometimes a corral was constructed on a permanent basis by making a wall of stones. There are the remains of such a structure about two miles north of the villages on First Mesa, which must date from the far past when the antelope still grazed near these pueblos. It is built clear across a narrow neck of the mesa

39

and if a band was spotted and could be driven through the opening they could either be killed on the spot, or forced to jump off the cliff, breaking their legs or necks.

The Zuñi also have a stone corral which is not only very old, but has become extremely sacred, so much so that the Indians hesitate to even approach the spot except under official and ceremonially approved circumstances. Stevenson mentions that she had seen both the corral and the sacred springs which surround it. These were probably the original occasion for its having been built on that spot. Her guide at that time reluctantly pointed out, "the corral in which Ku'yapalitsa, a female warrior bearing the name of tCha'kwena, and the mother of all game, kept game."[11] The first of these names is that of the goddess, the second that of the kachina who represents her.

The idea that all game was once impounded by a gamekeeper, most often a goddess in anthropomorphic form, is common to all Pueblo mythology and it finds expression in manifold ways. Similar ideas are of course worldwide, the best known example being Artemis, in one of her aspects, and the Cretan Mother of Animals who is her predecessor. In the case of the Zuñi corral the myth has become attached to a particular place, and one which is ideally suited to the content of the myths.

That this corral was not originally built as a shrine for the myths, we know from other Indians who remembered its use as an antelope trap. As it lies to the south of Zuñi, on the route taken by many peoples on their journey to the Zuñi Salt Lake, it is described by the Hopi, Don Talayesva, who mentions passing the place on a salt pilgrimage he took with his father. "The next day we climbed a steep zigzag trail into deep woods, passed waterfalls and came to an old corral, where the Zuñi used to catch antelope by the power of secret charm songs which drew the animals to them and caused the corral walls to rise up by magic."[12] Then, illustrating the equation of sexual and hunting power, his father mentions that the Hopi too know magic songs which are powerful enough to attract women as well as antelope.

While there is no settled view on the origin or creation of

antelope, it is certain that they did not exist in the Underworld as the Badger did. The Acoma account of this animal's origin seems to be a bit of primitive science. Badger's pre-existence was based upon mythical necessity, but Antelope arrived in the natural course of evolution. The Keresan sisters, daughters of the mother goddess, created the various kinds of animals by taking images of them out of the baskets the goddess had presented to these women. At first the sisters were small in size and thus able to live on tiny creatures.

Bashya, the kangaroo mouse, was the first to be given life and his flesh was sufficient supplement to corn. They prayed to him with bits of corn, meat, and salt at each meal. Next other tiny animals that live in the ground and require no shade were brought to life. For larger animals grass was needed, so seeds were planted to the four directions, causing grass to immediately spring up and cover the ground, providing food for the smaller creatures. When these asked why they were brought to life they were told that they in turn would give life to larger animals. After the mountains of the four directions had been called up, the seeds of trees were planted.

With this much of the world in shape, it was time to bring out the game, which was brought to life in two divisions. First the cottontail and jack rabbits, the "water deer," and the antelope. These were sent to live on the open plains. Then came the larger game, the mule deer, elk, mountain sheep for the mountains, and bison for the plains. Since there was now food for the beasts of prey, these were next brought to life, followed by the birds. Finally cactus and certain thorny plants were brought to life, a fact which seems odd, but explains the rationale of the whole sequence.[13]

This account seems to be based upon a combination of logic and a graduated scale indicating the importance of various items in the Acoma food supply. It begins with corn, follows with the small mammals that are always at hand, the rabbits which are basic game, then the antelope. The game of the distant mountains and the bison of the even more distant plains are next in importance, followed by the beasts of prey whose magic is useful in taking game. The birds, whose dietary importance is peripheral, came last, except that the narrator suddenly remembers cactus. The fruit of cactus and yucca was an important source of emergency food in times of drought, although it was eaten and preserved at other times as well, so he rather awkwardly includes these at the end of the list.

At Hopi the story of the creation of antelope is closely tied to mythology and the sanctions certain myths give to the worship of different goddesses. If ordinary logic were applied to mythology, one would be inclined to attribute a historical progression to these deities. The simplest is an anthropomorphic being—perhaps just an ordinary woman, as she does not have the attributes of a Mother of Game. During the period of migrations she gives birth to little antelope twins and presently she too becomes an antelope, thus becoming the spirit-animal who is the ancestress of the whole lineage of pronghorns.

The next most complex divinity is a true Mother of Game, who is responsible for the origin of deer, antelope, mountain sheep, and rabbits, which is to say all of the important Hopi game animals. Yet a third goddess is involved and she is unspecialized, being an earth goddess who gives birth to vegetation as well as all kinds of animals, not merely game. The curious thing is that all three of these possibilities exist simultaneously, so that one is forced to conclude that if one or another of these versions is more ancient, the old myths must be continuously revitalized.

The simplest myth tells that the people were in almost constant movement after the emergence, making life difficult for a woman who was pregnant. "She managed to accompany the wanderers only as far as Giant's Chair where she remained alone while the others went to a place by Corn Rock." Then some women went back to find out how she was and discovered "that she had given birth to twins which were like little antelopes with horns on their heads. They also found that the mother had become an antelope as well."[14] The Hopi took them to the village, but as they were unhappy there they took them back and made a hole in the ground for their dwelling, at the same time giving them prayer-sticks, for the increase of deer and antelope. This is the origin of that custom. The name of the place was *DIGI' i Wï'XDI*, which also became the name of the woman, so it would seem that a mother of game is called by the unlikely name of Giant's Chair.

The second goddess is called *Tih'kuyi wuhti*, or Child-birth Water Woman, indicating that she, like Artemis, is a patroness of human births as well as a source of animal life. "Tih'kuyi 'Wuqti is mother of the antelope, deer, mountain sheep and both kinds of rabbits. She gave birth to two antelopes, and the blood that issued from her during the birth she confined in a little puddle by raking up the sand around it with her fingers. Of this blood soaked sand, she made five little pellets and formed them into five rabbits and from these all rabbits are descended."[15]

This specialized Mother of Game is often confused or identified with another goddess, Sand Altar Woman, or *Tuwa'-bontumsi*, who represents all the moist elements in life, and is thus more of a female Dionysos than a counterpart of Artemis. "She is the mother of all living things, i.e. of all human kind, all animals and all vegetation; plants suck from her breast a nourishing liquid, it passes up from their roots to their flowers and fruit, and animals and man eat of the vegetation, hence *Tuwa'bontumsi* is mother of all life. This liquid the bees suck from the flowers and make into honey."[16] Clearly she is the earth itself and only in the most general way responsible for bringing animals, including antelope, into being.

These mythical accounts of the origin of pronghorns have served as a bridge from the consideration of the antelope in its economic aspect, as game, to its other roles in community life. Along the way each aspect of man's relationship to this beast has some kind of a myth to accompany it. As an example, there is a story at Zuñi which "explains" why they are killed by smothering. The War Twins, who are always good agents for setting

things in motion, hid behind a tree and sang a song to these
animals.

Antelope, antelope, antelope
Like cream is your skin,
Like charcoal is your snout.
Like piñon gum your eye,
Like cedar bark your sinew.
Antelope, antelope.

" 'Indeed someone is insulting us!' They said. They rushed
out.... They came up, and butted against the dead tree. A large
buck antelope thrust his foot into a knothole. The younger
brother grabbed it. ... He lay down on his neck and strangled
him. The antelope struggled for breath and died."[17]

Attribution of the practice to a god is sufficient warrant for it.
Sometimes the organization of a community is attributed not
directly to a deity, but to a spirit-animal and man's relationship
to that animal, as exemplified in myth. Thus the town chief of
the pueblo of Acoma must be of the Antelope clan. Numerically
this clan is not important,* but in both myth and ceremony the
Antelope people predominate. The town chieftanship is the
most important ceremonial office and this man is thought of as
the spiritual father of his people. He is also "father" of the
kachina dancers who form a link between the community and the
spirit world represented by the masked impersonators of gods.

Since the kachinas are the essence of most ceremonies the
town chief is the ritual leader of the pueblo, and as initiation
into the kachina organization is felt to be equal to initiation into
the "tribe," he is in charge of that rite. In addition he has authority over the medicine men and the kiva chiefs. The annual
selection of the War Chief is either in his hands, or that of the
Antelope clan. Today the war duties have lapsed, but he is in
charge of preserving and encouraging the old ways, of guarding
the village and of protecting the people from witches.

---

* In White's 1927 census there were 26 antelopes in a population of 826.

44

Since the antelope, as well as clansmen by that name, is woven into this structure and these duties, there are a number of myths which relate the various pieces together. The first of these explains the origin of the Antelope clan and also why they are in charge of the kachinas. It begins much like the Hopi account of the origin of this animal. After the emergence, the Keres people were traveling southward, when they camped near Laguna. There, a chief's daughter was about to give birth, so her father commanded her to stay behind.

When she again catches up her father asks if she has had a child. " 'Yes,' she said to him. 'Dead was the child I gave birth to, so I buried it.' " The abandoned one, which was of human not animal form, is found by a deer who scoops up the child on his antlers, taking him to the doe who nurses him. Seemingly the deer and antelope lived together in a village. The boy is raised with a fawn who is his racing companion, but one day he asks, "Father, why am I naked and my brother is very nicely dressed?"

The deer does not know, saying merely that he came to them that way. As the youth grows he becomes a herder of antelopes, whom he releases in the morning to run hard at their head during the day, bringing them back in the evening. Meanwhile the deer-father becomes troubled. "How is this now, my child is a man? It is unfortunate. Some time later he will do something unfortunate. He will mix his blood with that of the antelope. That will not be right. I wonder who would tolerate the existence of half human flesh and half game as food?"

The deer chief is now faced with two problems: getting some clothing for the boy, and returning him to his rightful mother and grandfather. For the first he travels to Wenimatse, the home of the kachinas and the dead.* From the kachinas he borrows clothing such as they wear. "Early in the morning he

---

* The name Wenimatse is derived from "matse"—"blood." The connection of blood with kachinas will appear shortly.

went again to herd antelopes. Then he looked very nice like a katsina." While herding, the youth is spotted by a man from Acoma. "Someone like a human being, he walked ahead of the antelopes and like that of the katsina was his dress. Now you will announce that after four days we shall go to hunt antelopes. Let us catch the poor one, that one who goes with them."

In the following hunt many antelope are killed, and the youth is captured by his uncle, tied up, and brought back to Acoma. At first he will not eat wafer bread, so the uncle gathers grass. Every morning the uncle would take him to the foot of the mesa where he raised a great dust. But after a time he begins to eat normally and speak the Acoma language. Then he tells his story to the assembled people, ending with the fact that the chief must be his grandfather.[18] Thus it is explained how the chief of the antelope also came to be the town chief of Acoma. The relationship of this officer to the kachinas is implied in the myth, but the details are explained in another narrative.

The second myth, entitled Antelope Man Brings Back the Katsina, continues a larger story which was in part revealed in the Badger chapter. There, in the Laguna version, it was told that the Kachinas had been locked up. More often the kachinas are said to have run away, because of insult or neglect, causing a period of evil times. Since the ceremonial organization differs in the two pueblos, at Acoma it is the Antelopes who find and release the imprisoned kachinas.

Both clown-scouts and the Antelope people were out searching when the two groups met and decided to ask Spider Grandmother where the kachinas could be found. She does not know, but thinks that Mina Koya, Salt Woman, might have the information. "Yes, I know what place they stay, those katsina. You tell the Antelope man and scouts to wait until the horns of the antelope are ripe." During this time the people hunt deer and rabbits so that they will be able to feed the kachinas when they are released.

Then after all was ready the group assembled. First the

46

scouts, who are warriors, dug a little with their flint knives. Next Antelope Man, who only carries a staff as a badge of town chieftancy, is given the knife and he too digs a little. "Then the Antelope man told Badger to dig down to the door. The Badger dug down until he got to the door. The door was a thin rock. Then Antelope man told the Antelope to break the door with his horns. The Antelope backed off and ran toward the door and hit it with his horns." When they break in Antelope Man finds the head kachina, Kimasho, as well as lots of flowers, corn, and melons—these as well as the rain that had been withheld from the people.

The kachinas promise to come out and drop these good things right by the pueblo. The exchange of food is arranged and a procession starts for Spider Woman's house. At its head was Antelope Man, followed in order by Antelope, Badger, the kachina chief, and the kachinas, with the scouts guarding the rear. At Spider Woman's house the kachinas are fed the meat that had been killed for them and promise that when they get back to Wenimats, "we are going to make rain for the whole world."

"Next day the clouds came from Wenima and it rained like everything. The people had a meeting at Shipap. They made the Antelope man, the headman, to call out the katsina. No one else could. The people, everybody, made prayer-sticks. After the rain, in the morning, Kimasho came to the Antelope man's house and said, 'Well, we are finished now. You can tell your people to plant tomorrow.' . . . The people came in with prayer-sticks to give to Kimasho. Kimasho told the people that the Antelope man was their headman because he was the one who had brought them back. He would be cacique [chief]."[19]

There is yet another myth in this semicycle which would perhaps be fitted in the middle, or even the beginning, if they were all arranged together. It tells of a great battle between the kachinas and the Indians and accounts for the disappearance of the former. When the great goddess, Iyatiku, left the people shortly after the emergence, she told them that the kachinas, who were very powerful spirits and must be respected, would come in a few days to dance. Since the kachinas are also called shiwana, which means rain or storm clouds—and sometimes the dead as well—there is always an undertone indicating that what has fled from the village and must be brought back, are these clouds.

In expectation of the kachina visit, the women bake bread, the men hunt deer and rabbits, while the War Twins show the people how to make prayer-sticks as offerings to these spirits. When the real kachinas came they were dressed as the dancers are today, but they wore no masks as their faces actually looked the way present masks do. They brought with them buckskin bags of useful things such as arrows, pottery, clothing, and flints, which multiplied when poured out on the ground. Instructions were then given in their use.

The War Twins next told the people that they must 'believe in the katsina,' as they were powerful and were rainmakers. Then the kachinas danced all day in the plaza. These dancers came often after that, but the people became so high-spirited that one day, after the dancers had left for their home at Wenimats, someone began to mimic their dance with exaggerated motions. Others joined in with gaiety and laughter. Then, suddenly someone left hurriedly. It was a kachina who had been left behind. When he told his fellows how the people were behaving, the kachinas decided to return and kill all of them.

"The morning following thousands of katsina were seen running toward Kashikatshutia from the west, raising a big cloud of dust. They were met by the people of the village, the women behind, the men in front. Many people were killed. If a katsina was killed he immediately came to life again and resumed fighting. At nightfall the fighting ceased and the katsina returned to Wenimats. Most of the people had been killed. The rest were very sad. And they quarreled among themselves, blaming each other for their misfortunes."[20]

As a result of this battle the real kachinas never came back, but they agreed that if the people wanted them to come in spirit the dancers could imitate them by making masks that resembled their features. Some people thought that it was improper to imitate the spirits, and these split into bands that migrated away, becoming those Indians who have no masked dancers.

The role of the Antelope clan in this battle is expressed in an elaborate ceremony in which the Antelopes and the Warrior Society defend the pueblo from attacking kachinas. Before describing this great battle it will be well to revert to the animal himself briefly. Ordinarily one does not think of the antelope as any kind of a fighter, much less as a symbol of warlike activity. As a matter of fact all horned animals are prone to heroic combat during the rutting season, and as antelopes were the most numerous and frequently seen of the horned creatures, by the western Pueblos, it was this species rather than elk, mountain sheep, or deer that impressed them. An antelope buck actually becomes "locoed" during rut. He continuously twitches his skin, hair, and mane, he starts erratically and his eyes bulge out abnormally and ferociously. There is a continuous wild activity in the herd at this time, raising up clouds of dust like those seen at the approach of the kachina warriors.[21]

Like the elk, the antelope buck then gathers up a harem which he protects jealously. It is in this latter habit that the Indians of Acoma have found a close analogy with the duties of the Town Chief, while the actual fighting is a secondary arrangement. While this particular ceremony belongs to Acoma alone, the close association of antelope with warriors is widespread among the Pueblos. At the Tiwa pueblo of Isleta, also located near antelope country, the Town Chief, who also acts as War Chief, wears antelope horns; he has charge of the scalps. All this despite the fact that he is not supposed to kill anything, "not even an insect."[22] Among the Hopis, a helmet with antelope horns is worn by scouts as well as the War Chief.

The Hopi Horn Society members wear antelope horns and carry elk antlers in their hands during their policing actions, and when we come to the Hopi Antelope Society it will be found that they are connected with the Snakes, a sometime warrior group.[23]

Returning to the Acoma ceremony, "the kachina are going to fight us," it is seen as largely a dramatization of the last myth. There is one important variation, however, as in the myth it was the people who were killed. In the ceremony the kachinas seem to have the worst of it. Like the kachinas in the myth, those in the ceremony come to life again and return to their home at Wenimats. It has been a long time since this ceremony was held, since defense of the village is a thing of the past, and these rituals were in part a kind of "war games," such as other armies use to prepare themselves. It was not always so, the most famous, or infamous, of the assaults on the Sky City having been that of Zaldivar in the year 1599.

In the past the ceremony was held in the spring at five- or six-year intervals. The Town Chief asked the War Chief to select certain young men to act as the attacking kachina warriors. These young men practice running and jumping, and drink herb emetics night and morning. The Antelope people and the Opi, Warrior Society, members make preparations for defense of the village, calling upon young initiates to perform the actual fighting. The struggle is so realistic that those who are to represent the kachina warriors conceal the mask they are to wear, lest an enemy might take advantage of the melée and actually kill him. To obviate this possibility friends arrange mutual signs by means of which they may stick close together during the fight.

Each kachina warrior then kills a sheep whose blood he saves in a clean bowl. The blood from the sheep's heart is sealed up in a piece of gut which is worn around the neck. The Antelope people have meanwhile prepared the village for defense, and scouts close the village from outsiders. On the seventh day, shortly after midnight, the kachina warriors leave their wives and mothers whom they may not see again. Doubtless the danger of death is exaggerated to simulate the feelings of real warfare.

"Early in the morning of the eighth day two red scouts arrive in the pueblo, crying 'Ah-a-a-a Ai!' the war cry. The war chief meets them. The red scouts warn him that the katsina will soon come and destroy the village." At the same time there are a few friendly kachinas walking about the pueblo, as it is said that in the first battle some of these spirits fought on the people's side. Two of these representing the War Twins go about pressing bows and flints against the two walls at each corner of the houses to strengthen them. Others give herbs to the children so that they will not be too frightened, for they alas think that the kachinas will bring them presents in the usual manner. Their consequent terror when they witness the unexpected and realistically portrayed turn of events must be considerable.

White scouts next arrive in the plaza with word that the kachinas are coming to bring presents as usual, but the red scouts dispute this and a group of men begin erecting a barricade to the west of the village. This is made of hides and birch poles which are kept on hand for the purpose. Soon the white scouts return to announce that everyone is to be killed or taken to Wenimats, and at that word tumult breaks loose, rocks are thrown, and preparations for the fight begin in earnest.

The Antelope people are painted pink all over, except for reddish brown faces with black, sparkling streaks under the eyes, and in their hands they carry canes rather than weapons. The Antelope women have their faces, arms, and hands painted yellow with pollen. The Opi, on the other hand, are properly painted as warriors and carry flints and knives. To meet these defenders, the kachina warriors come running and yelling toward the village. At one point they must leap a deep chasm, in which two men once fell to their death during this ceremony. As they near the pueblo they pull up young trees and shrubs and brandish them.

When the kachinas reach the mesa the Town Chief goes down to meet them and gives them smaller, less dangerous clubs than the ones they hold. The chief and the Antelopes then hold back the kachina band with their canes, but despite this the barricade is reached and struck four times by each kachina. The barricade is then moved back in successive stages, until at the third stand some of the kachinas have their throats slit by Opi warriors—an event which has been carefully prearranged.

"When the Opi cuts the gut of blood at the katsina's throat the blood runs out onto the ground, where it remains. This is a sacrifice to the earth. If a katsina has more than one gut of blood he will have his throat cut again. They lie face downward on the ground after their throats are cut, and pray." The War Twin impersonators then touch the slain kachinas with flints and bows which slowly restores them to life again, whereupon they stand up and fight with renewed fury.

Neither the Antelopes nor the Opi are "killed" in these fights, only the kachinas. At the fourth station, many throats are cut, and at the seventh station, the Opi seize the white scouts, who have guts of blood concealed in their breechcloths, and castrate them. These men do not rise but writhe on the ground in feigned agony. "When the fighting is finished at the seventh place, boys arrive from the house of the Antelope clan with baskets of prayer sticks which have been made by the Antelope people. . . . The Antelope men go to the baskets and get their prayer sticks and give them to the warrior katsina, placing them in their hands and holding their own underneath, praying."

The kachinas then depart as the people return to their homes or ceremonial house. Everyone who has participated in the fight must be continent for eight days before and after the event, and there are also taboos on salt and meat during the four days preceding it. Afterwards an air of sadness is maintained in the village for several days. The dried blood is left lying in the plaza.[24] The various strains interwoven in this ceremony, as well as those related in the myths, all express the functions of Antelope clansmen as personified in the Town Chief. Like the buck antelope, he is a protector of his herd. On the one hand, this protection is expressed through the guarding of fertility, while on the other, he assures, through the War Chief, the physical defense of the people. Holding both of these responsibilities together he is the intermediary with the spirit world of the kachinas.

The state of affairs at Hopi resembles the Acoma arrangement, in which the Antelopes are not actually warriors but closely associated with them. At Hopi the famous Snake-Antelope ceremonies are the joint responsibility of the two societies and the relationship is one of supervisors to active warriors. Wiki told Stephen, "We never call the Snake father. The antelope is called father by the Snake men. The father of Snake maiden is father of the Antelopes, and Antelopes are fathers of the Snakes."[25] Without stopping to untangle all of the ramifications of this statement we may merely note that the fact that Snake men were fathered by Antelope men is intended to be taken as a reflection of a social condition. The Antelope men superintend for the simple reason that they are too old to fight, or for some other reason do not actually take part.

Stephen's informant puts the matter quite plainly, although he probably shifts history about a bit to bring it into conformity with ceremonial logic. "Long ago the Snake society and Antelope society were confined to men of the Snake clan. . . . In the old time the Snake society were actual warriors and when they went on the war trail they carried neither spear nor bow and arrow. They had the battle axe and the nodule club. They knew no fear and marched up to the enemy and seized him by the throat (as we seize a snake) and knocked him on the head with axe or club. The Antelope society were old men, they remained in the kiva and sang and prayed while the snakes were fighting."[26]

There is a bit of natural history which may perhaps throw some light on the link between these two societies. In his paper, *Mammals of the Boundary*, Baird quotes the following statement. "The antelope is said to have an abiding hatred for the rattlesnake, which it decoys first into a striking attitude, and then utterly annihilates by leaping into the air and coming down upon it with its four sharp-cutting hoofs placed together."[27] While this relationship is positive and negative, rather than complementary, so striking a natural trait would hardly have been missed by the observant Indians.

The Snake-Antelope ceremony is a rite in which fertility motifs mingle with war elements. One man told Stephen, "that all these ceremonies are for rain to fall to water the earth, that planted things may ripen and grow large; that the male element of the Above, the *Ye*, may impregnate the female earth virgin, *Naasun*. The Snake men are warriors; they must not, can not, sing or speak, they must *do*."[28] In this ceremony the Antelopes are the peacemakers: "and the Antelope men stay in Antelope kiva and pray that the snakes remain peaceable."[29]

During the Antelope ceremony, which is held in alternate years, the same theme is carried into the dance. Corn stalks, not snakes, are placed in the mouths of the novices that they may grow fast, as corn does. "At the Antelope dance, corn stalks are carried with prayers that vegetation may be abundant; they also pray that sickness may not come to children, that young people may grow thus."[30]

A race is run as a part of this ceremony in which the starter must be of the Horn clan, or at least have some affinity to it, "so that he may *properly* tell the youths to run fast like an antelope."[31] This race begins at 4 A.M., beyond Sun spring, where the starter gathers up a little water from each spring and puts it into a gourd which he has brought from Antelope kiva. Just as the sun peers over the horizon, he dashes this gourd to the ground, breaking it with a prayer that the rain may speedily fall, and the runners start off at full speed.

The Horn clan is rather obviously associated with the antelope as an animal, a fact which comes into prominence during the Hopi solstice ceremony. At that time there is another mock struggle, but this time related to the Sun's hesitancy in beginning his northward journey. At the point of decision, members of the Singers' society attempt to detain the shield-bearing impersonator of the Sun by seizing his feather-rayed shield, but the struggle, although seemingly violent, is in mimicry only.

Just after this combat twelve men from Nasha'bki, which is

the home of the Horn clan and is also called Chu'bmo, or Antelope Mound, enter the kiva followed by one who represents an antelope. This Antelope Man wears an elaborate headdress called "many flowers," which is adorned with real antelope horns and squash blossom effigies. After intoning for some twenty minutes he is handed a black shield on which is painted a very good likeness of a pronghorn antelope.[32] There follows another struggle in the same mock fashion as that for the sun-shield.

Later in the same ceremony, three antelope heads are placed on a mound of sand and prayer-sticks are offered to antelope and other animals. The symbolism here is uncomplicated, relating to the increase of game during the enlarging new year that begins with sun's northward journey. A similar thought is carried out in the Game dances that are held in the Río Grande pueblos shortly after the beginning of the year, often on January 6 by our calendar. In these, men dressed in skins with the horns still on them, lean on canes to imitate all of the game animals, including antelope; these dances will be described in some detail later.

A retrospective view of the antelope's role would seem to indicate that his organizational functions at present outweigh his importance as a game animal, but most probably this appearance is only a result of mythic sublimation, which is to say, the antelope has gained his important ceremonial position, at Acoma and Hopi, precisely because he was the most important species of larger game for these two groups of Indians. For Acoma's fellow Keresans of the Río Grande area, it is the deer rather than antelope who stand first, as would be expected in that more mountainous country. Thus it is emphasized that in former times antelope were the fleeting cloud shadows of the plains, for even the relatively limited mountains about Zuñi were sufficient to shift the center of attention there to deer, a fact which is reflected in the minor importance and early extinction of the Zuñi Antelope clan. By the 1880's there was only one family, or perhaps one man, of the Antelope people remaining at Zuñi. If the animal had been of sufficient importance, a way would surely have been found to perpetuate its role through a sub-clan or society.

As the fleeting and graceful antelope vanish from the horizon of our interest, there appears in its stead a perhaps more fundamental game animal—the deer.

Chapter III

DEER

IN ANY PART of the northern hemisphere, whether the terrain be woodland, desert, steppe, tundra, swamp, high mountains, or valleys, there is likely to be some member of the deer family within easy hunting distance. Deer do well in boreal and scrub areas in which they require but the smallest space for a living. The white-tail, for example, can make a living on an area a half-mile square.

In the Pueblo area mule deer are divided—the Rocky Mountain and the desert races. The Rocky Mountain mule deer is very large, weights of up to 400 pounds field-dressed being claimed.[1] The desert mule deer, which prefers a broken country, pinyon-juniper habitat, is considerably smaller, seldom exceeding 160 pounds dressed. The white-tail deer of the Pueblo area are likewise divided in two races, the Texan and the Sonoran white-tail. The Texan race has settled in two quite different habitats, displaying once again the deer's great adaptability. One group formerly inhabited all of the plains of eastern New Mexico. The other group formerly inhabited both sides of the Sangre de Cristo Mountains along the eastern bank of the Río Grande. This form is quite large for a white-tail, weighing about the same as the desert mule deer.

Gradually both the numbers and the territory inhabited by the Texan white-tail shrank, those on the eastern plains disappearing entirely. Vernon Bailey states that, "in 1904 the Taos Indians told the writer that white-tailed deer were then very rare on the west slope of the mountains but still fairly common along the east slope."[2] Both the Taos Indians and the Tewa to the south of them distinguish these white-tail with a separate name, that from Taos meaning "stream deer" from

57

their preference for water courses; mule deer will live content without any water nearby.

Sonoran white-tails are a dwarf race, the biggest bucks seldom dress out at better than 75 pounds and does are exceedingly small. At one time this deer ranged as far north as Acoma, always on the west side of the Río Grande, and in that pueblo they give it a separate name meaning "water deer"; it is said to have been created at the same time as antelope. In northeastern Arizona, including the Hopi area, there were never any white-tail, although the mule deer, of the race now called *crooki*, were abundant in many parts of the area.[3]

While the white-tails have not done well in population, the mule deer have prospered. In New Mexico, white-tail numbers are stationary at about 18,000 head.[4] In Ligon's big game survey for the year 1926–1927 he estimated that there were 41,000 deer of both kinds in the state, the majority in national forests. At the same time he calculated the desirable populations for various kinds of game, estimating that the state could support 200,000 head of deer.[5] As an illustration of how much of the deer's recent progress is due to human effort, the numbers had risen by 1950 to somewhat above 260,000 head, and by 1964 it consisted of about 300,000 mule deer alone.

One indication of prehistoric relations between Pueblos and deer is provided by the bones excavated from various ruins in Chaco Canyon in northwestern New Mexico, where deer have only recently reappeared, which yielded a great many bones from the past. This pueblo was abandoned during the drought of 1276–1299. According to Judd, "Deer furnished not only hides for clothing but meat for the table, sinew for bow strings, and bone for implements. Hence it is only natural that the mule deer, which frequents upland country, should be conspicuously represented among mammalian remains."[6]

Directly to the south of Chaco Canyon there are ruins on the Zuñi Reservation which were inhabited in 1015 A.D. These were excavated by Roberts who lists the game animal bones found as from mule deer, antelope, and jackrabbit, with the deer bones extensively used for tools, such as awls and daggers made from the ulna.[7] The ruins of Paa-ko, which was abandoned about 1540 A.D., lie over the mountains to the north and east of Albuquerque. Here the "Bones most frequently found were cotton tail, jack rabbit, mule deer and turkey."[8] That the Paa-koans were heavy meat eaters, as compared to other Pueblo groups, is shown by the fact that as much as forty per cent of the materials removed from the various areas during excavation consisted of food bones.

Turning next to the northern Río Grande, the ruins of Riana in the Chama River valley, which was destroyed by burning shortly after 1348 A.D., we find unexpected results. Sixty-eight per cent of the bone remains are from antelope, followed by a small percentage of mountain sheep, a few cottontail, and lastly but two per cent of mule deer bones. Apparently antelope were abundant on the *llanos* nearby, even though this valley is surrounded by mountain chains, and there is a report that they lingered on until late in the nineteenth century. Mule deer must also have been abundant close by, but as they have to be taken singly, antelope were preferred when available.

In Arizona a particularly large number of bones were collected from eleventh- and twelfth-century sites at Winona and Ridge Ruin near Flagstaff. From this large collection it was possible to identify 221 individual animals, which were divided as follows: 97 jackrabbits, 39 cottontails, 30 mule deer, and 3 antelope.[9] Results of a different kind appear from the ruins in Big Hawk Valley, about twenty miles north of Flagstaff, now in Wupatki National Monument. The surrounding area here was covered with a blanket of black ash from the eruption of 1067. Thereafter a number of agricultural groups moved in to take advantage of this soil. The meat bones found were mainly cottontail and prairie dog; antelope were well represented. Deer and mountain sheep, however, occurred rarely.[10]

The implication of game bone finds seems to be that an agricultural people is likely to concentrate on the rabbits that they find nearby during the course of their labor. Then, whether they hunt antelope or deer depends upon the availability of the former animal. If antelope are handy they are preferred, as they can be taken in numbers. There is information from one Hopi ruin which seems to have taken a balanced number of both deer and antelope. Awatovi lies near the First Mesa and was occupied from prehistoric time through the seventeenth century. The following remarks on bone remains of this site were made by Lawrence. "As would be expected, deer and pronghorn were both extensively used before the introduction of domestic animals. There is no evidence that either was preferred. . . . Cranial fragments are relatively scarce, suggesting that the animals were brought from a distance and at least partly butchered where killed."[11] She further notes that these bones became far less numerous after the introduction of sheep and goats, but that they are never entirely absent. Rabbits were used extensively, while prairie dog and porcupine bones were occasional.

The lack of cranial fragments among these finds does not indicate that the heads were left in the fields where butchered, since the ceremonial treatment of the head is a matter of great ritual importance to the Pueblos. The disposal of antelope heads was mentioned in the last chapter. The fact that deer bones equaled antelope in number would seem to indicate that formerly mule deer were common enough in the woods of Black Mesa.

Indian deer hunting shares a number of qualities with the same activity when undertaken by white hunters: the release from the tedium of the normal daily round, the excitement of pursuit, the exercise of special skills, and the final confrontation with the game. There is one great difference, however, in that Indian hunting is throughout surrounded by magical activity. The root of magic is a view of the world that is based on the unity of all life, and as life, in this view, is not confined to the biological world but includes other phenomena of nature as well, there is nothing that may not be linked. Since all of the parts have but one breath any one of them can affect any other, and we find that a stone fetish or even a color may act upon a living animal. Man's role in this animistic world is to utilize these interconnections to influence the course of events. If his approach is rash, the whole system may break down and he will be punished, but if he can arrange his desire to fit into a course of mutual benefits, much good may come to him.

The influence to be drawn from magic is promoted by a number of simple correspondences. Song and talk, which men use in communicating will have a similar effect on the larger world. The system of the six directions, which is the framework of the cosmos, may be called upon to aid with its sets of mountains, colors, animals, and trees, all of which combine to aid the hunter, if he has a good heart. Other powers, such as sex, may be especially directed into channels which will aid the hunt, and even plants and stones have powers that may be called upon. Then too, there are devices: smoke may blind the deer, or bits of turquoise and shell attract him. Another effective way to attract game animals is to imitate them in dances.

While this elaborate panoply of magic aids man in his hunting, it at the same time involves a number of logical extensions which find expression in myth. These have little to do with hunting proper, but nonetheless derive from man's relationships with the animals. Since the magical view is not our own, it will be helpful to discover something of its appearance to a Pueblo Indian. In Don Talayesva's autobiography he tells us that he was born with a special relationship to deer and antelope. He was in tune with them in a remarkable way. "As soon as I was old enough to wander about the village my grandfather suggested that I go out to the Antelope shrine and look for my deer people who were invisible to ordinary human beings." Sometimes he would see these animals change into people, or dream that antelopes lived in the village. When he was five he would wander off to a place where "the spirits of deer and antelope gathered to give birth to their young and to feed on the sunflowers."[12]

When he came home with the stains of sunflowers around his mouth it was noted, as though perfectly natural, that he had of course been feeding with his deer and antelope relatives. No one doubted that he could see these spirit deer and antelope, for the magical power had been granted him by his birth. His power derived from the fact that he was a twin, and twins naturally are related to twinning animals, such as deer and particularly antelope. How delicate the bond may be that is sufficient to establish a magical tie is shown by the fact that Don was not literally a twin; he was not born with a sibling, but only had a faint mark on his back indicating that a sister had been carried with him in the womb.

When associations so slight can be the basis for special powers, it is plain that the Pueblos will be on the lookout for every possible sign of interconnection and for every device that will lend its influence in shaping events. In this respect song is a more powerful variant of speech. Talk is an effective means of communicating, but song has a creative power. Creative deities sing over medicine bundles, and we are told that Thinking Woman brought the mothers of mankind to life this way. When the spirit, Badger, brought the dead maiden to life this act was done by singing over her bones. In mythology the animals themselves do a great deal of singing, and dancing as well, for the two forms of compulsive magic are closely related.

Hunting is but a single instance in which the power of song is used to good advantage. While we think of hunting as almost entirely an act of silence and stealth, the Pueblos are committed to the belief that the game wants to come to their village and that it may be drawn directly to them with songs that call the animals and show them the way. White sums up the attitude of the hunters of Keresan Santa Ana. "There are songs to enable a hunter to locate deer, songs to be sung while tracking a wounded deer, a song to be sung when the hunter first touches the fallen animal, a song to be sung while skinning the deer, while cutting up the carcass, and still another while carrying the deer home."[13]

These songs are not an expression of joyous feeling on the hunter's part, although he very well may feel happy enough, but are an attempt to completely encompass the deer, both when alive and after death, in the ritual power of these songs. Many of the songs will have a ritual orientation in which the singer addresses first one and then another of the directions, calling in toward the center, which is the village of Santa Ana, both the deer and the powers that aid the hunter. Since magic is treated with strict economy it may at the same time serve a second purpose and the clouds that hang about the mountains where the game is hunted are enjoined to return with the game to Santa Ana, that the rain may descend and the rivers begin to flow.

One such hunter's song from Santa Ana invokes both the aid of Gotsa, a spirit gamekeeper and patron of the hunt, as well as the colors of two directions.

> *I am going to Gotsa's home*
> *And ask him for his game.*
>   *Thus I sing.*
> *Let me go to the Blue Land*
> *Where the deer fawns are born*
> *And the clouds hover over them*
>   *And the rain descends.*
> *Let me go to the Yellow Land*
> *Where the antelope fawns are born*
> *And the clouds hover over them*
>   *And the rain descends*
> *And the rivers begin to flow.*

At Santa Ana, and generally elsewhere, blue represents the West and yellow the North, red the South, and white the East. In the case of this particular song the two directions may represent the actual area of the hunt, as we have seen that antelope were once abundant in the Chama valley to the north of Santa Ana and deer would of course be found in the Jemez Mountains to the west and north.

Often, however, the directions may not be literal, since the invocation is for magical encirclement by the colors and the beasts of prey of the directions, who thereby surround the game and force it into the center which is the village. The beasts of prey are Mountain Lion for the North, Bear for the West, Wildcat for the South, and Wolf for the East. Eagle stands at the Zenith and Shrew at the Nadir. In another song the hunter calls upon these beasts in turn to aid him in hunting deer.

> *You are the only mountain lion Shaiyaik, (hunt chief)*
> *You are the only mountain lion Shaiyaik,*
> *There is a middle road to the North,*
> *The deer has taken me along that road,*
> *Now he has left me far behind.*
> *You are the only mountain lion Shaiyaik,*
> *You are the only mountain lion Shaiyaik,*
> *Get ahead of him and stop him.*
> *Bring him back on the middle trail from the North to me,*
> *Bring him back on the middle trail from the North to me,*
> *So I can see him.*

The song is then repeated to each direction, naming the appropriate beast of prey each time, which when the Eagle and the Shrew are included makes a perfect sphere rather than a circle about the village of the hunter.

At Zuñi a hunter sings a song as he offers shell bits, cornmeal, and pollen, scattering these in the deer's tracks.

> *This day*
> *He who holds our roads,*
> *Our sun father,*
> *Has come out standing to his sacred place.*
> *Now that he has passed us on our roads,*
> *Here we pass you on your road.*
> *Divine one,*
> *The flesh of the white corn,*
> *Prayer meal,*
> *Shell,*
> *Corn pollen,*

Here I offer to you.
With your wisdom
Taking the prayer meal,
The shell,
The corn pollen,
This day,
My fathers,
My mother,
In some little hollow,
In some low brush,
You will reveal yourselves to me.
Then with your flesh,
With your living water,
May I sate myself.[14]

For such a song to have full magic power, it must be sung exactly, without varying a word. As an aid to the hunter's memory there are a number of poetic devices used in the native text of the song, which include internal rhymes, alliteration, and the like, but even so it is hard to get any song just right, and we hear in folk tales of hunters who forget their songs and thus have no success.

Talk is closely related to song as a form of compulsive magic. Hunters will recount to one another their past hunting experiences, which is encouraged by the hunt chief, if it is to be a communal hunt, for, "by talking of hunting men 'draw the game toward the pueblo.'" When the Santa Ana Indians go on a communal hunt that may take them into the Jemez or the Sandia mountains for a week or so, another element is introduced. After supper these men sit around the fire telling more stories, or singing hunting songs. "They tell stories about their love affairs, about their sweethearts and mistresses, their conquests in love. This is done 'to give them good luck in hunting.'"

Sexual power, as used for magical purposes, is as reversible as a good raincoat. Here the positive side is worn; this bragging has suggestive magic, just like the talk concerning previous hunts, to bring the game in closer. More often the reverse side is present and continence is invoked as a part of the hunt.[15] The Indians explain this taboo by saying that contact with women is weakening, or that deer and antelope detest the smell of women and babies.

At Isleta a hunter is said to remain continent for a month before he goes on a hunt, which would certainly seem to be an extreme case, violating the normal four-day Pueblo pattern. He also takes a purge of cedar leaves each morning and on leaving admonishes his wife "to plaster the walls, to keep herself very clean, not to scold the children, not to quarrel with the neighbors or gad about among them."[16] As a reward for her care, which is aimed at not disturbing anything at home lest that have the effect of stirring up or scattering the game, she is given the buckskin.

The kinds of magic that have so far been recounted are based on either similarity of human behavior, or that of beasts of prey, to the end desired. There are, in addition, correspondences deriving from plants and stones. Magical plants are used more often in war than on hunts, but at Zuñi the blossoms and roots of te'nastsali are kept by the hunter's fraternity "because it is good medicine for game."[17] Since this plant is eaten by game, prayer plumes are offered to it as a part of the ritual treatment of dead game. At Hopi red gilia is ground up for use as an offering when hunting antelope, as these animals like to feed on it, making gilia powder attractive to them.

Stone fetishes are a fixture in all Pueblo hunting. These are of at least two kinds: large representations of the beasts of prey which are used about altars, and the small personal fetishes which are carried by individual hunters in buckskin pouches. The latter derive their power from having been set in the proximity of the larger fetishes. According to Zuñi theory all animals were of vast size in beginning ages and were hence a great danger to man. The War Twins, sons of the Sun, either touched them, turning most into stone as a protection to mankind, or the same results were obtained when in a fit of anger the Twins set the world ablaze. Some of the animals became the huge rock formations, while others were shriveled to the size of stone fetishes.

Certain animals escaped these catastrophic events and these became the source of present animals, while even those that turned to stone were not actually killed, as their hearts continued to live, thus giving power to the fetish. For hunting deer or elk, the Zuñi prefer a stone resembling a mountain lion. While a natural stone may be used, the common ones are carved from low-grade turquoise, with short legs and ears, and a long tail lying along the back. A small sliver to represent an arrow is usually tied to the back of this fetish. After the kill these fetishes are dipped into the warm blood of the heart of the slain animal to "feed" the fetish.[18]

Yet another method is used for drawing in the deer. At Isleta, after the harvest is over, the hunt chief holds a ceremony which he begins by going into retreat for four days. At noon on the fourth day, "He blows smoke into his medicine bowl, and he smokes toward the mountains, to blind the deer."[19] The chief then whistles, which will draw in the deer. At the actual leave-taking of the hunter, the chief will sing and again blow smoke in the direction of the hunt. Correspondingly, when the hunter sees a deer he will act as if blind, put down the offering he has brought from the hunt chief, and smoke to all the directions.

Magic does not cease as soon as the deer is shot. At Zuñi the last breath of the dying animal is inhaled and a prayer is addressed to A'wonawil'ona, the Zuñi high god and creator.[20] The words are freely translated as, "This day I give you my thanks for your rains, your seeds, and the mysteries of life which I inhale." The hunter then digs a hole, which represents the entrance into the underworld, into which he places *klo'o*, which is a mixture of micaceous hemitite, ground abalone shell, and turquoise, to which corn pollen has been added. "We did this to get deer again easily."[21] These rites are performed to make the deer live again, which is also the rationale for smothering the beast when possible: that keeps the breath, which is the life principle shut up inside the animal so that his life will not escape and drift away.

How literally these magical practices are interpreted even at present is illustrated by an account from Isleta. Deer meat is often required for ceremonial purposes, and one February not too long ago it was found that no venison was available for a ritual, so the hunt chief was consulted. He first made a circle of pollen, leaving a gap toward the east. Then, waving a feather in circular fashion as he talked, he concluded with imitative calls of mountain lion and wolf. "He told one of us to open the door. He began to sing. In came a big deer with big horns." While Wildcat Boy, as the hunt chief is called at Isleta, kept on singing he motioned for the door to be closed. "The deer walked into the circle of pollen." Then the chief closed the gap in the pollen circle, tapped the deer gently on the forehead and it dropped down dead.[22] This story was repeated by an eyewitness.

One of the most effective forms of imitative magic is to impersonate the animal desired in a mimetic dance. These game dances are a ceremonial adaptation of actual hunting practice in which the hunters wear the antlered head and skin of the deer. If the wind is blowing toward the hunter, game animals will often pay no attention to a horned figure on the horizon. With some skill and a bit of luck a hunter so disguised may creep in close enough for a kill. Hunters "stalked deer in the guise once familiar at Zuñi and elsewhere—with their face and arms painted yellow and white and the hide and antlers of a deer over their head and stooping back."[23]

When the Zuñi needed venison for a ceremony, they were required by the logic of their belief to make certain that it was killed by smothering, rather than an arrow. To assure this outcome they used traps somewhat on the order of the brush corrals built to take antelope, except that in this instance gaps were left along the runway and pits were dug at each opening. These were then covered so that the deer, sighting freedom, would try to escape, only to fall into the trap where he could be dispatched in proper ceremonial fashion.

After placing prayer-sticks to the gods in each pit, two hunters are sent out to start the deer. These men have painted arms and faces while the head is concealed under that of an antlered buck, tied on with thongs. "In this dress the two huntsmen imitate as closely as possible, even to browsing, the game they would catch."[24] When these or similar hunting methods are translated into ceremonialism we have the famous deer dances of the Río Grande pueblos in which mimesis of great elaboration is displayed.

In deer or game dances, which also include representations of antelope, elk, and bison, all of the hunt elements are summed up for the benefit of the entire population, many of whom have no role in actual hunting. These dances are usually held at mid-winter, sometime between Christmas and King's Day on January 6. The first to appear in the plaza are the singers, who build a "hunt fire" and begin the songs that call in the game. The arrival of those representing the animals can be a most moving sight as their shadows appear on the ridges of surrounding hills in the first light of a very cold dawn.

At Taos, where the dance is held in conjunction with the Saint's Day on December 25, the entrance is particularly effective as only the antlers appear over the surrounding wall when the dancers enter the pueblo. Two files of deer dancers are led in by watchmen. Behind these follow the two Deer chiefs in white kilts of the Hopi style; their bodies and antlers are entirely whitened. Then follow the deer, with bits of spruce in their mouths, antelope, and a few bison. Lastly two wildcats and two mountain lions enter.

In the plaza the dancers are joined by two Deer Mothers, spirits who lead the two columns of animals. These mothers are so sacred that none may touch them during the dance and simulated hunt, for which reason two members of the Big Hail society hover about them throughout the ceremony. The

"Deer," who include both aged impersonators and the youngest members of the pueblo able to perform, are directed in their dance formations by the Deer Mothers who use gourd rattles for the purpose.

The impersonators of wildcat and mountain lion act as the hunters in this dance, laying their hands on some chosen "deer," which signals to the members of the Black Eyes society, who have been clowning, and one of these then shoots a little arrow into the hanging pelt or head of the selected deer. Then he must throw the game over his shoulder and run off a way, which depends upon the weight of the victim. Meanwhile the spectators try to get a solid hold on the hunter and if they are successful the latter must drop his deer. After more dancing and hunting the Black Eyes give the other dancers bits of raw venison. In the evening there is a brief ritual of feeding the deer heads that have been used, by rubbing meal on the head and giving it pollen.[25]

At Taos the deer dancers are completely covered by the animal's pelt, so that all in all they seem to be very realistic representations of deer. In other pueblos the costume worn in deer dances becomes progressively more stylized. At San Ildefonso the dancer walks with two short sticks representing the forelegs of the animal, while wearing only the antlers. In place of the pelt he has a short feathered cape. At San Juan only the antlers remain to suggest the deer, while among the Hopi an antlered helmet mask, with squash blossom ears and a spruce collar is worn. This dancer is naked to the waist and wears the very undeer-like fox pelt for a tail. In short, he no longer represents a deer of the wild, but is a kachina spirit deer.[26]

Bringing in the deer can be thought of in two ways: most simply as the hunter bringing in game, or more complexly as a spirit who brought all of the deer for the people's use. While the first order of relationship is straightforward, the second is not, for the reason that to an agricultural people the necessity for game is something that must be explained or rationalized. Both the Zuñi and the Keres of Cochiti have myths and ceremonies in which a Bringer of Deer kachina appears. At Zuñi it is Saiyatasha, or Long Horn kachina, who sends the deer.

Saiyatasha's long horn indicates that he brings long life to all of his people. He has a mask and collar made of elk hide, a buckskin shirt and leggings, the latter white, and he wears a fawn-skin quiver over his right shoulder. In his right hand he carries a rattle of deer scapulae, while his left hand grasps bow and arrows and many prayer-sticks. Saiyatasha sends the little deer kachina called Natsiko. The latter, who stands for the deer dancers elsewhere, may appear at any time, for it is said at the end of his myth, "any time the kachinas go there [Zuñi] for the mixed dance you may go with them if you wish."[27] Natsiko has a black nose, antlers, and a green face painted to resemble a young deer. At the back of his head are eagle tail-feathers and owl feathers that are placed there to bring rain.

According to this myth, the Zuñi at first had no big game, but lived on corn, wild seeds, and rabbits. After surveying the situation, Saiyatasha spoke to Pautiwa, telling him that it was hard for the Zuñi to live mainly on corn. "They do not look well because they always eat only one kind of food. What do you think? Our people ought to have fresh meat . . . especially on their feast days they should have something to make them feel better. Now they have only little animals and they last only one meal. What do you think about their having deer?"

The chief of the gods objects on the grounds that the Zuñi have never asked for deer in their prayers. They did, however, know about the existence of deer, since they were mentioned in songs. To remedy this the gods made them think about deer and then to imagine creating one, bit by bit, in song. So they sang, "Now we have all the clothing of the deer; here is a deer horn; here is a deer ear," and so on until they had mentioned all of its parts.

The gods then call in this deer, "who took off his skin and turned into a person," which is to say he became the little deer kachina. Natsiko is then told to go to Zuñi so that the people, "will have good luck with your flesh and find deer everywhere."

They also say that someone will pretend to kill him, but that like the kachina he will not really die, but come to life again. This statement refers not only to Natsiko but also to the real deer whom he represents. At the same time it is decided that he shall carry a white cane and lean on it, which is a recollection of the realistic deer dancers and ultimately of hunters.

At the Keresan pueblo of Cochiti it is Heluta, or Heruta, who brings the deer.[28] Here the story has even more of an agricultural bias, as this kachina raises deer like corn. "Heluta told them, 'My seed is dewclaws. Whenever you kill a deer, do not throw these away, because they are my seed. Watch me and you will see my field.' " He then took a cluster of dewclaws, dug holes and put them one by one in the earth. "When he had finished, the first he had planted were already coming up above the ground. The people watched the first small antlers grow until they were full size and the deer ran off to the mountains. Heluta called them all together and took them to Shipap where he shut them up. When they were mature he let them out in the mountains, 'So he is the father of all the deer.' "[29]

Heluta is also the supernatural father of all the kachinas, who are rainmakers, and as their father he leads in any line of masked dancers. There is nothing deerlike about his mask, but he does wear a buckskin. His account of the way to raise deer came about as a result of a contest in which the people of Cochiti challenged everyone to a display of food crops. First they proudly exhibited rooms full of different colored corn, melons, and other good things. Then, "When they had looked at everything Heluta said, 'Is this all?' " As they said that it was he replied, " 'Now it is my turn to show you how I live.' He opened his little fawn-skin bag and took out a piece with two or three kernels sticking to it. 'This is what I live by.' "

Naturally the people laughed at him, but he said, "Wait. You will see which one makes the best living; you by all your work, or the man who has the power himself." He then went back to Shipap, the entrance to the underworld, and as punishment for the people's hubris sends four rainless years. Since their crops have dried up and they are now starving, they send a fly as a messenger, but Heluta pulls out his tongue—therefore flies only buzz nowadays.

Next a hummingbird is sent with a message. "The people need you. They want you to forgive what they have done to you. . . . Now they have learned that it is by your power that they live." At this Heluta repents and says that he will come back, but that first they must hunt and bring him a deer from the north side of the mountains, where the sun has never shone upon it. After they bring him such a deer he returns to the village, planting the dewclaws for their increase.

As is so often the case, the rite that this myth justifies is not in exact correspondence with it, as the focus is on the increase of crops rather than game. Heluta brings the shiwanna, the rainmaking masked dancers from the underworld, to dance for the people of Cochiti. To make the ceremony realistic, a ditch is dug at night from which the dancers will seem to arrive. A tree is planted in this ditch, possibly in recollection of his having formerly brought in deer, as trees are often planted about the plaza for deer dances. First, this spirit comes to ask the people if they want him to bring the dancers, then a clown pulls up the tree, letting the dancers emerge from the trench as though from the underworld. Next the leading dancer—or possibly Heluta himself—points to the line of shiwanna and says: "My sons and daughters, think of nothing else but of our *yaya* [mothers] the shiwanna. It is they who give us health, life, abundant harvests of corn, wheat, watermelons, etc. Be careful to think of nothing else."[30]

The kinds of magic that we have been following are all closely related to the single purpose of hunting and may be presumed to have originated in that activity, but there are more complex kinds of magic in which deer figure. Hunt magic has a peculiar viability in that the other end of the relationship also has a life of its own. The animal world has desires of its own, as well as the powers it lends to man, and in the exchange of influences a spiritual alternating current is set up which accounts for the magical qualities that animals so often display in myths and stories.

One of the most interesting products of this interrelationship is the transformation of men into beasts and of beasts into men. Animals, as we know, are much like men; often they merely take off their skins, which are their clothes, and become ordinary humans. Some transformations are little more than story devices, but behind these is a vista of witchcraft. One who is ill or in difficulties may suspect, or know, that his troubles are caused by the magical power of another used for an evil end.

Deer often figure in these stories of witchcraft. The Tewa tell a number of stories in which Olivella Flower is married to Yellow Corn Girl—a stock figure in this case—who is a witch. Every day he would go hunting and every night he would bring home a deer. Every day his wife would make wafer bread, which is the proper food for hunters, but she would feed him only gruel, saving the better food for a witches' gathering at night. After he is asleep she takes out her real eyes, places a skeleton, or two black corn ears, beside her husband and repairs to the witches' kiva.

Deer may appear in two ways in these stories, either metaphorically, "Here is your deer," meaning "Here is your meat," or more literally when the witch actually takes the form of a deer. When the witches see Olivella Flower they say, "This is our deer. Tonight we will eat him up." Fortunately Spider Woman warns him in time. "Oh my boy. . . . They are going to kill you today when you go up the mountain. They will send a big deer, but it will not be a real deer, but a witch." With Spider Woman's aid he kills it and appears before the expectant witches. "Olivella Flower brought the big deer and threw it down into the kiva. 'There is your deer! Catch him!'"[31]

Since there is always this possibility that an ordinary looking deer may be a witch, or a person bewitched, a certain anxiety is aroused in connection with eating venison. While the fear has not given rise to any actual taboos, it does find expression in tales. Two from Taos illustrate this point. The first story is based upon the possibility that the deer one kills may somehow be a close relative, a difficulty which the tale unravels and rationalizes.

Little Dirt is one of the Pueblo waifs who are also semispirits, but he has actual standing in that hunters pray to him for luck, despite the fact that he lives under refuse in the corner. Little Dirt's grandmother taught him the tracks of all the animals. First he tracks and kills a rabbit, which is mysteriously cooked for him, then he kills a big buck. It transpires that the cooking has been done by a doe. "Before you go," she says, "I want you to come with me. I am your wife. I want you to see the children that have been born from you."

Little Dirt is led to a trapdoor under some soapweed and there he finds two little deer who call him father. Then mother deer warns that the people will be dangerous to him, as well as to these deer children, whom he is to save when the people come out to hunt. Everyone will get a deer, but the two little ones will run up to their father and he is to take them home.

When Little Dirt goes home the people threaten to kill him if they do not get a deer on the following day's hunt, so he reveals the whereabouts of the deer. The hunters each bring home a deer, but Little Dirt manages to save his two deer children. His problems are not over, however, as the envious people immediately call him to the kiva where a grim proposition is made. "Sit down in the middle!" they tell him. "Tomorrow morning we are going to have an around the world (long distance) race. If we beat you, we are going to kill you and your children and grandmother. If you beat us, you may kill us. We will start just as the sun rises."

These people, it seems are "a bunch of witches," which is a transformation made so that the entire population will not suffer when the race is lost to the deer boys, and lose it they do. The witch racers are big raw-boned men, who change into hawks as soon as the race is begun. The deer boys resort to magic tricks, such as causing a big rain—deer are always rain bringers—which wets the hawks' wings and thus equalizes the race. "The foot of the little Deer boy was bleeding. 'Try for the sake of our father and mother!' Now they had to run back as human boys." After the deer boys win, the envious people and the hawk boys are killed. Then the story takes a neat twist which establishes when it is all right to kill the deer.

"They went to their house and said, 'Now, we shall live without fear of the envious people. Now you are little deer and will live in the mountains and I am Little Dirt and will live in the corner, and whoever wants to be a good hunter he will address me. I will stay here to be asked.'"[32]

Thus the doubt about killing deer is resolved by placing the hunt in the charge of this minor spirit to whom one must make application. Since Little Dirt is married to a doe and as the deer are his children, he knows who the real deer are. But the anxiety lingers on and we find another tale where the only point is to express the fear that the deer one eats may be a human being.

A pretty maid marries a witch boy who causes her to fall ill and die. The witches dig her up, taking the body to the boy's house. "The witch chief rolled a wheel over her, and she came to life and said, 'Oh, I am so tired!' The people said, 'Hurry up, roll the wheel again!' He rolled it. Then she turned into a deer, and they shot her with arrows, and the women who came in had big bowls to cook the meat, after men cut it up." A little girl, who happened to observe this evil work, went home and warned her mother. "When a woman came into their house with meat, she threw it at her and said, 'You cannibal! I would not eat that, you eat it yourself.'"[33]

Transformations do not necessarily have such unpleasant results; one may merely be changed into a deer, then back into a human being again. Presumably such an experience would justify a special position, or indicate special knowledge on the part of the individual involved. In the Tewa village of Tesuque they tell a story about the son of a Taos chief who went hunting, but forgot to take along any water. When he stopped to drink from a spring he was immediately transformed into a deer, quite possibly a "water deer." His hunting companion reported to the chief, who suspects that the son has been killed in the mountains and threatens to kill all the people of Taos unless the son returns.

The youth's grandmother gives the companion a magic reed filled with water. After waiting at the spring he shoots the deer as it comes to drink, then gives it the water from the reed. Thereupon the deer becomes a man again, by merely taking off his deer hide. Before returning to the world of men he must undergo a period of isolation for four days, a rite which we will meet again. "He took off the hide, he became a man again. He went to Taos. They put him in a place where they never made a fire, where there was no smell of smoke. He stayed four days."[34]

That men can change into deer and back again has its parallel in the fact that a deer can change from one life into another, if they are only given the proper rites after they have been killed. A myth which involves both of these transformations at once is told by the Tewa who live in the Hopi country. Hence the myth may reflect either Tewa or Hopi practice, possibly both. This myth, Deer Boy, very much resembles the myth of Antelope Boy, which explained the clan of that name at Acoma, but here the purpose is quite different.

The daughter of the Crier chief at Walpi was a very reserved girl who never took part in the dances. Despite her reticence she was visited one day by a young man who, although unknown to her, was the son of the sister of the Town Chief; he would thus be next in line of succession. Then one day in February a rabbit hunt was called in which girls were to take part. Whenever a man would kill a rabbit, a girl would run up to him and take this game. After a time this girl could no longer keep up with the others and, falling back, she delivered a baby. Not knowing what to do with it she left it in the grass, then rejoined the hunters.

By and by a coyote came along, heard the baby crying, picked it up and carried it in his mouth as far as a spring. As he was by then tired he left the baby and went off to tell his grandmother.

"At that place lived a woman who was a deer, and she found the child and took him to her house. There was high grass growing there and that was her door. She took away the grass and there was a hole in the ground to her kiva. The deer woman had lots of milk."

As the deer boy grew he played with his brothers until he became strong and a good runner, but one day a hunter found a strange track, so the next day a large group of both men and girls set out on a combination rabbit and deer hunt. The deer woman told the boy about this hunt: "If anybody catches you, it will be your father. Your mother is coming too. If your father does not catch you, run to your mother and say 'My mother.' " When the hunters saw a boy running with the deer they were much surprised and this surprise grew when he ran up to the girl, embracing her and calling her "mother."

After recounting these experiences he tells his parents that the deer woman had said he should be placed in "a room without window or door where nobody can look in. If anyone looks in before four days, I will go back to my mother," meaning the deer woman. So they locked him up and counted the days. "On the fourth day about sundown the mother of the boy said, 'It is time for me to look in where my son is.'

"About midnight there was a big noise up the ladder. Grandmother said, 'There is a big noise. Did anyone of you look into the room? 'Yes,' said the mother. 'I looked in through a crack. It was sundown, and I thought we could look.' " The next morning the grandfather went up to look, and there in the middle of the floor stood a big deer. "He went down and began to make feather-strings for him. Somebody called out for the people to come. So they all came with feather-strings and meal. Grandmother went up and opened the door. The deer began to run. 'Grandchild, do not run. I am going to tie something on your horn.' The grandfather led him by the horns and the people came up and tied their feather-strings to both horns."

Deer Boy then ran north to his deer mother and his brothers who were waiting for him. "Then all of them went to the mountains. 'Hereafter we shall live in the mountains,' said Deer woman. So they went west to the San Francisco Mountains."[35] These mountains, in addition to being the habitat of real deer, are also the spirit home of both deer and kachinas. The spirits of deer that the Hopi kill go there to live for a time, if their horns have been properly decorated with strands of prayer-feathers, and are then born again as the kind of deer we see and hunt.

In Pueblo thinking there is a very close relationship between kachina dancers and deer, since both of them are rainmakers. We have seen how the hunter prays to the spirits of the directions that they send the double benefits of game and storm clouds to make the rivers flow. These gods and deer share the same spirit homes in the mountains. As a result of these identifications it is not altogether suprising to find that one of the most complex transformations results when a kachina is killed. He becomes a deer.

Why a kachina, who is a god, should be killed at all raises some interesting questions. Is it an instance of a "dying god," a type of fertility spirit? Does it, as Bunzel thought, imply a ritual sacrifice of human beings at some past date in Pueblo history? Before these questions can be answered we will have to examine some specific cases of kachina becoming deer and the rites which stand behind these myths.

Parsons says quite definitely that, "When Zuñi kachina die, they turn into deer." Benedict likewise says that, "The kachina when they are killed become deer, therefore in this tale the usual gathering of the kachinas in Kachina Village is made a gathering of deer."[36] There are at least three individual kachinas who as a part of their myths are killed and then undergo transformations into deer. These may be considered in the ascending order of their importance.

The first is Atoshle, who is sometimes called Suyuki as she utters that word as her call. She wears coarse, grey hair with eagle-down in it and has a white-spotted, black mask. She carries a stick which she shakes, and a basket in which she puts children, for she is a cannibal woman. "Even though she was evil she was a kachina." In actual practice the Atoshle kachina is proscribed from touching babies or children, lest she frighten them to death as happened in a tale.

In myth there is no such inhibition and the theoretical role is acted out in full. The story of the Rabbit Huntress contains a number of elements and is also found outside Zuñi, but we shall confine our attention to this girl's experience with Atoshle. One day while the maid was on a most successful hunt, having killed a deer as well as twelve rabbits, she retired to a cave to cook her game. "She was still eating when she heard Atoshle calling in the distance. Atoshle was calling, 'I smell rabbits cooking. I smell a human being.' "

The huntress is forced by this ogress to hand out her rabbits, one by one, then Atoshle asks for her woman's garments which are also handed out piecemeal and eaten in the same order by the kachina. At the moment when Atoshle is using her crook in an effort to catch and eat the girl herself, the War Twins arrive and make short work of the kachina. "They let fly their arrows, and she fell, a deer."[37] They then gutted her and retrieved the game. There may be no significance in her transformation, other than the general rule that kachinas when killed become deer, for there is another tale in which she pursues fawns and is killed by being tossed from one deer's antlers to another until dead, at which point she does not become a deer.

A second group of kachinas, that are reported to turn into deer when killed, has a ceremonial role of importance. They appear in a myth entitled, The War Twins Obtain Ceremonial Objects, indicating a more serious narrative than the light-hearted tale of the Rabbit Huntress. The Saiyathlia kachinas are four in number and appear at various times to exorcise by whipping. Sometimes they may be called in to cure nightmare, but more importantly they always appear at the Winter Solstice ceremony to dance for the old year, and again to perform the ritual whipping at the tribal initiation.

In appearance these kachinas are rather awesome, as the

mask has a large mouthful of teeth made of corn husks; it is covered with coarse, white horsehair. They wear two blue horns, a collar of coyote skin and, at such times as they are dangerous, they come wrapped up in large white buckskins. Their role is mixed, as they take away the bad luck of the old year, and at dawn they kindle a new-fire for the coming year. On the lighter side they also appear, for good luck, at the beginning of a rabbit hunt.

Apparently the Saiyathlia kachinas also have powerful rain-making objects—lightning frames, arrows, and thunder stones —since the stated objective of the Twins in the myth is to get these objects in order to cause a great rain. To begin with, the Twins are looking for eagle feathers with which to fleche their arrows. In order to get to the aerie of the eagles they kill two fawns, hide in the skins and wait for the eagles to carry them up.

After they get the feathers the War Twins want to reach the home of the Saiyathlia, which is called Heshoktakwi and is a dangerous place. They arrive there during the night while these kachinas are initiating four little boys. The Twins join in the ceremony, but are whipped so hard that they die. "Then the Saiyathlia brought out the stone knife to cut off their arms and legs to put into the pot for their little newly initiated Saiyathlia to eat." These boys ate the meat, but the voices of the Twins were still alive. The kachinas joined in eating the meat, but voices began to come from all parts of the room, including the yucca blades with which they were whipped.

In time the kachinas began to sneeze, until from their bodies the Twins appear with the sneezes. "The Ahaiyate [War Twins] caught up their bows and arrows and shot the Saiyathlia, and they turned into deer."[38] These two then find the "rain-making things," stuff a big buck with twigs and leaves, and ask their grandmother to beat it until she is exhausted. They then "play their rain-making game," causing a great flood. While all of the elements in this myth sound as if they are derived from ritual, it is not possible to say how the parts are fitted together. It is evident that whipping the initiates brings rain, or is a rain ritual, but whether or not that result is related to the fact that the whipping kachinas become deer is uncertain.

The third kachina is one that we have met already as the bringer of Little Deer, Natsiko. Saiyatasha's role is open to closer examination, as he appears in the highly important Shalako. This very complex ceremony will be discussed here only in so far as it relates to deer, an important qualification since the reader may gather that it is merely, or principally, an elaborate hunt ceremony.[39] Like any major ceremony, the Shalako combines a number of ideas, and these are subject to various interpretations. For one thing, it is a harvest home and feast for the living, while at the same time at least one night among the fourteen days is devoted to the dead. On, " 'shalako night,' the belief is general that the spirits of the dead are actually present,"[40] or as Stevenson was told, "They will see you, but you will not see them; they will not be in the flesh, but in the ghost self."[41]

The Shalako kachinas who give the ceremony its name are the most impressive of Zuñi spirits, since they tower several feet above ordinary mortals. This great height is achieved by means of a device which Stevenson calls an effigy; it is a structure resembling a hoopskirt with a mask on top, so built that the impersonator can step inside, grasp the central pole and hoist both mask and cape above him. He and the effigy then resemble a great masked kachina. The mask has a large, upward-curving horn on each side of the head and a beaklike snout of a nose, causing some to speculate that he might be a giaint eagle connected wth the sun.

The Shalako itself is preceded by a year-long series of preparatory rites, beginning shortly after the solstice and continuing until the Shalako proper is held during the first weeks of December. Since our interest stems from the killing of kachinas, and the resulting transformation of these spirits into deer, we may begin our account at the end of the ceremony. After their many public appearances, these "couriers of the gods," return to Kothluwalawa, the home of the gods in a lake at the junction of the Zuñi and Little Colorado rivers. Stevenson, who seems to have been the only white person allowed to see this retreat, describes the events.

"All of the Sha'lako now appear on the field at once, running as rapidly as possible. . . . The Sha'lako are followed by a number of gaily dressed young men, and when these gods are a distance from the village . . . they are pursued by the young men. When a Sha'lako is caught, the bearer of the effigy throws it upon the ground amid great excitement. The one who catches the effigy exclaims: "I have killed the deer." He sprinkles it with meal, praying that he may be successful in the hunt. The catching of the effigy is indicative of success in the coming hunt, and great efforts are made to get ahead of one another to capture the so-called deer."[42]

It would seem then that the mask and its attached apparatus definitely represent a deer. Parsons adds the further relevant information that when the young men strike the Shalakos, the effigies are then placed on the ground with the heads facing the east in the same way that the dead, both human and deer, are placed.[43] It is in connection with this closing ritual that Bunzel detects a sinister note, and indeed those familiar with Frazer's *Golden Bough* will at once be struck with the similarity of the opening passages and the Zuñi rite. Frazer describes a priest of Diana, who guarded a grove sacred to the goddess, until a candidate priest succeeded in slaying him. There are a number of parallels, including the importance of fire in the ceremony, so it will be well to let Bunzel state the case in her own words.

"There are hints in ritual that ideas of human sacrifice may lie but a little way beneath the surface in the concept of masked impersonation. The great ceremony of the Sha'lako opens with the appointment of a group of impersonators of the gods. For a year they are set apart. They do no work of their own. In the case of the Saiyatasha party they even assume the names of the gods whom they are to impersonate. At the end of their term of office they have elaborate ceremonies in which they appear in mask; that is, in the regalia of death. After all-night ceremonies they depart for the home of the dead. 'Everyone cries when they go.' ... The final ceremony of the departure of the sha'lako is especially suggestive of this interpretation. When out of sight of the village the Sha'lako are pursued by young men. When caught they are thrown down and killed, and the mask is treated like the body of a fallen deer."[44]

The implications of human sacrifice in the descriptions of events in the Shalako ceremony seem to me to be exceedingly slight or nonexistent. All kachina masks represent spirits who live at the home of the gods, which is also the home of the dead, but to call them the "regalia of death" is to ignore the positive and life-orientated aspects of kachinas—and these predominate. It is through the rainmaking powers of the dead that the kachinas become related to them. On the other hand, there can be no doubt that the ritual killing of a god is involved at the time of the Shalakos' departure. What this particular instance means I hope to set forth presently.

Meanwhile, some mention should be made of Frazer's theories concerning dying gods. He examined a number of myths relating to Tammuz, Adonis, Osiris, and Dionysus, to name a few, and discerned a pattern behind the myths, based upon the annual death and rebirth of vegetation, the death of the god signifying the closing of the year, or in some climates the burying of seed in the earth. The death is often violent and sometimes brought about by the worshippers, who tear the victim into pieces and devour him. There was an even earlier pattern, according to Frazer, in which the god was killed in animal form; bear, stag, fox, or other animal. This was thought to derive from a time when the god was still in animal form and had not yet developed anthropomorphic characteristics.

As an instance of this stage he cites Dionysus; "The Bacchanals of Thrace wore horns in imitation of their god. According to the myth, it was in the shape of a bull that he was torn to pieces by the Titans; and the Cretans, when they acted the sufferings and death of Dionysus, tore a live bull to pieces with their teeth."[45] Some of Frazer's sources here are very late, as in the case of Nonnus, from the fifth century A.D., and gods also die for other reasons; both Apollo and Zeus had tombs but they were hardly vegetation spirits.

Returning to the Zuñi material at hand, we have already seen that the War Twins were eaten by initiates, although when their voices refused to die, they were sneezed back into existence from within the body of Long Horn, who brings the deer and flagellates those who reach manhood. Whipping is a rite that promotes growth, either of crops or of human beings, and it is for this reason that it is used on initiates. The reborn Twins then whip the stuffed effigy of a deer, promoting not only rain, but a great flood.

Let us next follow the deer-hunting theme through the Shalako ceremony. In the olden days, at least, this rite was preceded by a deer hunt, for there is to be feasting for all, outsiders as well as the Zuñi, and meat as well as a great store of corn breads are necessary. The first step in the ceremony is the appearance in town of the Little Fire God, Shulawitsi, whom we have met in the Badger chapter. He is led in, to light the ceremonial fires, by his ceremonial father who wears no mask, but has a dressed deerskin hanging from his shoulders. That the fire he now lights is comparable to a hunt-fire is shown by Shulawitsi's dress: "A fawn skin filled with seeds, supported by a strap over his shoulder, hangs in front; two cottontail rabbits with a fringe of rats (Neotoma), which are procured by Shulawitsi's father and paternal uncles, hung over the back."[46]

In Stevenson's day he was met first by three He'hea kachinas, but these did not come when Parsons observed the ceremony in 1915. "I was told that they only came out when a clansman had killed a deer for *shulawitsi*. The *hehe'a* carried it."[47] The next to arrive are Saiyatasha and his party. Saiyatasha, Long Horn, is second only to the Shalako kachinas in importance. Of this group Parsons says: "Some of the kachina are possessed of features of the hunt: Long Horn who sends the deer; the two kachina in his group who represent trees, perhaps the forest home of deer."[48]

According to myth, Saiyatasha's call, Weanna-hu! hu! hu!, will protect a hunter from bears, which must have been a useful service in earlier times. "Now if the hunter is out and is frightened, if he will make the call of father *sayatasha*, the bear will hear and run away to his home in *shipapulemi*."[49] This kachina is accompanied by "warrior" kachinas who wear white buckskins hanging from the waist and who carry small deer antlers in their left hands.[50] At the rising of the morning star—a hunting as well as war spirit—Saiyatasha and the pekwin, deputy to the Sun, repair to a rooftop where they hold a rite and offer prayers.

The clowns, who are fertility spirits with a zest, play a relatively minor part in this ceremony, but when they come they are dressed in deerskins and they have a fawnskin with its head attached thrown over one shoulder. This skin has been sewn up to form a pouch in which they carry seeds or wafer bread; if it is the latter this is given as an offering to the dead. While this short list of elements related to deer and deer hunting has been selective, when it is joined with the final act of killing the Shalako effigy and treating it like a slain deer, we see that a central strand in the ceremony is somehow based upon the hunting and killing of deer. Since the Shalako ceremony is considered by the Zuñi themselves to be the most important of all those held during the year, how do we interpret these facts?

The question that arises at this point is why a predominantly agrarian people places such an emphasis on deer hunting in rituals that mark the close of their agricultural year. Certainly the Shalako impersonators who are touched and ritually killed are not in themselves symbolic vegetation spirits. To explain this seeming discrepancy we must go back to Heluta, who planted the dewclaws of deer in the Cochiti myth. He, it will be remembered, is the same spirit who led in the shiwanna, the masked rainmaking spirits, and "It is they who give us health, life and abundant harvests of corn." Nor should we forget the Santa Ana hunter who sang to the directions, to "the Blue land where the deer fawns are born," who ended his song with;

And the clouds hover over them
And the rain descends
And the rivers begin to flow.

Bringing in the deer—killing it—is associated in the Pueblo mind with bringing in the clouds, who are the collective spirits of the dead, and they are brought in from the home of gods and ghosts. These clouds that come to the center, the village and its fields, bring the rains that feed the life-giving crops. And so a cycle is completed and another transformation made from life to death to life again. When it comes around to the full at the end of each year, all of the forces involved are called together for a great feast: the living, the dead, and the gods. Since the deer and its hunting has also played a part in keeping the cycle spinning, its role too is noted. Immediately after the Shalako, the Molawia ceremony is held at Zuñi to memorialize the flight and return of the Corn Maidens and this might be considered the agricultural adjunct of the Shalako.

There is a Zuñi myth in which the deer were once locked up, because both the black gods and the white gods had called a hunt in the same place at the same time. When the winning group locked up the deer in a corral there was not only no game, but there was no rain either. Shitsukia finds out where the rain has gone and he knows that the deer must be nearby. So there he plants his seeds, finds the impounded game and is thereby able to dress himself in deerskin clothing and moccasins.[51] In short, the deer provide all of the necessities for civilized living: clothing, meat, and water for cultivated fields of corn, squash, and melons.

It is no wonder then that it is good luck to "kill" the Shalako effigy, so that he will turn into a deer, and it should be evident by this time that there is no need to search for sinister explanations. Touching and laying out the Shalako effigy brings good luck to the hunter in the coming year, so that he may again bring in deer, with all the attendant benefits of such a hunt. The deer, it is true, is sacrificed, but not as a human surrogate, and in this optimistic view the animal too will be renewed and live again.

87

Chapter IV

BISON, OR AMERICAN BUFFALO

In range the bison was only on the fringe of the Pueblo world; these animals occurred in the mountains east of Taos, and the extinct pueblos on the eastern side of the Manzano Mountains probably overlooked these great beasts grazing on the plains, but the present Pueblos lived outside the bison's range. Nevertheless, so great an animal had an impact outside its actual range, as is shown by the fact that it was kept in Montezuma's menagerie, far south of its range. In the next two decades the Spaniards heard much more of this animal and of the seven cities in the north which were named Cibola, after the great cows that were thought to graze in the area. These cities of Cibola were occupied by the ancestors of the Zuñi Indians of today, who still live in a nearby town. Fray Marcos de Nizza made an expedition into northern Mexico in 1538 and there heard more of the New World buffalo from the Opatas, who were accustomed to trading shells and parrot feathers to the Zuñi in exchange for buffalo hides, which they of course got from the region farther east and north, either by hunting expeditions or by trade.

Fray Marcos obviously did not get a look at these beasts, as his fanciful account demonstrates. "In this valley they brought to me a hide one and one half times larger than the skin of a cow; they told me it belonged to an animal that had but one horn on his forehead; this horn bends down to the breast and then rises in a straight point, which gives so much strength to the animal that there is no object, no matter how hard it may be, which it cannot break."[1] Strong these animals certainly are and in a charging herd unstoppable, but they are neither rhinos nor unicorns.

When the "cities" of the Zuñi Indians were discovered by the Spaniards, there were no buffalo nearby, but buffalo hides and articles made from them were abundant. For war there were buffalo shields made from hide with the hair scraped off and figures of animals painted on the bare surface. Helmets were also made of this heavy hide and toward the end of the century Espejo reports that buckskin moccasins had soles of buffalo hide, while buffalo robes were much prized and sometimes the skins were actually worn as garments. Some idea of where the source of these hides was located is supplied by Castañeda, the narrator of the Coronado expedition. While the Spaniards were at Zuñi a group of Indians arrived from the pueblo of Pecos: "They brought a present of tanned hides and shields and headpieces, which were very gladly received. . . . They described some cows which, from a picture that one of them had painted on his skin, seemed to be cows, although from the hides this did not seem possible, because the hair was wooly and snarled so that we could not tell what sort of skins they had."[2]

These Pueblo Indians from Pecos were living on the edge of New Mexico's buffalo country and made frequent hunting expeditions into the plains. Even at this early date the eastern slope of the Sangre de Cristo was the western limit of buffalo range. In the first part of the nineteenth century two of the beasts were reported to have been killed at Santo Domingo, but these must have been strays. In the drainage of the Pecos, bison were abundant, but by the beginning of the seventeenth century —possibly before—hunting there was dangerous because of other warlike tribes who made a claim to the animals. The Taos Indians reported that there were once two kinds of buffalo, a smaller variety in the mountains and the larger plains variety.[3]

The fact that buffalo hunting was never quite integral for the surviving Pueblo groups, and the circumstance that these animals had disappeared altogether before modern times, puts a special character on the nature of buffalo ceremonialism. Those pueblos that would have been most actively engaged, as the large town of Pecos and the various Saline pueblos, are extinct, so the picture is one of importing a hunting dance which often incorporates elements from Plains or other Indians. As would be expected the buffalo is most important at Taos where the Indians frequently hunted them, then it becomes of less importance, traveling westward, until we arrive at Hopi. There it is the Buffalo dance that was imported.

Because hunting these animals was also a journey into alien territory, war elements are sometimes introduced into the Buffalo dances, and an unusual type of interpueblo endeavor, even including different language groups, was sometimes organized. "The Cochiti formerly went into the Pecos drainage to hunt buffalo. Occasionally buffalo were found in the Estancia Valley. On hunts east of the Pecos, the Cochiti usually joined hunters from Santo Domingo and the Tewa Pueblos.... Active hunters appear to be no more recent than the great grandfathers of today's generation. This would place these expeditions no later than 1880."[4] The enemies indicated are the Comanche, Jicarilla, and Mescalero Apaches. The weapons used for bison hunting, in addition to bows and arrows, were the iron spear—of Spanish origin—and toward the last an occasional rifle. Since these expeditions had to be licensed by Spanish authorities, it is possible that interesting information may one day turn up from that source.[5]

If we begin nearest to the sources of the myths and dances in which the buffalo figures, which is to say Taos, we find there a myth to account for the introduction of the dance and accompanying ceremony. "Coyote was roaming about the big plain in the east, in the buffalo country. He went about from place to place in the plain. One day he found a bunch of buffalo. Then he made up his mind that he would take them to the people of Taos. So he kept on rounding them up, herding them for three or four days. On the fifth day he began to drive them slowly toward the west. They went walking slowly and gently when he wanted them to go."

Coyote is most often a negative figure to the Pueblos, but he does sometimes fulfill good offices and the is certainly a wizard of sorts. On the literal side coyotes were often seen in the company of buffalo, where they ate the wounded and fed on carrion. People, including Indians, were often selective in the meat they could carry away from a buffalo hunt and a bountiful supply of the lesser cuts was left. This Coyote drove his charmed herd first to *kankaba*, "buffalo-when-at," apparently a nearby hunting ground for the people of Taos, and then on toward the village itself.

He sang,

> *Hia hia a a*
> *Yaia eya eya*
> *Heya heya*

"Then the buffalo went dancing, turning their bodies, they went forward and back again, while Coyote sang. Then he would stop at places and dance a while, then at the end of his song he hollered,

> *Kancho chilowe*
> *Buffalo-hunt-dry-out-that one hollering*
> *A a a a*
> *A a au'*
> *A au'*

Then he began to sing, and the buffalo danced. When he hollered, the people of Taos heard him and they went on top of their houses to see if Coyote was bringing buffalo to them. He was just a little way off on the east side of the village and he sang,

> *Hia hia a a*
> *Yaia eya eya*
> *Heya heya*

and the buffalo were dancing. They danced harder when the Taos people were looking at them. Then he started down, still singing, and the buffalo were still dancing."[6]

Then Coyote took these buffalo to the chief of the Big Earring People so that in the future he would make the Buffalo songs and dances. Next he went to the Day People, as they were to be companions in this dance. Lastly he went to the Old Axe kiva People and told them the same thing. These three groups that Coyote talked to about the Buffalo dance are from three of Taos's seven kivas. The Big Earring chief is also chief of all the kivas on the north side, the town being divided into two sections by a pleasant river. The Old Axe People were once associated with buffalo hunting and they now perform in the dances, and have power against drying winds in spring, buffalo being associated with winds. A buffalo skull is burned for a smoke against drought, high winds, or severe cold.

The Taos Buffalo dance is mimetic in character, which is unlike the Hopi counterpart farther west, and its central function, like the Deer dance, is to promote the increase of game. It also has, to be sure, the attendant weather connotations which relate to snow, cold, and wind, rather than rain. Rain belongs more to deer, but the Old Axe people do initiate the summer rain retreats at Taos. There are several possibilities in mimesis, one of which will appear in the Zuñi and Hopi imitations of mountain sheep where the performers leap and bound over obstacles or cavort on rooftops. These impersonators are imitating individual animals. The outstanding characteristic of buffalo, however, is not individual but group behavior, and it is to picture the vast extent and collective movement of these animals together that the Taos dancers have chosen their steps.

A great number of dancers is required to represent a herd, so all male members of Taos pueblo are supposed to take part in the Buffalo dance. In one dance the north side kivas turned out seventy-two buffalo and one deer, while those from the south side had sixty-nine buffalo and a deer. There were also four hunters who from their shrill cries are probably to be associated with the Coyote of the myth, and there is also a chorus of twenty-five singers, indicating that most adult males take some part. It is of great interest that no Mother of Game appears in the Buffalo dance, while she is a regular part of the comparable Deer dance here and in the other Río Grande pueblos. This would seem to indicate that the increase of game—or at least buffalo—is no longer the major aim of this ceremony.

At one time real buffalo heads were worn by the dancers, but as time passed these were hard to come by, at least in large numbers, so the Taos Indians used bear's hair and cow's horns to make up an artificial head. Downy feathers are attached to the horns to represent snow and a beard of hair is worn around the neck. The bodies, arms, and legs are painted dark red and blotched with white; a buckskin kilt is worn.

Much of the dancing is semistationary, the dancers sway from side to side to the beat of the music, or from time to time rotate in the same spot, all with the intent of suggesting the internal motions of a grazing herd. After a time the dancers form into four lines and perform a quadrille-like movement, the lines passing through each other and reforming in different positions in the plaza. Altogether the effect of the dance, which lasts about an hour and a half, is subdued and its present purpose is to bring snow, an intent which is likely to be successful since it is performed in January.

The Buffalo dances of the Keres pueblos differ in a number of ways from that of Taos, and they also exhibit considerable variety even within a single village. A primary difference is that there is no attempt to reproduce the movements of a herd; instead there are only two, or sometimes four, buffalo represented. Secondly, they are general game dances which often include deer, antelope, elk, and at times mountain sheep, although the buffalo always takes precedence and the dances are called "mo'shatsh," the Keresan word for buffalo. As a part of the hunting orientation of these dances they include a Mother of Game, or Buffalo Maid in an important role, though in some cases her function seems to have been forgotten and there is merely a woman dancer. As a result of the diminution in importance of the original ceremonies there appears to be an increasing tendency to divide Buffalo dances into two separate groups: the sacred and secular performances.[7]

One indication of this split is the use of either real buffalo heads, or imitations, the latter being more spectacular but not sacred. White makes the following comment on the real heads that are used at Santa Ana. "The buffalo heads are 'alive'; each one has tsats-winoshk (literally 'breath-heart'; translated by informants 'soul,' or 'spirit') and a name. When a new head is made, animated and named and established in the household of its 'owner,' or custodian, it is treated 'just like a new-born baby'; all the relatives of the custodian visit the head."[8] The source of these new heads was for a time a small herd kept by the Taos Indians, in part at least so that these animals could become the fountain head of the Buffalo cult.

The Buffalo dance of the pueblo of San Felipe is still in its sacred phase, probably because other kinds of game are included. This status is indicated by the fact that performers must fast for four days and practice ceremonial emesis. The hunt chief has lost much of his former position, but the 'old man' gathers together all the males of one kiva group and they then decide who will act as animals—there are two of each kind—and who will represent the hunters. The hunt head brings his paint and grinding stones, fetishes, and the like to a room for his retreat. By the fourth day everything has been prepared for the dance; spruce has been brought from the mountains, the costumes are ready and the dance steps have been practiced. The hunt chief then makes a line of meal from the altar to the door.

"The girl who is to be the mother of game is there. The 'hunters' come in. The Shai'yak start singing hunting songs. The 'mother of game' is standing by the door. When the hunting songs are started, she starts dancing sidewise towards the altar. She dances slowly. Whenever in the songs the Shai'yak say 'hiyani' (road), the girl sprinkles corn meal taken from her basket along the road which the medicine men have made for the animals on the floor. Then the Shai'yak sing songs for dancing, and hunters, animals, all dance."[9]

The next day the animals and hunters go out early and wait until they are called in by drumming and singing. The animals dance first, with the two Buffalo taking the lead. They are led into the plaza by the Shai'yak headman, who would once have been chief of the hunting society, but that is now defunct. He carries spruce branches in one hand and a small mountain lion fetish in the other. The Mother of Game also carries a small lion effigy which she keeps pressed close to her abdomen during the dance. As she comes out into the plaza she sprinkles a road of meal for the animals to follow. These then dance while the hunters sing for them. The Mother of Game wears a black leather cap with two small horns on the top of her head; her face is painted with white clay and she wears a white manta and buckskin leggings. She dances between the two Buffalo and in the quiet intervals runs down the line of dancers, shaking a wand with rattles at the dancers. This dancing proceeds at intervals throughout the afternoon and in the final appearance, after supper, the animals flee only to be captured by the hunters.

There is another type of Buffalo dance described from the pueblo of Santa Ana in which two Buffalo were the only animals represented; as usual a girl danced between these, while two other male dancers appeared in beaded aprons and non-Pueblo moccasins. Their bodies were painted green and a crest of brown hair was worn down the middle of the head. There was also a hoop dancer. Altogether the group is supposed somehow to represent eastern or Oklahoma Indians, which is of interest as showing outside influence on Buffalo dances and myths.[10]

The Santa Ana Buffalo dances may be asked for by anyone who is willing to get a group together to practice, thus the dance is outside the official cycle, though not quite secular since the heads of the animals used are very sacred.

At Sia the Buffalo dances may only be called by the Masewi, or war captain, when they are sacred; others may be asked for by any officer. In either case the dance is held for the increase of game and to give hunters power over game, and as a side effect it is supposed to bring snow. For the occasion the dancers' lower limbs are painted with red ochre, while both the chest and back have a red disc painted on them; these are surrounded with white eagle down, suggesting the sun tablets of the Hopi Buffalo dancers.[11]

The Buffalo dances at Cochiti follow the general pattern. The costumes vary, but the group includes drummers and singers, two Buffalo and a Buffalo Maid, and one Shai'yak or hunter. Early in the year the body is painted black and eagle down is daubed in the dancer's hair, but this snow-bringing feature is dropped if the dance is held later, as no one wants snow in the springtime. The body paint is also changed from black to red in these later dances, perhaps to suggest the summer sun.

A different aspect of the Cochiti Buffalo dances is their curative power. Someone who is ill may request that the dancers come to his house to perform one round. This is spoken of as bringing good medicine.[12] The snow-bringing theme that runs through all of these dances has a dual implication, that of bringing moisture and of bringing game. Game animals are driven down from the higher mountains, because of winter snows, to where they are more accessible to hunters. While this would scarcely apply to the buffalo itself, these dances are held not so much for that animal as for the deer, elk, and possibly mountain sheep whose movements are affected by the weather.

There are likewise weather elements in the Hopi Buffalo dances, as indicated by the use of lightning frames and sun-shield symbols, but before discussing these there is the question of how Buffalo dances came to the Hopi in the first place, since they live so far from the former range of that animal. Parsons thought that the Buffalo dance came to Hopi by way of Zuñi, in part because the dancers in both places wear unusual hair bangs that hang down as far as the mouth, but there seems to be more evidence that these dances were imported directly from the Río Grande pueblos. One of Stephen's informants settled two points quite definitely. "In 1888 Ha'yi said: 'Buffalo dance we copied from the village people on the Rio Grande. . . . Here we imitate the buffalo with sheepskin and ox horns. We never hunted the buffalo.' "[13]

There is a myth to account for the introduction of these dances which is something of a counterpart to the one already given from Taos, except that it extends the process much farther westward. "Two real bisons came from the far east, halted at Keam's Cañon and hung up their skins in a ledge recess and became youth and maid. They had many buckskins. They came to the villages. Bison (Buffalo) was danced, and the Bison youth exchanged the Bison maid for the Tewa youth's sister. Bison youth and Tewa maid then went to Keam's Cañon, put on the bison skins and became real bisons and galloped back to the far east. Bison maid who had become a Tewa maid stayed with the Tewa."[14]

The Tewa referred to here are those of the village of Hano on Hopi First Mesa, descendants of a group who left their Río Grande homes about the year 1700. Inferably they brought the Buffalo dance with them, from whence it spread to the Hopi villages. Since the dances are not indigenous, they became a gathering point for other outside elements, such as the Comanche dance step, and they may be held at times when the only purpose at hand is to express the pure joy of dancing. In kachina dances only the men perform, even when the figure impersonated is female, but in the Buffalo and the Butterfly dances an equal number of men and women may participate. Their secular nature also allows them to be held at any time of year, which is again unlike the sacred kachina dances.

Even rehearsals for Buffalo dances take on a gay nature and, so that no one may be left out, the first day's dancing may be by children. That night the girls who will dance the following day gather in the kiva, where their behavior is subdued in contrast to the boys, but it is the girls who choose partners. The dances are performed by groups of four of each sex, who dance in the plaza for about fifteen minutes, then the next group takes over. In the nighttime preparations and choosing of partners there is no dancing, "but for a brief, high-stepping caper, the Buffalo caper, by four men on their descent into the kiva."

The girls who dance wear the bare-shouldered black manta, their hair flows loose and their faces are covered with the odd, artificial bangs. They wear a man's dance kilt as a bodice and a large wedding sash, all covered with as much turquoise and silver jewelry as they can borrow from relatives. They dance barefooted and wear on their backs the sun-shield on which is painted the sun's face, surrounded with red horsehairs to indicate his rays. On the top of their heads are bunches of downy eagle feathers, while an artificial squash blossom adorns the right side of the head. Their faces are painted white with two black stripes slanting across each cheek and in their hands the girls carry wands, which are notched sticks called cloud ladders, or sun ladders. These are diminutive replicas of the notched poles that were once used for climbing out of the pueblo houses when these had no door. The suggestion is that the clouds should use these to climb out of the nearby springs, or that the sun should climb the sky.

The boys who are to dance wear a woman's white blanket as a kilt. The Buffalo headdress is made of a heavy sheep's pelt and like its eastern counterpart contains downy eagle feathers, but these are cloud symbols, rather than snow bringers. There are numerous dance steps available, in some of which the boys spring in front of the girls, where they bend forward and perform a very spirited dance while the girls' steps are subdued. After the girls withdraw from the plaza the spectators pick up anything that may be at hand, swing it around their head four times and then fling it after the departing Buffalo. This gesture is to indicate that the retreating Buffalo should take away sickness from the village, as the dance was given in part for someone who was ill. A final gesture in the dance is to send the Buffalo back to their home in the east. Two of the dancers retreat to a kachina shrine where they take off the headdress and wave it in a sinistral circuit about their heads four times as they say to the Buffalo, "You may go home."[15]

Fewkes mentions a different kind of Buffalo dance that was held in one of the Hopi villages on January 15, 1900. It involved two men who appeared in masks, that is to say, as kachinas, which the Buffalo dancers are not. Colton likewise mentions that Buffalo kachina may appear in mixed dances on First and Second Mesas.[16] Fewkes here explains the notched wands as ladders for the sun, in a Buffalo dance held during March. These were to aid the sun in climbing back from his winter house, so it may be supposed that the sun-shields on the backs of the maids have the same purpose, although Fewkes explains this in connection with the bringing of the dance from the east. "There is a tradition that a Buffalo maid was brought to Tusayan from the Eastern pueblos by the Sun, whose emblem she wears on her back in the dance."[17]

Since we have found other connections between Buffalo and the sun, notably the red discs painted on Sia dancers, and will find them again in the myth, it is of interest that Fewkes found some very old masks that were kept at First Mesa, although they were no longer used. "The former use of these masks in sun worship and their antiquity give them a particular sanctity. . . . Objection might be made to this identification, for these clan masks have two horns, which are absent in Hopi sun masks, and the facial markings are different. The author theoretically connects the horns with those of the bison, and believes that the clans which once had these forms of sun masks derived them from those tribes which practiced a sun ceremony."[18]

If we look back over these Buffalo dances, we will find that they are based on a very similar set of ideas which will shortly be of use in interpreting the Bison myth. The first point in common is that when origin is mentioned, both the Buffalo and his dance are brought to the West from the East, which may be connected with the journey of the sun across the sky. The Buffalo, or Buffalo Youth, is always accompanied by a female attendant, who may be either a Mother of Game or a Buffalo Maid—consorts have a way of alternating between mother and wife. In the Río Grande dances there is always a hunter or hunt chief, who among the Keres is called Shai'yak. The original of this office was a Keeper of Game, as well as supernatural patron of the hunt society, and he was as well the consort or husband of the Mother of Game.

When we come to the myth of Buffalo Man, or White Bison as it is called at Taos and Zuñi, a special problem has to be faced: the myth, like the Buffalo and its dance, quite evidently is an importation from the East. In the Taos version the hero of the story is an Apache chief. There are similar tales from the Cheyenne, Wichita, Northern Shoshone, Gros Ventre, Arapaho, and other Indians, and it is also found in Europe. In fact, Europa herself mated with the white bull, later said to be Zeus in disguise. The offspring of that union was Minos, who married Pasiphae; she in turn conceived an unnatural lust for a great bull sent by Poseidon. Quite obviously any general discussion would take this chapter far afield, but there is one version of the myth, from Acoma-Laguna, which is well integrated into the Keres pantheon and does illuminate the Buffalo dances.

One would expect to find Buffalo dances at these western Keres pueblos, comparable to those held by their related Keres-speaking people of the Río Grande. Acoma does have such dances, but they are purely for pleasure. "During the four days that follow [Christmas] there is much dancing in the church. They dance buffalo, eagle, Comanche dances, etc. No masks are worn. These dances are not esoteric, and are not connected with the k'atsina. They are danced merely for pleasure."[19] There was once a Buffalo clan at Acoma, as at Sia and the Tewa pueblo San Ildefonso; no such clan is listed for Laguna. There is no particular evidence then, of any rite of the western Keres that might once have been connected with the myth of Buffalo Man.

One version of this myth, from Acoma, is a romance recorded by Gunn.[20] Arrow Youth is a daring hunter who overcomes all rivals to marry Kochinako, the most beautiful maiden of Acoma, but unfortunately for both she is vain and fickle. Shortly after their marriage, while Arrow Youth is away on a hunt, she goes to the spring with her water jar and there is approached by Mushaitch Hutch-tsi, the Buffalo Man. "She did not seek to avoid him, for, to speak the truth, she rather admired his appearance; and when he spoke to her, she answered boldly. He proposed to her that she accompany him to his home. She readily consented, and directed by the Buffalo Man, climbed upon his back. Then he started swiftly away in the direction of his own country in the northeast." It will be noted that the direction taken here is naturalistic, toward the actual range of the animal.

Arrow Youth sets out to find his wife and after many adventures he finds Buffalo Man with his head pillowed in Kochinako's lap. He rescues her and another woman, then flees with the Buffalo in pursuit. When overtaken the three climb a tree, from which Arrow Youth shoots all the Buffalo, including Buffalo Man. He then broiled the meat, which the other woman ate, but Kochinako refused. "Is-to-a-moot waxed very angry. 'You still love the buffalo man. Then die that you may still be with him.' With that he drew an arrow from his quiver and shot her through the heart. She died and Is-to-a-moot married the other woman whom he had rescued from the buffalo man."

All that we learn from this story is that there was a rivalry between a youth and a minotaur for the former's wife. When rescued she betrays love for the bull, whereupon the husband slays her and marries her shadowy counterpart. Fortunately there is yet another version in which we can identify the characters, their characteristics and perhaps some of the implications of the myth. The narrator of this version lived as a baby in Acoma, but when his father died his uncle took him to Laguna where he was raised. Let us first follow this myth in some detail.

Arrow Youth was a deer hunter, not a farmer, and he was married to the daughter of Chief-Remembering-Prayer-Sticks. His wife was Yellow-Woman, or Kochinako, who is not a forward woman. When she meets Buffalo Man at the spring she first says she cannot go with him, because of her water jar. He tells her to put it upside down by the spring and let him carry her on his back. "Then westward they went," through a mountain gap to a sky high mountain on top of which was his home. "Up on the trail they went out and up." From that day onward Arrow Youth could kill no deer.

While on an unsuccessful hunt Arrow Youth awakened early one morning. "Then in the east came up his friend the Big Star" who spoke to him. " 'I'll tell you this,' said the Star, 'yesterday morning,' said he, 'Buffalo-Man stole your wife, Yellow-Woman, therefore you cannot kill any deer.' " Having learned this Arrow Youth returns home, gathers up his quiver of many arrows and a flint knife. He finds the water jar upside down, then follows the tracks to the westward. By and by he comes to the cottonwood tree and engages the aid of Old Woman Spider, who offers to help by making the trail short and by providing him with four kinds of medicine which he is to blow on the guards of Buffalo Man, as well as the Buffalo. Then he may bring back his wife and "the other Yellow-Woman."

These guards prove to be the beasts of prey, Mountain Lion, Wolf, Bear, and Wildcat, as well as rattlesnakes. The medicine not only pacifies these guards, but changes them into helpers of Arrow Youth. "Go ahead, you must bring her here. From here on we shall help you." When he arrives Arrow Youth blows the medicine on the Buffalo, putting them tight asleep. With his flint knife he cuts his wife's bonds. Next he calls on the help of Eagle Man to quickly take them down from this mountain in the sky. The Eagle is, of course, the beast of prey of the Zenith and Eagle Man is the Acoma Hunt chief. When they reach the bottom they are told, "You will run. When you get through this mountain you will run, for the Buffalo-Chief has supernatural power," so spoke Eagle Man.

Then the buffalos awakened, discovered the escape and began a pursuit. "They went with the Wind. Then Arrow-Youth looked backward and he saw the wind. Quickly he chewed medicine and then he blew on it. Then it stopped." When they reach the guards, these urge the escaping party to hasten.

"After some time again the Buffaloes came behind them. With hail they were going. Then Arrow Youth looked backward again. He saw the hail-storm behind. Again quickly he chewed medicine and again blew it Arrow-Youth upon the buffaloes. Then it stopped."

The cottonwood tree, which is a sure sign of a spring in that country, appears again, offering the fugitives a haven from the pursuing buffaloes. Most of the great animals passed this tree. "Then one, the last one, was a young buffalo. He stood up under the cottonwood tree." At this point Yellow Woman is forced to pass water. "Underneath was standing the young buffalo. The water sprinkled on the back of the young buffalo." The young calf then calls out to the other buffalo that sister-in-law is sitting in the tree. In other versions he looks into a pool of water by the cottonwood and sees her reflection from above. The Buffalo Men decide then to cut down the tree. Arrow Youth pulled out his bow and took out his arrows. "Buffalo Man he butted the cottonwood tree, but he shot him and he fell down." One by one Arrow Youth kills all of the animals.

" 'I'll tell the people to come for buffalo meat,' said Arrow-Youth. Then after some time his wife was crying all the time. 'Why are you crying?' said Arrow-Youth. 'Because,' said Yellow-Woman, 'did you not kill my husband, Buffalo-man?' 'indeed?' said he. 'Did you love this man very much?' said Arrow Youth. 'Yes,' said Yellow-Woman. Then in his turn down there he killed his wife. Then he took the other Yellow-Woman." The two of them then went to the town.

" 'Father,' said Arrow Youth, 'I did not bring your daughter, Yellow-Woman here.'—'Why?' said her father, the Chief. 'Because,' said he, 'I killed her.'—'Indeed, why did you kill her?'—'Because,' said Arrow-Youth, 'because she did not want to come this way. She loved her husband Buffalo-Man very much, so I killed her.'—'Indeed?' said the Chief. 'All right,' said he, 'never mind.'

"Then again thus spoke Arrow-Youth, 'Now go ahead, tell the people, all the men who live here, to go for buffalo meat.'

Then the Chief spoke thus, 'let me tell them.' He spoke thus, 'From here men and young men, go ahead to get buffalo meat. ... There in the corner in the north under the cottonwood tree,' said the Chief, 'There Arrow-Youth killed all the buffaloes.' Then the people said, 'let us get it,' they said. Then they went to get buffalo meat."[21]

The reader of this myth realizes at its conclusion, if not before, that the story is not, after all, a romance. This is brought home to one by the response of the chief to the news of his daughter's death: "Indeed—all right—never mind." The chief is more concerned to tell his people that they can now go out and bring in the buffalo meat. Certainly that suggests that we have been listening to the account of a hunting rite, whose goal was meat and whose protagonists fitted somehow into this intent. To begin with, let us examine the actors. The chief, Holding-Prayer-Sticks, is the mythical founder of Acoma and a chief by the same name is supposed to have founded Laguna.

Arrow Youth is a supernatural hunter whose role we learn from another myth. Mountain Lion Man tells him to make prayer-sticks for the animals. In exchange for these he is to get as much game as he wishes. "Then after a while thereabouts they went up and he [Mountain Lion Man] gave him control of all game."[22] These prayer-sticks are for a number of deities: for Mountain Lion Man, the original of beasts of prey; for Shai'yak, the original of the hunt chiefs who are still called by that name; for Kochinako, or Yellow Woman, and for two unidentified deities. Big Star, who told Arrow Youth why he could no longer kill deer, is the Morning Star who is the patron deity of hunters. Among the Tiwa he is called Dark Star and plays the same role. At Hopi the relationship is the same. "On first Mesa Morning Star is himself associated with all the animals and asked to give them to men, both hunt animals and domestic."[23]

Yellow Woman is a less stable character, in that the name is sometimes used generically to indicate all of the women who appear as spirits in myths and tales. As one of the directional sisters she is Yellow Woman of the North. The Mountain Lion is the Beast of Prey of that same direction. The myth is set in the supernatural world where the mountains of the directions are the homes of animals as well as the Chiefs of each cardinal point. The guards that Arrow Youth meets are a part of this mythic, directionally oriented landscape. They are the Beast Gods who are first guardians of the Buffalos, then the helpers of Arrow Youth, which is logical since the Mountain Lion has in other myths given the hunter-spirit two crooked canes with which he is to herd all game animals.

The Yellow Woman of the second account is identical with Kochinako of the romance. The two names are linked together in other pueblos as well. At Sia we find the statement: "Ko'chinako, a virgin (the yellow woman of the north)."[24] From Cochiti, Dumarest explains the schemata of the directions as a male *shiwanna*, or rainmaker, for each direction. Each of these is accompanied by a woman who acts as intercessor with them and who, when the clouds come, are traveling behind them. One is, "dark yellow woman, *koshinako*. . . ."[25] Rain as we have seen is closely related to the game animals and particularly to deer, which was Arrow Youth's first choice. The buffalo, on the other hand, had power over wind, hail, and snow. On this point the rites described earlier, such as burning a buffalo head to allay the drying wind in spring, agree with the myth in which the buffalos travel with the wind. One suspects that the connection between buffalo and the wind is a result of the fact that dust clouds raised by the beasts make the winds visible.

Kochinako has a dual role that ties two ideas together. She is an intercessor for rain, which is indicated by her water jar that is turned upside down in the myth and the incident that brings on the climax of the narrative. She is at the same time a Keeper of Game, in which role she is usually the sister rather than the wife of Arrow Youth. She gives this game as well as protects it. "Whatever animal suits yourself, that you will kill, thus said Yellow Woman."[26] We are reminded of the Greek goddess Artemis, who similarly was a protector of wild things and at the same time a patroness of the hunt. Artemis in time became associated with the moon, at least in the Roman view in which she is Diana. As we look further into the nature of Yellow Woman we find that she too is identified with the moon and is additionally associated with the sun.

Yellow Woman's moon identification appears frequently in other myths. In these she is killed, which invariably ruins Arrow Youth's hunting, and then revived to live only at night. In one account she is merely blind during the daytime. In a myth which is often parallel to the one just presented, she is killed and her brother watches over the buried body for four nights—possibly an extension of the ceremonial period to the dark of the moon. He seeks her. "Only at night was alive Yellow Woman, but in the daytime she was not alive."[27] It appears that she has fallen into the hands of witches and from this strait the animals of prey undertake to help Arrow Youth retrieve her.

". . . then to the north west corner, there where the bad people lived; then downstairs on the corner shelf, on that was a beautiful water jar. There they kept Yellow Woman's heart. They arrived there. They went in. When they had gone in, they grappled and fought. Violently they fought. Then mountain lion, bear, cat and wolf fought. Then they killed them all. At that time they took down the water jar. They broke it to pieces. . . . The heart was quite ready."[28] First an arrow was stuck in the middle of this heart, then it was taken back and by the power of Iatiku, the Mother, given to Yellow Woman again. "Yellow Woman put on her dress, and so she was alive in the daytime."

Kochinako has another important role in which she is a consort of the Sun. While she is sleeping, the sunlight falls upon her and from this impregnation is born the War Twins, the sons of the Sun by Yellow Woman. At Acoma she is sometimes kidnapped by a bad kachina who kills her, but it has no sooner been said that she has been killed than it is stated: "In the daytime slept their mother, but at night she walked about."[29] As a moon woman she is not only a bride of the Sun, but is constantly killed by his agency, only to be reborn again.

By thus outlining the characters that appear in the myth of Buffalo Man, we have to a degree explained the Pueblo view of its significance. The unexpected remark of the chief—"never mind . . . go ahead to get buffalo meat"—is not the heartless remark of a father, but a chief's expression of the purpose behind whatever rite was justified in the myth. The fact that all the spirits involved in the story are related to supernatural justification of hunting customs confirms the direction of both myth and rite: buffalo meat. As patroness of game it is logical that Yellow Woman would love Buffalo Man, chief of these animals and symbolic representative of buffaloes. It is also natural that Arrow Youth would have to kill her before Chief Holding or Remembering-Prayer-Stick's people could get the game she protected.

There is of course the implication here that a sacrifice of a maiden, whether real or symbolic, took place in the rites to which the myth was attached. Such a conclusion is plausible enough, as a maid was almost certainly sacrificed to the minotaur in Minoan times and there are plenty of instances in the New World. But since we do not know what the rite was, or to whom it originally belonged, it can with equal logic be interpreted as only a story of the moon in a role as Mother of Game, whose monthly death makes it impossible it to kill game. When she is gone Arrow Youth can kill no deer. After her death he took "the other Yellow Woman," which is to say the new moon. The rite then becomes one of the death and rebirth of a goddess who is favorable to both animals and success in hunting. She is a "giver of herself" along the lines of Salt Woman and other personifications of necessities bestowed by nature.

Since the myth fits so well into the Keres pantheon, it must have been reinforced by actual rites, even if these were borrowed. What these may have been like is difficult to tell, as they would have become increasingly less meaningful by the close of the eighteenth century, but it is natural to suppose that the present Buffalo dances are relics. Perhaps the dance described from San Felipe would be the nearest to the original, as there the Mother of Game comes in with the two Buffalo. She is Kochinako. This group is led into the plaza by a Shai'yak carrying a mountain lion effigy. He like Arrow Youth is the archetypal hunt chief. The drummers and the singers are the townspeople who sing for the four: Mother of Game, two Buffaloes, and Shai'yak.

Perhaps the Sun was also included in the rite, as the red solar discs still appear on the chests and backs of the Sia dancers, as they do on the backs of the Hopi maidens in the Buffalo dance. In the myth the journey to the west seems to be a Sun journey and the Buffaloes themselves live in the sky. Certainly the Sun presides over the weather aspects of the rites as he makes his own journey through the seasons, bringing snow, hail, drying winds, and then the fertile summer rains. Into this cosmic picture the alien buffalo has been fitted as neatly as the neighboring deer.

Chapter V

AMERICAN ELK AND
MOUNTAIN SHEEP

THE AMERICAN ELK has had a variety of names. The term "elk" is applied to the moose in the Old World, and our elk is really a variety of red deer. However it is named, the elk has an admirable ability to reproduce its kind at about the same rate as domestic cattle. Thirty-seven head were released in New Mexico in 1915. By 1947 the New Mexico herd had grown to 3,000, and by 1950 that number had doubled. It doubled again by 1962 when there were 12,500 elk in the mountains of that state.

It is the size of the American elk that makes it the most impressive of our game animals and, befitting its height, which is about the same as a horse, is the set of truly magnificent antlers that are regrown each year. Since the body of the bull may be seven to eight feet long, the antlers are not out of proportion even though some reach sixty inches in length. These antlers curve upwards and over the back with six branching tines that are distinctive enough to have individual names. The first two are the brow and the bez, which together are called the war tines. After the trez comes the royal and the final two are called surroyals, lending a nautical note which does not seem altogether out of place when a group of bucks sail by. These solid antlers are shed annually.

As compared to the elusive mule deer, the elk is a very noisy and careless animal. The cows with their calves keep up a squealing and barking that indicates the position of the herd, and the bull has quite a variety of sounds, ranging from the explosive grunts and barks of the danger call to the intense bugling of the rutting season. This bugle has been described variously, but it begins on a low note, rises to a high, clear, brass trumpet, or shrill whistle, then falls to guttural grunts.

Elk were thought of as another and larger kind of deer by the Pueblos. The elk were scarcely more than a memory to the Indians by 1890, but their horns were used in ceremonies. A remote indication of elk hunting appears in a tale from Laguna-Acoma. The hero of the story is a Zuñi, and in fact the drift of the story is a modified version of the Zuñi tale of a youth who so loved his eagle that he went to her home in the sky. However, inset into this is an account of an elk hunt.

"I'tiwai' said, 'I wonder, is there not below in the north any game? I think I shall go hunting,' said he. Then his eagle said, 'Indeed,' said he, 'There is plenty of game, but it is very dangerous.'" The question of how dangerous an elk can be is of interest, since it comes up again in another context. A bull elk in captivity can be as dangerous as a dairy bull. There are numerous accounts of bulls in the wild, especially in rutting season, suddenly turning and attacking a human being. Thus, while they are not a ferocious animal, an attack is always a possibility.

The youth of the story finds in the north, "a flat surrounded by mesas," and from Spider Woman he gets some medicine that will pacify dangerous animals. "I shall help you from now on. When first you try to kill it, there in the middle of the north wall, there in the west stands the tallest, largest elk. You will kill it.' . . . Then he chewed the medicine. Indeed then the elk was going to attack him already. From the middle of the north came the largest elk with very sharp antlers in front. He blew the medicine on it and shot the very large elk. It fell down and did not gore him. Then he killed it. He skinned it with his flint knife. After a while he skinned it entirely. Then he tore off the leaves from a piñon tree and put the meat down on them."[1] This account next mentions jerking the meat, then drops the subject to return to the youth's relationship with the eagle people.

A more evident reflection of elk hunting appears in the game dances of the Río Grande Pueblos. Usually the role of elk is minor—he trails behind deer and antelope—but the Tewa pueblo of Nambe has an Elk dance devoted to these animals, as is appropriate for the northerly Tewa. Rather curiously, the people of this small pueblo bought the Elk dance from the Taos Indians at some time in the past, probably not altogether as a means to increase that game, but as a rite of regeneration for themselves, as they were very close to dying out. As a part of their payment the Nambeans gave "a promise that the ceremony would always be properly or strictly performed, lest the pueblo of Nambe die out."

In order to raise money, they first sold some land to Spanish Americans and with the funds thus gained bought ten turquoises, five hard red beads, twelve dance blankets, and twelve deer skins, with which they then bought the dance. It is held on the Saint's Day, October 4, and when properly performed two deer impersonators observe a twelve-day retreat in the mountains before the dance, during which time the War captains take them food, consisting of rabbit meat and bread made without lard. Hiding away in the mountains is related to the thought that game itself is kept in the mountains in some kind of a compound, perhaps like that described in the antelope hunts. When these animals come to the village they of course bring the rain clouds with them. In the Nambe dance there are supposed to be ten Elk impersonators and eight of Deer, but the population of the village is so small that neighboring pueblos have to join them in presenting the dance.[2]

At Keresan Cochiti an Elk dance is held regularly as a part of the game dance cycle, occurring once every third year. Cochiti is divided into two kiva groups, the Turquoise and the Pumpkin. One year both kivas will hold a Deer-Antelope dance in mid-winter, while the next year both groups will hold a Buffalo dance. Then in the third year—1956 was one—the Turquoise kiva presents an Eagle dance and the Pumpkin people an Elk dance. This performance included two Elk impersonators and fifteen or twenty "Comanche" dancers, dressed in the feathered bonnets of the Plains warriors, who dance and mimic the actions of hunters.[3]

At Sia the Elk are included in the Buffalo dance, which is the collective name for any game dance. Here there are two groups of dancers, each composed of two buffalo, three or four deer, one or two elk, and four or five antelope. These Elk are kachinas, called Shkisha, who belong to the Fire society, as does Shakak, the supernatural of the North, and Heluta, the one who brings the deer. Curiously the Deer kachina does not belong to the group, but to the Kwiraina clown society which also provides a mountain lion to act as a side dancer.[4] As a sign of the scarcity of elk from the 1880's to the middle of this century, the Elk kachina has wooden horns.

It is the Beasts of Prey who act as supernatural patrons of the hunt, and at Acoma-Laguna there is a myth which tells how each species first took game. As everything is balanced in Pueblo thought, each of these prey animals selects a certain type of game, the elk being associated with the east direction and the wolf who also represents that cardinal point. At Hopi too the elk is a "pet" of the spirit chief of the east direction. The other associations are that the mountain lion is to hunt the Deer People of the north, the weasel to take the mountain sheep of the west, while the wildcat of the south is to take antelope. Because of his gluttony Coyote is not given any big game, but condemned to be a scavenger. In the myth of the origin of hunting customs each of these prey animals is in turn given his chance.

" 'Next it is Coyote's and Wolf's turn,' said Shaiyak [the supernatural patron of the hunt], 'Coyote and Wolf it is your turn.' Then they said let us go. . . . Then they went out up. To the east they went. Above in the east they came out. Then below on the east hillside was an elk, and a reindeer, a jackrabbit and a rabbit. Eastward down they went. Then said wolf, 'Brother,' said he, 'Coyote, I shall take the elk,' . . . Then wolf started to catch it. Eastward he pursued it. Southeastward he pursued it. Southwestward he pursued it. The sun was already rising and then he killed it. Then he ate one half of it."[5]

The selections of predators and prey are quite sound; while

a mountain lion can kill an elk at times, they seem to much prefer deer for their diet. The weasel may seem like an odd predator for mountain sheep, but the logic here is that this is the only pair that can be found together on the alpine peaks of mountains. Wildcat will kill either deer or antelope, but in the Pueblo country they may have had a better chance with antelope.[6] While wolves undoubtedly killed more antelope than elk, their ability to take the latter game was almost peculiar to them. In his study of wolves, Young quotes from a Biological Survey employee to the effect that wolves "seem to be able to kill elk at will. . . . They usually hamstring the elk, and after felling them make a meal from the eyes, the udder, and other choice parts, and seldom return to the carcass, preferring a fresh victim.[7]

Elk was desirable not only for the abundant meat, but also for its very thick hide. This could be used for such practical matters as the soles of moccasins, or more importantly for the helmets on which many kachina masks are built.[8] As the skin becomes part of a supernatural, so also is elk hide used to wrap up the image of the Hopi goddess Tuwa'bontumsi—Sand Altar Woman—the mother of all living things.[9] Another supernatural usage of elk skin is recounted in the Acoma origin story. Iyatiku told Oak Man that he must make a drum and a rattle. For the drum he was to use a segment of a certain tree. " 'Knock the center out and use the outside cylinder. Cover both ends with the skin of the elk.' She instructed him how to lace the skin on. Then she taught him how to make the drumstick out of wood of the same tree. When the drum was finished he was taught how to make the rattle. 'Take the scrotum of the elk; take the hair off and stuff it with dry sand and let it dry, tying a stick in it first. When it is dry, pour the sand out. Then put some agave seeds into the rattle.' "[10]

The great antlers were much prized, along with the horns of mountain sheep, by the Al or Horn society of the Hopi who carried them as a part of their ceremonial gear. This warrior-watchman group has as one of its duties the closing of all trails into the pueblo during certain ceremonies. The old elk antlers, along with the more plentiful ones from deer, are whitened with clay before each use, such as the one described for an initiation ceremony. "Several of the *Tu-wa-la-tu*, or watchmen of the Horn Society, carrying each an elkhorn, went out before sunrise as sentinels, and placed the horns upon different trails. This signal is perfectly understood among the neighboring tribes, and no one ventured to pass it."[11]

In this same ceremony the effigy of Sand Altar Woman, which is a figurine about eighteen inches high, is brought in with torchlight by a Horn man dressed in buckskin, wearing a helmet made from a female mountain sheep scalp. All in all this is one of the least agrarian rites recorded from the Pueblos. When the Horn priest comes in he carries "a huge bunch of goat and sheep hoofs, jingling it as a bell, and the other followed in the rear, carrying on his left arm a large elk antler. With his right hand he jingled a large bunch of elk hoofs."

Since the prosperity of game is so closely linked with that of the people in such a ceremony, and as the elk's antlers are used to protect the village by closing its trails, it is then very surprising to find that in myth Elk is one of the monsters which assault them. All of the Pueblos, as indeed people everywhere, have ogres of various sorts. Some of them are simply people-eating monsters. While these spirits are evil, all know that they will not injure people in real life—as witches do—but only in myths and tales. Since they pose a psychic rather than a real threat, we can look for an explanation in that realm.

The group of monsters of particular interest here is one which includes Big Antelope of the Sia stories, dangerous Deer and Antelope of Cochiti, and Big Antelope and Elk of the Hopi. The elk is admirably suited to the role of monster, being an oversized deer with some ferocious aspects, but the same thing can hardly be said for the antelope. What this group has in common is that they are game animals; people eat them. These cannibal monsters are said in story to eat people, until the War Twins, who are also hunters and patrons of hunters, slay the evil creatures and save their wards, the human beings. Often some form of Eagle monster belongs to the same group, possibly because he too was often killed by the Indians, or because he is a keeper of game. In Cochiti myth he is guarded by a vicious deer and antelope.[12] Possibly the Zuñi ogress, Atoshle, whom we met denuding the rabbit huntress of her game and clothing, while preparing to eat the girl as well, is also a kind of gamekeeper or Mother of Game.

At Sia, Big Antelope is a cannibal monster killed by the Twins, and as often happens in combat myths the monster can change roles, shifting from evil to good. One of the Twins, Masewi, "cut the breast with his stone knife, passing the knife from the throat downwards. The boys then flayed the antelope; Masewi cut the heart and flesh into bits, throwing the pieces to the north, west, south, and east, declaring that hereafter the antelope should not be an enemy of his people, saying, 'His flesh shall furnish food for my people.' Addressing the antelope he commanded, 'From this time forth you will eat only vegetation and not flesh, for my people are to have your flesh for food.' "[13] Clearly the issue here is whether game should eat people, or people eat game, and that issue is decided by the hunter gods.

At Hopi there were four of these cannibal monsters: Kwa'-toko, a monster eagle similar to the Zuñi Knife-Wing; Chaveyo, who jingles a metal whip and has a heart like a stone war-axe. Then there was Wulo Chubio, Big Antelope, who can be identified with the Sia counterpart, and Wuko Chai'zrisa, Big Elk. "The giant elk was of form like the modern elk, but of stupendous size, and exceedingly fierce; he slew many people with his horns. . . . The giant elk also devoured the bodies of the people he killed, and goring and thrusting with his horns seems to have always been his method of dispatching his victims."[14]

The Little War Twins first kill Kwa'toko and his wife with lightning; their children become owls and crows. Chaveyo is found near a pool on Mount Taylor. He throws lightning at them, but they catch the bolts, sling them back, and kill him.

This demon would seem to be based on a weather spirit of evil intent, whose metal whip indicates the destructive force of lightning. Giant Elk was more of a problem and the Twins required the aid of small animals—who usually fight on the side of man—to bring about his death. The scene is again Mount Taylor.

"Big Elk was one day lying down in a valley near Mount Taylor and the Twins went out against him. Pocket Gopher met them and said, 'Do not go alone against him; he is very fierce and strong and may kill you; wait here and I will help you.'" Gopher then dug four caverns and made the Twins remain in the upper one, then he dug a long tunnel. "Coming up under Elk, he plucked a little of the soft hair over his heart region, and Elk turned his head and looked down." Gopher said, "Oh, do not be angry with me, I want just a little of your soft hair to make a bed for my children." Elk allowed him to continue until he had the region quite bare, then gopher told the Twins who threw their lightning at Elk. The latter sprang up and charged, but they hid in the upper cavern. As he gored at them they retreated from one cavern to another and from the fourth level they killed him.

Chipmunk then came scurrying up and with his sharp teeth he showed the Twins how to cut up the monster. "Pookong [one of the Twins] thanked chipmunk, and stooping down he wetted the tips of the two forefingers of his right hand in the blood that issued from Elk, and, drawing his fingertips along the body of Chipmunk, he made the marks which he still carries. After the monsters were slain, the village people became numerous."[15]

In addition to absolving the guilt and settling the rightness of eating game, these stories of monsters also express a fear. The roots of this fear are in the child's view of the world. Even relatives are monsters which sometimes threaten him. This fact is recognized in the use of bogeys to discipline children. The Little War Twins, although gods, are also children. Once when they went out to slay a monster that had been eating Oraibi children they said: "He is our uncle and he is bad." While Indian parents are kind to their children, the uncle may not be. Talayesva's uncle took him along when he was altering goats and as a joke went through the motions of castrating the terrified child. To the adult it was a bumbling prank, but to the child sheer terror.

When the child is grown the outside world which surrounds the pueblo is also monstrous and threatening. Dangers from storms, human enemies, and sometimes animals were real enough and the community had no defense against them, except their gods and rites. In one monster story the Twins are actually swallowed by the earth, but they then kill our globe by finding its heart and piercing it; thereafter they crawl out through its nose. "The old people say that this monster was really a world or country, as some call it, similar to the world we are living in."[16]

The awe and fear of the child for the bigness of things outside himself is remembered by the adult and equated with his own doubts concerning the vastness which surrounds him on every side. These powers are then personified and slain by protecting gods. The earth as a monster has a double role, for the earth is the mother of game. Antelope, deer, and elk are her creatures. The feeling that is made explicit in the story of Big Antelope doubtless applies to Big Elk as well. When this child of earth is slain, its heart and flesh are divided to become the creatures which provide food for mankind, the living game we see and take.

Mountain sheep are most often thought of as semilegendary animals which inhabit only a few of the highest mountains in the West, but they once also inhabited desert and plateau mountains as well. Their meat is by consensus pronounced the most delicious of all game. They were a staple item in the diet of the Pima and Papago Indians and the Hopi hunted those that inhabited rough country nearby, well into this century. In the mountains of the Río Grande country mountain sheep were apparently plentiful, as the Riana ruins on the Chama indicate that more mountain sheep than deer were eaten.

The horns of mountain sheep are large, but they are not so large as reported by Coronado's men. Castañeda gives the earliest description of these horns. "The men in advance guard saw a flock of sheep one day after leaving this place. I myself saw and followed them. They had extremely large bodies and long wool; their horns were very thick and large, and when they run they throw back their heads and put their horns on the ridge of their back. They are used to rough country, so that we could not catch them and had to leave them. Three days after we entered the wilderness we found a horn on the bank of a river that flows in the bottom of a very steep, deep gully, which the general had noticed and left there for his army to see, for it was six feet long and as thick at the base as a man's thigh."[17]

Castañeda's final statement is correct, as large horns measure 16 or 17 inches around the base, but he should have deducted two feet from his other measurement, as 49 inches is a record, and even large horns seldom exceed 40 inches around the outside of the curve. The horns are yellowish brown in color and are heavy, one set having weighed 28 pounds, while Audubon took a ram's head that weighed over 44 pounds. That is quite a burden for the animal to hold, even for the 344-pound animal recorded by Audubon.[18] Rams of the Rocky Mountain race weigh up to 285 pounds, on a body five feet in length, while those of the desert race are much smaller, the average for Arizona rams being 170 pounds.

Mountain sheep were found on both sides of the Río Grande, at least to the neighborhood of Albuquerque. On the west side of the river skeletons from modern times have been found near the Riana ruin,[19] and the Cochiti Indians are reported to have hunted them in the Jemez mountains until 1880.[20] In the Sandia Mountains on the opposite side of the river their bones were common in the rooms excavated at Paa-ko. While the flesh of these sheep was doubtless relished, they also were incorporated into the ceremonial life from an early time, as Hibben noted from Riana. "Mixed with the debris of the burnt roof and scattered over the whole kiva space were the fragments of a beautifully worked Wiyo bowl, and the head of a mountain sheep with the horns attached.... The sheep head was fragmentary and badly burned but enough was recovered to show that it was worked and cut on the skull and that the horns were wrapped with fibre. The piece was undoubtedly a remnant of headdress or ceremonial paraphernalia used in connection with kiva ritual."[21]

The desert bighorn is smaller in size. It inhabits the southern part of New Mexico and is probably the race once found in the Zuñi Mountains. In Arizona the desert race extends from the international boundary to the Alpine zone of the San Francisco peaks. According to Mearns this Mexican race is the *Pang-wuh* of the Hopi.[22]

In 1889 Merriam reported mountain sheep as common on the rim of the Grand Canyon and he sighted a small flock on the main peak of the San Francisco Mountains.[23] These sheep also roamed out onto the Painted Desert country wherever there were grass and springs. Don Talayesva records memories of the days when they were hunted in Hopi country. The region mentioned is in the area of the highway junction near the present Tuba City.

"We came abreast a sacred spring, deposited a prayer feather opposite the spot, passed another spring with similar sacrifices, and arrived at the shrine of Mountain Sheep, nine or ten miles from Moenkopi where our ancestors used to hunt. There were antelope tracks set in soft mud which the War Twins had turned to stone. We placed a feather on these, prayed to the Mountain Sheep for success in hunting, and asked them to come back so that we could hunt them again."[24] At the time of which he is speaking—probably in the 1920's—the last surviving bighorn might still have been somewhere about, for the demise of the final sheep in the Hopi country has been recorded by the Arizona hunter, Jack O'Conner, who saw one near Oraibi in 1924.[25]

Mountain sheep are very gregarious but do not form large flocks like domestic sheep—or antelope in some seasons—but congregate in small bands of up to thirty individuals. When feed is scarce these may break up into even smaller units. Sheep are subject to predators other than man. Golden eagles have easy access to the rocky country inhabited by sheep, and in southern New Mexico they raise their young at the same time and in the same place as the desert bighorn. The most serious eagle depredation is upon the young of these sheep.[26]

Mountain lion and wildcat also took their toll and, while the coyote can scarcely get at them in their craggy escarpments, he may be more successful in winter, as Bailey noted. "The deep snows of winter often force them down into lower country where food is obtainable and where numerous enemies surround them and sometimes in soft snow destroy whole herds of defenseless animals."[27] The Hopi were aware of the coyote's sheep hunting and used it to explain the hardness of the animal's horns. One day "coyote and other Hopi" went hunting on a mountain side some 125 miles from the villages. For Coyote it was a great success. "He went hunting again, this time for mountain sheep. He killed one and skinned it. This one had horns filled with fat. The next one he killed had big horns filled with fat. Coyote buried these horns."

Apparently Coyote's success made the other Hopi jealous, for when he killed two more and was about to take the horns, his companions said, "Oh, you do not get any. Your turn comes last." Coyote was angry at this and whispered *E'katdini*, "become bone." One of the Hopi heard him whisper this. "The man was trying to cut through the horn but could not do it. The inside of the horn was solid bone, a horn should cut easily. The man grasped his knife and tried to cut it. He tried again and again, but the inside of the horn was as hard as bone. Then he became angry at Coyote. Coyote was a clever fellow and had made the inside of the horn solid bone. A long time ago the mountain sheep had fat in its horns."[28] As might be expected, the next two rams that Coyote encounters rush together, crushing him between their great horns.

Because of its early disappearance there are few references to mountain sheep hunting by the Pueblos. From the Río Grande area there is one account of Cochiti hunting in the Jemez Mountains, which would probably apply equally well to the other villages of the area. Big game hunts were communal and led by a "Cougar Man" as hunt chief. As described by Lange, "Pit traps for game can still be seen in a narrow trail on a promontory (Bandelier's 'Chapero?') east of Bland, above Cañada de Cochiti. The pits were located where the mesa top reduced to a narrow trail, with very high and steep walls on either side. Traps in the trail were covered with grass matting and dust, and hunters drove the deer and sheep onto the mesa and into the pits. Pits were never equipped with sharp stakes in the bottom; hunters shot the animals that fell into them."[29]

From the Hopi country one account of desert bighorn hunting was recorded by a very old man living on Second Mesa. These Hopi hunts were not only communal, but included men from several villages. Sheep were hunted in September, at which time they were the fattest. The hunt chief, who is an elder, but not the member of any specific hunting society, makes prayer-sticks for six hunting deities: Mother of All Animals, Masau'u, Sparrow Hawk and Eagle deities, Gray Fox who in modern times stands in for Wolf, and Mountain Lion. These sticks are first taken to the Badger clan chief as recounted in the chapter on that animal.

When the mesas or canyons are reached a fire is built and shelter huts for the men are constructed. From the fire "each man took ashes in his left hand and circled them over his head six times in an anti-clockwise motion. The ashes were thrown away and with them the odor and contagion of women." Early on the morning of the hunt another fire is built, this time with grass and animal droppings, and each man runs his hands and weapons through it. The hunt itself is a drive by men and dogs who make as much noise as possible as they progress in two wings. This is to overcome the tendency of sheep to sit tight when danger threatens. "They tried either to drive the sheep into a cul-de-sac canyon or else drive them over a mesa edge in such manner that the animals would be killed outright or severely injured. The incapacitated animals were choked to death or else shot with bow and arrow. Those that took refuge on inaccessible rock ledges were lassoed with ropes of braided wool, hauled to the top of the cliff and then choked to death with their heads turned in the direction of the villages."[30]

The meat was divided equally, with the killer getting the skin, hooves, and horns, which are not only a trophy but have an important role in ceremony. The blood is saved in stomach bags, the internal organs are eaten immediately and only the offal is given to the dogs, as the bones must be treated as sacred. That evening the men eat roasted sheep-heads. The hunt is continued for four days, during which time some of the bighorns are kept alive until the last day when all but two, a ram and a ewe, are killed. These two are freed to reproduce as a physical symbol of rebirth.

Before leaving the hunt camp, the men who have actually killed mountain sheep make a kind of giant prayer feather, by tying individual feathers at intervals on a long cotton string. This is then laid out on the ground with the sheep skulls on top, each skull facing toward the rising sun. Meal is then sprinkled over them and prayers are offered to the spirits of the animals. On returning home each hunter is purified in juniper smoke, after which the meat is cut in strips and dried, although there is of course a feast on fresh meat as well. The bones that were also brought back are in time painted with red ochre and placed in a shrine. The latter practice accounts for an error by the mammologist of the Awatovi excavations, when she states, "Mountain-sheep remains are also few; probably no very serious efforts were made to hunt them."[31]

While we will later come to the ceremonial use of mountain sheep horns, there was also a practical reason why the killer was allowed to keep them. These horns are composed of a substance called keratin and the Hopi had learned that it had a value to the hunter that was comparable to our fiber glass. Instead of using the sinew-backed bow the Hopi used this substance for reinforcing. The process is described by Beaglehole. "Mountain sheep horn was melted to a sticky gum which was rubbed along the bow. Wet strips of tissue were bound around the bow at regular intervals. Gum was applied on top of the tissue and the bow was left to dry."[32] Yet another reason existed to link the hunters to the horns of sheep, which was that wood intended to be used for arrows was straightened with a wrench made of mountain sheep horn.

There are very few representations of mountain sheep in Pueblo murals or pictographs. Stevenson noted that the walls of the Zuñi Hunting society were painted with scenes of the beasts of prey engaged in the pursuit of elk, mountain sheep, deer, and rabbits.[33] In his survey of the animals included in mural decorations, Watson Smith mentions only one other instance where bighorns were represented, which was on the wall of a ruin in Chaco Canyon and thus dating from the twelfth century or before. It included "ten human figures with bows and arrows, shooting deer or mountain sheep. All were solid white and very crudely executed."[34] In the recent study of pictographs of the Navajo Reservoir district, none of the Pueblo animals was identified as a mountain sheep, although some could well be. Of interest, however, is the appearance of the flute player in the hunting scenes, since he will appear in Hopi Flute-Horn associations.

If the naming of clans is taken as an indicator, mountain sheep have a slight edge over elk, for whom no clans were named. As would be expected the Mountain Sheep clan, now extinct, appears among the Hopi, but only on First Mesa. This clan has a myth to account for its origin and migrations, and a figure called Mountain Sheep Hero who is the eponymous chief. There is a possibility that this clan was a lineage of the Horn clan with which it is certainly associated. The picture is complicated by the fact that there are both Horn clans and a Horn society, and a Flute clan as well as a Flute ceremonial group, while the figure of Mountain Sheep travels in and out among all of them.

On First Mesa there is a phratry, a group of related clans that have similar associations: Horn-Deer-Flute—Millet. The wild millet, which is also the name of a clan at Oraibi, is thought to represent the food of the horned animals of the Horn and Deer clans, while the flute is related because of the association of a humpbacked flute player with hunting. Within this group was also a Mountain Sheep clan whose myth was taken over by the Horn clan on the extinction of the former.

This group, whether clan or lineage, was living outside the present Hopi country in a pleasant valley where they grew corn and hunted game, but after the death of their chief, dissentions arose that resulted in fighting and the movement of various splinter groups. Such inner divisions and the resultant founding of new pueblos have been a constant part of Pueblo life throughout its history. According to this legend the chief of the Horn people said: "My people, we must leave, for nothing good will ever grow again where so many bad people live." Their instructions were to travel until they found the footsteps of the god Masau'u, which is a metaphorical way of saying that they should go to the land of Masau'u, the Hopi country.

Troubles followed the migrating people who could not find an acceptable chief, so it was decided "that a youth be appointed who should be taught all the customs of the people—all that people know—so that when he should become a man he would be able to talk to the people and teach them how to do. . . . This youth belonged to the Mountain sheep clan."[35] He led the people on a journey that took a century. It began near Jemez in New Mexico, continued to ruins near Fort Defiance in Arizona, then to Canyon Bonito, Canyon de Chelly, Keam's Canyon, and lastly to Hopi First Mesa. Possibly the legend was invented to account for various well known ruins, although people from the Río Grande did flee to Hopi at various times.

Fewkes, on the other hand, maintained that these clans came from the south and were associated with ruins in the neighborhood of Winslow on the Little Colorado River. "This Alosaka cult . . . is in someway connected with the Mountain-sheep clan of the Flute group. . . . In the enumeration of the clans belonging to the Ala-Lenya [Horn-Flute] group, there is a Panwu or Mountain-sheep clan. This fact is significant, as the Aaltu or Alosaka wear artificial horns and personate Mountain-sheep in several ceremonies."[36] The god Alosaka is the patron of the Horn society on other mesas, and it seems possible that in some villages the same associations can be related to either the clan, or to the society.

Wherever they came from, the legend of the Sheep Hero justifies a rite, the Flute ceremony, and on First Mesa that rite re-enacts the coming of the Sheep clan or lineage. As a musical instrument the flute has symbolic value. Flutes represent the sounds of locusts who are regarded, rightly, as the harbingers of summer. When discussing ancient pictographs, Parsons mentions that, "Between Locust and Mountain Sheep there is a conspicuous association which intrigues us because of contemporary association on First Mesa between the Flute ceremony in which Locust figures and the Horn clan."[37]

The Flute ceremony is the major vegetation ritual of the Hopi, which is held in years that alternate with the summer Snake ceremony. That it is concerned with vegetation rather than hunting is not surprising, since we have already seen that game such as deer play an important part in rainmaking. On First Mesa the Flutes take over Sun watching as soon as the Sun turns back from his winter solstice position. The Flute ceremony is thus complementary to the Winter Solstice or Soyal ceremony.[38] On Third Mesa where there is no Horn clan, the Oraibi Horn society chief is the Sun watcher.[39]

In the Flute ceremony there are impersonations of the horned fertility deities, Muiyingwa and Alosaka, as well as Masau'u, god of both crops and the dead. There is a form of sun handling, in that the Flute standard which is stuck into a pedestal called "flower mound" is painted black on its lower third to represent night, then blue above for daylight. Skins and feathers are hung on the pole to represent the various phases of dawn, while before the Flute altar hangs a kind of stick-mobile to represent the sky. When brushed with an eagle feather this "sets the 'sky' aswinging." When the morning star arises at 3 A.M., a procession with flute accompaniment is made to Sheep Spring and cloud symbols are made along the trail. While the procession is making this journey, younger men run to the fields and bring back large armsful of cornstalks, sunflowers, and other vegetation. On the following day races are run in which the participants, with a sunflower over one ear, carry green corn and chili. The lead runner carries a bottle of water which he must surrender to any other runner who overtakes him; all of this racing is to make the crops grow fast.[40]

If this pleasant rite of summer seems at some distance from the subject of mountain sheep, it is not really so. The Mountain Sheep Hero was the young chief to whom the knowledge of these rites was entrusted and it was his people who brought them to the Hopi country. The standard of the Flutes represents the consultation between the sky god and the earth god Muiyingwa, the two-horned deity of germination. "This was shown to Mountain sheep (Panwa) hero who went to the south."[41] There is a specific reason for associating mountain sheep with the growth of crops. Not only is racing good for the crops, but leaping is thought to be particularly efficacious, in that it suggests that the plants spring up quickly, an idea that found its classic expression in the Roman Lupercalia.

At the present time the Horn clan provides the town chieftancy on First Mesa, and a part of the Flute ceremony dramatizes the coming of the Horns and their acceptance of the chiefly role. Previously the Bear people had been the town chiefs, but one day Bear and Alosaka, who always sat on the housetops, spied these new people approaching. These said, "We had lived (elsewhere for) a time and we longed to know where other people were, and Mountain sheep (Panwa) went forth and circled around and returned to tell us that people dwelt at this mesa."[42] The chief of the Horns then said to the Hopi, "We carry on our backs the wood of the Flute altar, and we can cause the rain to fall," and surely enough, as soon as they were allowed to enter and set up their altar rains began to fall.

As it has been suggested that leaping is a fertility or growth ritual, it can be expected that other Pueblo groups would also imitate mountain sheep, and this proves to be true. One instance occurs at Zuñi in connection with the Shalako ceremony, where deer play a role similar to that of the mountain sheep in the Hopi Flute ceremony. During the Zuñi rite it is the clowns who are called *Haliliku*, which is the Zuñi name for mountain sheep. It is in part the words that they say which have given them this name, but their speech has unfortunately not been recorded for a technical reason: "the words were unintelligible to the writer because of the mask."[43] All is not lost, however, as their actions speak for themselves. "They are supposed in this progress not to touch the ground, no matter how high or rickety the places they must climb."[44]

These Koyemshi clowns, who are impersonating mountain sheep, must visit each Shalako house in a course that carries them over the rooftops of the town of Zuñi. This romp requiring the agility of a bighorn is undertaken realistically enough to include the possibility of a fall, perhaps a serious one, and any such accident is thought to indicate a breech of continence on the part of the performer. While on the rooftops, over the harvest home feasts that are taking place in certain houses below, these sheep-clowns sing and are then invited to come down and join in.

There is also a more elaborate dance ceremony at Zuñi that goes by the name of Haliliku, or mountain sheep, but details concerning it are scarce. In Cushing's account of Zuñi creation myths, he makes one brief mention of this dance. "They settled at Kwaikina, where the Brotherhood of Fire (Makekwe) had its place of ancient origin in wonderous wise—told of by themselves—and where originated their great dance drama of the Mountain Sheep, and the power of entrance into fire, and even of contention with sorcery itself."[45] Thus we learn only that there was such a dance and that it was in the hands of the Great Fire Society. Stevenson makes no mention of this dance in her account of that society, perhaps because her studies were made during single years. If it was a biennial or quadrennial ceremony she may have missed the particular year. That there was a Mountain Sheep Dance is certain, for Parsons notes that it was performed in April of 1917, although she gives no further information.

There is one possible clue as to the meaning of this dance. The Great Fire Society is a curing order divided into a number of subdivisions, such as the "sword swallowers," those who hold live coals in their mouths, and others. The Beasts of Prey are associated with curing. Individual Beast Gods, such as Mountain Lion and Wolf, are hunting deities, but as a group these beasts of the directions bring their powers to cure the sick. Almost incidental to her long account of the rituals of the Great Fire Society, Stevenson remarks that, "The animal fetishes by the altar influence the spiritual presence of the Beast Gods."[46] The idea would seem to be that images of the game animals, including the mountain sheep, are placed about the altar because they will suggestively bring in the Beasts of Prey whose power is needed for the cure.

There are both mountain sheep kachinas and impersonators of this animal in various game dances. The people of Acoma have a kachina, Kashko, who represents the bighorn.[47] A whole company of these appear in connection with the winter solstice, when they are driven about in a flock like domestic sheep. At Jemez there are two mountain sheep impersonators in the Deer Dance,[48] and at Santa Ana sheep may be impersonated in the Buffalo Dance, but apparently they seldom are. Santo Domingo and San Felipe seem to lack these impersonations, as does Cochiti, but in the Buffalo Dance there, a mountain goat appears. One suspects that what is being impersonated is the female mountain sheep. Coronado thought that he saw mountain goats, but since the home of these animals is far to the north it has been suspected that these were mountain sheep ewes.[49]

The Hopis make frequent use of helmets with small ewe horns on them, which may explain the Cochiti goats, who act as side dancers or attendants to the line of kachinas.[50] It is among the Hopis, who had the most intimate knowledge of mountain sheep, that both kachinas and imitative sheep dances are most common. There are two versions of the Panwu or Pang kachina; the heads are identical, the mask being surmounted with two imitation ram's horns in black, with a green zigzag lightning mark along their sides. The head is black, with squash blossoms for ears, and has a short snout with the teeth painted on. One version is dressed in a buckskin shirt and a white kilt striped with red and black.

The second type of mountain sheep kachina is completely naked and is obviously a phallic sprite derived from the ram's promiscuous nature. His back and limbs are painted blue or green, while his ventral side is painted white.[51] According to Colton, these sheep kachinas appear in bands in ordinary kachina dances, where they have power over rain—being associated with the mountains—and over spasms.[52] The latter power may derive from the fact that when rams battle the powerful clash sends a spasm or shock wave the entire length of their muscular bodies.[53] Or it may be due to the twisting nature of the horns, since antelope and deer kachinas share the power.

Before turning to an account of the Horn Society's relationship to sheep, it may be noted in passing that like deer, the bighorn has served as a witch disguise. The Tewa who have moved from the Río Grande to the Hopi First Mesa tell the story of Handmark Boy. He is in reality made of ice and thus can only come to one end, but on the way he is subjected to a number of tests. One of these tests is to kill a mountain sheep. Alone he follows them into a canyon and to a very narrow place. "Handmark Boy took his medicine into his mouth and spat it on the sheep. The sheep turned and ran at him to toss him. He pulled his bow, shot and killed the sheep."[54] This it seems was not a real sheep, but a witch who had planned to kill him, so Handmark Boy did not go down to get the body. The stone mountain lion fetish in his wallet had warned him of this fact and when the youth placed it on the ground, "The little mountain lion turned into a big lion and chased a real mountain sheep and killed it." The lion then became a fetish once again.

Nothing so simple is involved in the role of mountain sheep in the Hopi tribal initiation ceremony. The ceremony is usually called the Wuwuchim. There are four societies involved in the tribal initiation and the roles of each have been likened to walls of protection about the people. The warlike Kwans are "the destroyers of the enemy" and compose the outer ring. Next comes the Al or Horn Society, which is not to be confused with the Horn clan previously discussed. According to Eggan, "The Ahl represent the horned animals, particularly mountain sheep, which are noted for their sharpness of vision and hearing."[55]

These two societies, the Kwans and the Horns, once joined together in defending the village against external enemies. The Horns were the second line of defense not only for the conceptual reason of their sharp-eyed sheep connections, but because as hunters they had weapons at hand. At Oraibi the Bow clan has charge of all weapons and controls the Horn society.[56] The inner defenders were the Wuwuchim society, composed of the ancients and councilors, and the Singers society who kept the myths of the people, which are central to the defense of a culture.

The core of this ceremony is the promotion of growth, but in this case it is primarily that of humans, as the novices are promoted during the nine days of the ceremony from the status of children to that of adults, and warriors if need be. During the rites the Horns imitate sheep and pray to Tuwabongtumsi, Sand Altar Woman, as she is the mother of all animals. Since human birth is very closely associated with animal birth, the Horn men also bring the image of Dawn Woman, Talatumsi. "While this image is being secreted the Horns scattered among the cliffs between the terrace and the summit, and bounded constantly back and forth among the crags, faithfully imitating mountain sheep."[57] The role of Dawn Woman in this ceremony is to act as the mother of the novices, who are being born again into their adult role, and the leaping about of the Horns as sheep will presumably speed this growth.

The Horn men who bear the image of this goddess wear an actual scalp of the female sheep with its small five-inch horns, and as a sign of their role they at one point give each of the novices a deer antler. The scalp of the sheep is affixed to a wicker helmet which Horn men wear. On the last day of the ceremony, four Horn priests (wrapped in rabbit skin rugs), with their helmets reversed, go out into the freezing November night to build three bonfires. "These four mimicked the actions of wild sheep with great fidelity; never remaining still longer than a moment, and never assuming their natural gait. They were constantly bucking and jumping, and always glancing sharply around."[58]

So the dance continues with the priests bucking and jumping over the piles of wood that are set about between the fires, until at last the cold dawn arrives and the Sun god salutes the joining of youth to age, which makes this ceremony a fitting counterpart to the Flute ceremony in which the youthful Mountain Sheep Hero brought fertility rites for the crops growing under the sun, by joining together the powers of sky and earth. How unfortunate that the mountain sheep no longer inhabit the mountains and mesas to enjoy the fruits of this union.

Chapter VI

RABBITS

WHEN THE PUEBLOS speak of hunting, without mentioning some specific kind of game, they mean rabbit hunting. Rabbits are nearly ubiquitous in North America, although the cottontails do not like the heavy, humid forests of Washington and there are no jacks east of the Mississippi. Neither elevation nor extremes of weather are problems to this order of mammals, as the pikas live the year around above timberline in the arctic zone, while members of the same genus, *Lepus,* inhabit the most arid parts of the Southwest and northern Mexico where their only water comes from the plants they eat.

In most areas there are always as many rabbits as the food supply at any given time can maintain. They are gifted with an amazing fecundity which places them almost in the same category as weedlike plants in their ability to take advantage of the first inclination of the scales in their favor, and this not in years, or even seasons, but in months. After a serious epidemic which has nearly wiped them out, a species that normally has four young will have eight or even ten in each litter until the population has been restocked.[1]

Of nearly equal importance to their plenitude is the ease with which rabbits may be hunted; their defense is reproduction, not cunning. The most primitive of weapons, such as the throwing-stick, are as effective in hunting them as anything, or they may be simply caught in traps, snares, and nets. They are thus ideal objects for community hunts in which women and children may take part. The steady availablility of rabbits has made a long continuity in the rabbit-to-human relationship and the consequent ceremonial elaboration of the hunt.

For an agricultural people some rabbit hunting is imperative as they are a pest in fields of young corn and other crops, unless their numbers are kept in check by community drives. For seed gathering peoples they provide a ready supply of meat when long and complicated hunts for large game were not practicable. A Zuñi Indian looking back on ancient times said, "Food was scarce. It was bad. They roasted cactus and wild grass. That only they ate.... Then in winter, when they killed rabbits, they dried the stomachs. They chopped up the intestines and the feet and hung it up with these inside. They would boil it with squash seeds and eat it with gravy. They would not throw away the bones. The grandmothers would grind the bones in stone mortars and dip up the mixture with their fingers."[2]

Perhaps this man was thinking of times of drought as well as ancient times, but in any case the dependence on rabbits is evident. Not only did the little beasts provide meat for the pot, but their furry skins were easily tanned and sewn together to make warm robes. The forerunners of the Pueblos, the Basketmakers, quite evidently took rabbits in great numbers for both food and clothing. One interesting proof of these prehistoric rabbit drives was found at White Dog Cave in northeastern Arizona. There a net was discovered which was made of nearly four miles of string, the string being spun from a mixture of hair and the fibers of a milkweed relative. This net was two hundred and forty feet long and about three feet high. It is believed that the net was placed across the mouth of a canyon and the rabbits, as well as miscellaneous small game, were then driven down into the net and there clubbed to death.[3]

The result of such a drive would be an immediate feast, much meat to dry, and a great number of skins for robes. These were made by cutting the skins in strips, then twisting the strips around yucca fibers to form fur ropes. Then these ropes were tied together by a simple looping stitch to form a sturdy robe, the advantage being that skins alone are very delicate and tear easily. These robes protected one from the cold and were also used at times for burial of the dead.[4] According to the archae-ologist Judd, rabbit fur blankets were still used by the Hopi when he first visited them in 1926.[5]

In modern times the ceremonial importance of rabbit hunting has gained in prominence, until now the religious significance probably outweighs the practical value of the animals for food, at least in the Río Grande pueblos. The food in this case becomes something of a communion as rabbit meat is an ideal ritual food, either to feed the performers in a ceremony or to "feed" the fetishes used in the rites. Other game is seasonal in nature and may not be at hand when needed for a ceremony held on a particular date, as we saw when a deer had to be conjured up by magic at Isleta. A supply of rabbit meat, on the other hand, can be brought in for any given day in the year.

The distinction between rabbits and hares is something of a problem in this country as we call them all rabbits, but in Europe and Mexico the distinction is kept in common speech. Strictly speaking the jackrabbits are hares and cottontails are rabbits, the chief difference being that rabbits are born hairless and blind, while the hares have their eyes open and are furred—almost ready to go.[6]

"There was a jack rabbit chief. Then where they lived a big snowfall came which was impassable. Then jack rabbit called out from the house top, 'Do not get up! Let the snow make a crust!' The chief said to the rest, 'Now you be ready to get up, and walk all over about the snow to leave your footprints all over the snow. Now be ready!' They left their tracks on the snow. The chief said, 'Now the hunters will not find us.'"[7]

There is yet another species that barely touches the Pueblo area. This is the white-tailed jackrabbit, the largest of American hares, who also wears a pure white winter coat and possesses an amazing bounding speed. These are said to be common in the valley near Taos, where they are given the name Ka-pap-tuna. Bailey mentions only two records for the state, but Ligon seems to have observed them often in the north.[8]

According to a Hopi Indian, "In the winter the men catch

rabbits by running them down in the snow. The men go out early and if they find a track, they will start following it and the rabbit is theirs when they catch up. There is a rule followed in such winter hunting. If someone is on the track of a rabbit no one else can pick up the animal and kill it.... A good runner can run down three or four jackrabbits in the snow in a day."[9] Rabbits caught this way are given ceremonial treatment and their souls sent home, just as with big game.

In the Pueblo area the black-tailed jackrabbit, which is the species of the hunt just described, and two species of cottontail are *the* rabbits. These are the prolific and widespread species that provide food in abundance. The black-tailed jack, also called the Texas jack, do not bear as many young as cottontails, but they have the speed of their bounding gait to protect them to some extent and it would be no slight trick to run one down.

Both kinds of rabbits breed the year around. However, there are limits to the stamina of the mothers and about four litters a year seems to be the usual rate. These jacks are common to abundant below the 7,000-foot contour, where they live on the scant herbs and grasses or the bark of shrubs and willows. They can be serious pests, particularly in newly planted areas. The jacks seldom drink water, gaining their moisture instead from the plants they eat. Speaking of those he found in the Painted Desert and nearby piñon and juniper belts. Merriam said: "During the intense heat of the day we frequently started them from their hiding place under the low branches of junipers or in tufts of greasewood. At such times they remain absolutely motionless, squatting close to the ground with their long ears laid flat on their backs. When in this position their colors harmonize so well with their surroundings that they are rarely seen until they start with a great bound and gallop away."[10]

The bone remains found in ruins confirm the importance of both kinds of rabbits. It has already been mentioned that, at Winona, of the 221 animals identified, 97 were jacks and 39 cottontails. In Big Hawk Valley cottontail and prairie dogs were the commonest bones found, while at Awatovi both kinds of rabbit bones were common. Bones of both were plentiful in the ruins of Pueblo Bonito and in the Navajo Reservoir district, slightly to the north, rabbits predominated in the more than 4,000 bones collected from sites dating from 1 A.D. At Riana ruin in the Chama River valley the remains of the Rocky Mountain Cottontail bulked large and were found in almost every room.[11]

The Zuñi have a brief tale illustrating the different habitats of the jack and the cottontails. "Anciently the Jack-rabbit lived in a sage plain, and the Cottontail rabbit lived in a cliff hard by. They saw the clouds gather, so they went out to sing. The long-legged Jack-rabbit sang for snow, thus:

> '*U pi na wi sho, U pi na we sho,*
> *U kuk uku u kuk!*'

But the short-legged Cottontail sang for rain, like this:

> '*Hatchi ethla ho na an saia.*'

"That's what they sung—one asking for snow, the other for rain; hence to this day the Pok'ia (Jack-rabbit) runs when it snows, the A'kshiko (Cottontail) when it rains."[12]

Cottontails face coyotes, wildcats, and foxes on the ground, hawks and owls from the air, but by keeping within short range of home base they may scurry to safety. For the species, rapid multiplication is the defense. It has been said that only one cottontail out of twenty has a chance to live out a full year. The young leave their mother at the end of two weeks. Sometimes the mother cottontail will breed again the day after giving birth. Cahalane estimates that if all the young of one pair and their offspring surivived for five years, the progeny would amount to 322,000 individuals—a most remarkable food-producing potential.

Since the cottontails are not travelers like the jacks, they do not often congregate in numbers. They can be pests, but local hunting is usually sufficient for control even when the corn is freshly sprouted. Don Talayesva mentions a kind of native pesticide that the Hopi used to check their depredations. "I probably made twenty-five trips to my cornfield to replant, chop weeds, poison rats, set traps for rabbits, and spray my plants with a mixture of powdered rabbit intestines, dried roots, dog dung, and water."[13]

One might think that the very ease of obtaining rabbits might curtail the use of ceremonies, calling for the help of the gods to obtain this game, but the very reverse is true. Because of the highly ceremonial nature of rabbit hunting, the old and seemingly primitive weapons have survived for the hunt, just as the fire-drill is still used to kindle hunt fires. At Taos guns are taboo on rabbit hunts, the bow and arrows being the only weapons used.

Except at Taos the universal and traditional weapon for taking rabbits is the throwing-stick, called *draits* by the Keres. These are made from some hard wood, such as greasewood, and sticks may be either curved or straight. The curved variety is the one preferred in the west, being used by the Hopi and Zuñi. It is known at Isleta, but is not much used there, although among the Río Grande pueblos it is used at Santa Ana.[14] The straight stick, called *wobaits* at Acoma, is used by the majority of the Río Grande Keres, by the Tewa, and at Jemez.

The history of the curved rabbit-stick is open to some questions. Basketmaker sites have revealed a common variety from that early age which characteristically has four indented lineal grooves. This may have been the prototype, since the Basketmakers had no bows and arrows. On the other hand it is very similar to clubs used by the Mayans as a defense against the atlatl. Arrows thrown by the atlatl travel at a slow pace, which makes a club for batting the missiles aside an effective defense. Actually there is no reason to decide on a specific use for these sticks, since a weapon at hand would be used in any way possible when it came to a fight.

The Hopi broad stick was thought of as primarily a weapon for rabbit hunting, but it was also used in war as Stephen notes in an account of a foray against the Apache. "They were armed with spear, bow and arrow, and *puchko'hu* (broad stick), a weapon that can be thrown so as readily to break an arm or leg and to kill if it strikes an enemy in the forehead. But it is most efficient to be thrown at an enemy drawing his bow or aiming; it is hurled so as to strike the enemy before he can recover."[15] This statement makes it clear that the same stick could be used as an offensive missile, a defense against either bow or atlatl, a rabbit stick, or simple club.

The Hopi theory is that the broad, curved throwing-stick was a gift from the Hawk deity, and that it was given to them after they already had the bow. This stick, which is painted with nonrealistic designs to indicate the rabbit's ears and eyes, came to the Hopi in the following way: "Kih'sha (Cooper's hawk or sparrow hawk) was the first possessor of a *puchko'hu*. He carried it under his wing and hunted rabbits with it. He plucked a feather from each of his wings and fastened them at the marks toward the point. (These are the ears) I find much reluctance to tell anything concerning this weapon. It is modeled after the wing of Kih'sha, and referred to as his wing. Long ago the Hopi had bow and arrow but no *puchko'hu*. Kih'sha is the great hunter. Eagle (Kwa'hu) and Kwa'yo are not very good hunters. Eagle, Kwayo, Lion, Wolf, Bear: all the preying animals have bow and arrow; so has Kih'sha, but he alone devised the *puchko'hu*."[16]

There are some oddities in that statement, such as the view that Eagle and Kwayo, which is a general name for hawks, are not good hunters. Kisha is a deity who is related to the Cooper's hawk and several falcons, and it is the swift darting flight of these birds which resembles the throwing-stick. The Cooper's hawk preys largely on birds, while the sparrow hawk is an insect eater, as the Hopi knew and explained in tales. The prairie falcon, not mentioned here, is also called Kisha and he is very skillful at taking young rabbits. Offerings are made to the Hawk deity in thankfulness for his gift.

The curved throwing-stick has one advantage over the straight, which is its magical power of drawing the rabbits toward the hunter. While the straight stick lacks this virtue it is more simply made. The Hopi hunter carries a broad stick and also tucks a half dozen pointed sticks in his belt; if these are lost or broken in the hunt they can be quickly replaced. To increase the virtue of any stick it is necessary to pass it through the hunt fire. The fire blessing is a reflection of the actual hardening of sticks and arrow shafts in a fire.

Among all groups of Pueblos a ritual fire is made by the hunt chief or other leader. At Acoma it is the War Chief who is in charge of the hunt. He calls the people to some chosen place where a fire is prepared with dry grass, rabbit manure, and some sticks. Around this pile he draws a circle of meal with four intersecting lines to indicate the directions. Fresh flowers are then picked and placed on the line and a bit of meal is sprinkled on the pile. "Then the war chief lights the fire. When the smoke begins to rise the war chief prays: 'Sun hunter, I wish you to help me today. Cause lots of cottontails and jack rabbits to come together here.' "[17] A theory connected with this fire and prayer is that before a person strikes a rabbit the sun will strike the animal and make him a little crazy.

The stated purpose of the fire is to draw in the game, by the power of the Sun's magic. In Hopi theory it is also the house of the rabbits to which they gladly return. "When everybody has come, the head of the hunt covers the fire, leaving a little opening at the top. Then we start off. O yes, the man put four prayer feathers on the ground in each direction and covered them with sand and on top made the fire. The fire makes the rabbits weak. Covering it keeps the rabbits there, that is their home."[18]

Speeches by the chiefs are a regular part of community preparations for the hunt. In part these involve the necessary mechanical instructions, dividing the groups for a winged drive, laying down the rules for disputed game and the like. But there is also a kind of formal permission and absolution from guilt. "He tells them that they are about to go out hunting and that they must kill anything that comes in their way; that if it is necessary for them to 'cut down a tree or uproot a plant' they should do it, that this would not be wanton destruction but quite legitimate, since it is a hunt. He tells them that their slaughter of animals is not to be regarded as cruelty, that the Masewi and Shaiyak have not summoned the people for an errand of cruelty's sake, but to kill game for the people to eat."[19] He then names all the beasts of prey, saying that each one gives his blessing and power to the hunters.

In communal hunts there is never a single motive, nor is meat for the table the prime reason for the hunt, as the hunters may get little or none for themselves. Sometimes they are given the rabbit "insides" for their own use, while the meat is reserved to feed the kachina dancers. At other times a hunt may be held to provide meat for the town chief, who does no manual work, he works only with his mind and heart for the good of the community. Sometimes a hunt may have the purpose of "feeding" the fetishes and kachina masks that are thought of as living, or again it may combine two kinds of practicality, that of ridding the fields of pests and of supplying a feast for the village.

There are degrees of ritual importance attached to various rabbit hunts and these may be indicated by the person who calls for the hunt. At Hopi where there is no hunt chief, many hunts are called by individuals—the laity—while the more ritualistic ones are arranged by the chief of the Rabbit clan. At Zuñi the most important hunts are called by the priest in charge of the ceremony to which the hunt is related, but others may be called by the governor of the pueblo. A brief description of a Zuñi hunt of the 1880's should suffice for all Pueblo rabbits hunts of the communal type.

This was a thanksgiving hunt, held to celebrate the completion of the harvest, but it involved a number of other rituals as well. Like similar modern hunts this one made use of horses, as the farming and hunting district may be far from the pueblo. Even the Hopi now hunt rabbits from horseback, although this is recognized as an innovation. No women were to accompany this hunt; special hunts in which women and girls may take part are often designated. Some days before the hunt a cottontail and a jack had been caught on the order of a Koyemshi, or clown, who was to be an official in the coming hunt. These were left hanging in the village "for good luck to the hunters," until after the hunt was completed.

The party made its first stop on a knoll at some distance from the pueblo, where three officials were sitting at the base of a piñon tree. These were the Great Father Koyemshi, his deputy, and a man of the hunt society. The two clown officers sat facing each other, one looking west and one east, while the Great Father clasped the hands of his deputy. When the hunters dismounted the Great Father whispered a prayer, put his hands to the mouth of his deputy, then to his own and "inhaled from him a breath of all that is good." Further prayers were followed by a smoke.

Then the three officials led the party on foot to a fire that was already made. This "was burning in a low and symmetrical cedar tree, the flames spreading evenly and beautifully. They must walk, because when the world was new the Zuñi had no horses. The three men stood near the fire, offering prayers to the dead and begging the intercession of their ancestors with the Council of the Gods that the rain-makers should water the earth. Bread was thrown into the flames, with a call to eat and convey the spiritual essence of the food to the dead."

There is a rite in connection with the fire, although it does not occur in this account, in which the members of the Fire order of the Hunt Society throw live coals to the six directions to draw in the game. For the horizon directions the game consists of both kinds of deer, antelope, and mountain sheep. Jack-rabbit is drawn in, or down, from the Zenith and cottontail from the Nadir.

In this instance the hunters threw bits of bread into the fire, for the dead, and then passed their rabbit sticks through the flames. They were next divided into groups and led to the hunt by the Great Father Koyemshi who remained with them until the first rabbit was killed. It happened to be a much bewildered cottontail, into whose blood the clown officer dipped his fetish.

The hunt was fruitful, but it was no mass slaughter. From a number of accounts it would seem that the average take per man on such a hunt is five or six rabbits.

The game this day was destined for family consumption—the hunt had been called by the governor of the pueblo, not a religious officer—so each hunter took his share home. A member of the household places the rabbits abreast and on their sides, with the heads facing east. An ear of corn is placed between the forepaws with the upper end to the animal's mouth. Each member of the household sprinkles meal and prays that the beings of the rabbits may return to their homes and send more rabbits. It is notable that each of these little creatures is given ritual handling equivalent to that for dead deer or other big game. At Hopi rabbits are the smallest animal so treated, and this is probably true elsewhere as well.

Next the game is flayed, leaving bits of skin on the paws, ear tips, mouth, and breast. Then it is cut and drawn, the forelegs crossed and the hind legs bent up over the back. Wafer bread is placed under the left foreleg and the rabbits are laid on the coals with their heads to the east, where they remain "until the first crackling noise, when they are removed, for then the spiritual essence of the bread has left the body and gone to feed the rabbits. If this is not done, the rabbits will not appear."[20] Any blood on the hands must be washed off over the fire, because if this is done at a distance the rabbits will go off, in which we see an analogy between this fire and the ritual hunt fire.

Since ritual is so highly developed in connection with these hunts, one might anticipate taboos on casual hunting, and, in that case, rabbits would lose much of their value. Fortunately this is not the case, and they may be hunted at will by farmers or by traders on long expeditions. Cushing describes such an expedition, on which he accompanied two Zuñi hunters.

Together they "set out one sandy morning for the far-away southern mesas. I say a 'sandy morning,' for the wind was blowing through the mountain funnels west of Zuñi such a terrific gale that not the least particle of landscape, except such as was flying through the air in the shape of sand, could be seen two rods ahead of us. Earth, sky, and the little river along which our trail ran were equally invisible." The three plodded ahead all day without food or water, until at sunset they descended into a white-walled canyon.

"No sooner were we well down before an exclamation from Pa-lo-wah-ti-wa caused me to look around. 'Supper is ready!' he cried, pointing to a little cottontail rabbit which was just scudding into a hole in the rocks. Forthwith Kesh'-pa-he dismounted, and cutting a slender twig, so trimmed the branches from it as to leave one or two hooks or barbs at the lower end. He then pushed the twig into the hole." This stick was twisted around and around until the loose furry skin was entangled and the cottontail drawn from the hole. "He was soon grasped by the hind-legs, hit a sharp blow with the open hand just behind the ears, and instantly his struggles ceased. Before he was fairly dead, the Indians drew his face up to their own and breathed from his nostrils the last faint sighs of his expiring breath. Thus they killed no fewer than three or four rabbits."[21]

A fire was built and snow piled on a sloping rock where it melted and ran into the single pot carried by the group. The rabbits were thrown into the fire until the fur was singed off, then taken out, skinned and placed on sticks to roast. A loaf of bread was made by wrapping dough around a stick similarly set by the fire and cornmeal was stirred into the boiling water of the bowl. According to Cushing the dinner was one of utmost delicacy and all that the travelers had to carry with them was a pouch of meal and a pot.

There are any number of ways to pick up a cottontail when a little food is needed, and some of these are so simple that children can use the devices. When necessary a snare can be made from one's own long hair, or a deadfall trap can be made from a rock slab. The latter method, which is particularly handy when one is camped about his cornfield, is made by tilting a flat rock on an upright stick. A horizontal tension stick and cord is placed against the stone, meal is sprinkled on the ground and when the animal enters he dislodges the tension stick, allowing the stone to overbalance and fall.

The fact that rabbit hunting is relatively easy makes it ideal as a means for the initiation of young boys. Before a Hopi youth can hunt larger game he must first be initiated in a rabbit hunt. His success cannot be based upon the cottontail, since that is too easy to kill, but must wait until he is sufficiently skilled to kill a jackrabbit, which means that he is then adept with the throwing stick. When any youth kills his first jack, "the hunt is stopped and all the men gather around the boy. His father, or a kinsman if the father is not present, chooses the best hunter on the field to act as hunt-father to the boy 'because he wants the boy to be as good a hunter as this man.' As in the old days the men hunted clad only in breech cloth, pigment and moccasins, so today the boy is stripped of his clothes. The men form a circle round him holding each other's wrists. A relative takes the boy by the shoulder and bends him forward with his back towards the north. The hunt father takes the dead rabbit and swings it across the boy's back from left to right leaving a blood mark on the flesh."[22]

The boy is then given the rabbit which he may eat, but he must abstain from salt for several days. For three days he undergoes sunrise bathing rites and prayer-stick planting. On the third day a special stew is made by relatives and a hunt is called for the next day, on which the youth is to act as commander of one of the wings of hunters. On the fourth morning there is a special feast at the house of his hunt-father's mother or sister, and at that time he is given a new name and gifts, among which are two painted, curved throwing-sticks from his hunt-father.

He is dressed in ceremonial attire, with bells about his waist, turquoise necklaces; parrot and white eagle feathers are tied in his hair. His body is painted and his face rubbed with meal. In this attire he appears at the hunt fire and announces to all his new name. Thus his passage into manhood is due to skill in the use of the throwing stick. This may occur at any age, but twelve seems average. It should be noted that he still must undergo tribal initiation which is not the same as initiation into the hunting group.

Many rabbit hunts are tied to a particular season and are involved in various kinds of weather control. At Isleta, as at Zuñi, there is a thanksgiving hunt expressing gratitude for crops. "Also it is to bring frost, to harden the corn and grapes which are to be dried. Therefore all crops, such as melons, which would be hurt by frost, must be gathered before this dance."[23] A curious feature of the hunt that accompanies this dance is that it includes in one day purposes that are ordinarily spread over a number of hunts. This is managed by having a series of hunts, the first of which is for the town chief, and all rabbits taken go to him. The second round is for the hunt chief, the third for the war chief and other officers; then the rest of the day is devoted to hunting rabbits for the laity. As women accompany this hunt the animals are given to the first woman to reach the slain game, for which she must pay the hunter on the following day with gifts of wafer bread and stew.

The winter solstice is a crucial season in many ways. The Sun is the great rabbit hunter who first makes the little creatures dizzy, then the hunters can kill them. The Sun is also the greatest of fertility spirits and as rabbits are emblems of fertility we can expect rabbits to be associated with the sun on that score. Further, the Sun exercises his power upon the earth, and rabbits are of the earth. As a result of these connections there are taboos on rabbit hunting either during the solstice ceremony, or on First Mesa during all of December, which is called the "dangerous moon." According to Stephen, "Rabbits during the December moon weep when hunted—during this moon there should be no hunt."[24]

On Second Mesa there is a closed season, but only during the time in which prayer-sticks are being made for the Winter Solstice and for four days afterwards. "During these days rabbits are supposed to have time to increase in numbers; this is in line with the fertility of all animal life. But since the ground is considered specially thin during this month called 'danger moon,' it is dangerous to break into the earth, so no animals, not even rabbits, should be dug from their holes during the whole of the moon."[25]

Apparently the thought behind this taboo, which seems more an admonition than a strict rule, is not so much one of conservation as a feeling that when the sun is weakest the earth is likewise frail and should not be dug into. Perhaps the taboo then applied more to cottontails who might be underground, for Stephen also mentions a rabbit hunt that was actually held on December 10, 1891. At Oraibi on Third Mesa the end of the Soyal ceremony is followed by three days of rabbit hunting. The game is brought back to the various kivas where it is placed to the north of the fireplace.[26] One would gather that the suggestion here is that the Sun too should make his way back to the north side.

There is another taboo, this time on eating rather than hunting rabbits, that may serve as an introduction to the relation of rabbits to fertility concepts. At Laguna and Cochiti the members of the Kurena clown society, and at Zuñi the members of Shi'wanakwe clown society, may not eat jackrabbits. Both of these groups are alternative clown societies of lesser importance than their counterparts, the Keresan Koshari and the Zuñi Newekwe. They are somewhat specialized for the promotion of fertility and weather control.[27]

The Kurena end all of their songs with the word "sunrise" and in mythology they come from the south, the land of summer and they traveled to the northeast into the forest. When they came from the south they were leading a group of people called She-kun who carried with them magical plants in full bloom. Sometimes the plant would seem to wither and die, but then it would suddenly revive and bloom again. There is also a taboo restricting all three of these groups from eating Rocky Mountain bee plant, an important source of boiled greens among the Pueblos. As they promote plant fertility they may not eat these, and the fact that rabbits nibble on such fresh greens makes their meat taboo. After the ceremonial rabbit hunts held in conjunction with the summer and winter solstices, the rabbits are taken to the clowns and placed in front of the sacred corn-ear fetish. The meat is then sent by the war captains to the houses of the shamanistic societies.

Rabbits are related to the spirits through their fertility, particularly the blood and skins, but they are not directly represented as kachina. In the account of the supernatural world there is no Hare cycle like the one found farther east, and there are no myths relating the little creatures to the events of creation. There are however kachinas that represent rabbit hunters. On Hopi First Mesa there is a kachina called Makto whose helmet has a broad face consisting almost entirely of a throwing stick, which matches the one held in his hand.[28]

At Acoma there is a figure—a single kachina rather than a group of them—who is said to have been modeled on a great rabbit hunter of the past, the far past probably as his story concerns rabbit-fur clothing. "One morning he went out hunting. He saw a jack rabbit. He was going to hit him with his throwing stick when the rabbit spoke to him. The rabbit said, 'Wait, don't hit me. Come here.' Nyenyeka went up to the rabbit and asked him what he wanted. The rabbit called Nyenyeka by name and said, 'I am going to make a bet with you. I am going off a little ways and sit down. You throw your stick at me. If you hit me you win my clothes, if you don't, then I win your stick.' . . . So the jack rabbit went off a short distance and sat still. Nyenyeka threw his stick at him and cut his head off. So he won the rabbit's clothes. He skinned the rabbit and wore his fur over his head."[29]

If the rabbits are not directly represented among the supernaturals, their skin and blood is important to several deities. The creation of rabbits is closely related to that of deer and other game at Hopi. Tih'kuyi Woman, the Mother of Game, gave birth to a pair of antelopes and the blood that issued from her during this birth, she confined to a pool in the sand. From the blood-soaked sand she made five pellets and from these created both kinds of rabbits; from these all others are descended.[30]

Blood does not occur in their Acoma creation, where cottontails and jacks are simply taken from the basket of images along with their close relatives, antelope and water deer, but at Zuñi birth-blood enters into the Mother of Game rites in a literal fashion. This blood provides the essential link between the concepts of game mother and the deity who confers the blessing of human birth. The personal name of the Mother of Game is Kuyapalitsa, but when she is impersonated—by a male—she is called Chakwena. A part of the hunt ritual consists in the lying in, for four days, of Chakwena in an imitation childbirth. The time varies in different accounts, but the point is the same. According to Parsons, a rabbit is killed four days before the hunt and the blood rubbed on the legs of the Chakwena impersonator.

"In the hunt the chakwena must take a straight course over all obstacles, so that the blood will be rubbed off on the plants and rabbits will be plentiful. If the hunt is not conducted strictly or the chakwena is not properly stage-managed, during the year there will be a paucity of both rabbits and infants."[31] In this rite we see an interesting agreement with the Hopi myth: rabbits are born from the birth-blood of the Mother of Game, but while the Hopi mother has been giving birth to animals, the Zuñi mother in this instance bears children.

The Zuñi rite is a fragment of an elaborate and important ceremony held quadrennially, or in times of drought or some other evil that requires exorcism. Like the Hopi first rabbit kill, child naming is involved, but on a community-wide basis and the children are four or five years old. Stevenson's account differs slightly, in that the Chakwena's legs have been daubed with a pinkish paint that is washed off by pregnant women before the hunt begins. Chakwena gives prayer-sticks to needful women who take them to the Great Mother, A'wan Sita, to be placed in a shrine at mother rock on Corn Mountain, the great

148

mesa behind Zuñi. This is an important pilgrimage made by women and their husbands, if they are seeking children.

As a central part of the ceremony there is a 'Rabbit Hunt with the Gods,' which is so called because the masked kachinas do much of the hunting. There are usual kiva preparations, with songs, rattles, and drums. Then at sunrise on the morning of the hunt, Chakwena makes a ceremonial circuit about the plaza four times, this circle symbolizing the world. Next she enters the chambers of the rain priests and sits on a sacred, embroidered blanket on which there are meal marks to indicate the cardinal points. The Sun priest motions her to the six directions and the Bow or warrior priests make fire with a fire-drill. From this flame a cedar-bark torch is lighted and given to Chakwena who then leaves the village by the western road in the company of two clowns likewise carrying torches. These clowns set fire to the grass and brush as the party proceeds.

The Salimobia, warriors and seed bearers of the six directions, are very much in evidence, acting as both ritualists and policemen for the large party of those both on foot and mounted. Maidens ride behind their fathers or brothers. One of the cedar torches is used to fire a tree, which becomes the hunt fire. Chakwena then prays to her counterpart, Kuyapalitsa, to send many of her "children," which is to say rabbits. A large circle is formed around the hunt area, and the Chakwena and members of the hunt society stay within this to drive the rabbits out with their firebrands. The surrounding "gods," or kachinas kill the driven rabbits with throwing-sticks. "When a god fails to kill a rabbit which runs between himself and another man, and the man kills it, the latter strikes the god over each arm and leg; but should the god slay the rabbit he whips the man; if both fail they whip one another." All carry yucca whips for this purpose.

In this account the blood ritual takes place on the first kill, rather than four days before the hunt. "The first rabbit killed has its nose cut and is handed to the Chakwena by a maiden, and the Chakwena rubs the bleeding nose down her legs on the inner sides, that the A'shiwi (Zuñi) girls may hasten to arrive at the age of puberty and that they may be prolific in childbearing."[32] After this hunt the game is treated in the ritual manner previously described and for four nights the Chakwena circles the village depositing prayer-sticks for safe parturition, long life for children, and the like. She then spends four more days lying in, while women who have lost children at birth may lie down with her on a sand bed that she prepares. Afterwards the goddess is bathed and dressed in a new gown with embroidered sash, white buckskin moccasins, but with the Chakwena mask on "her" head and a fawn skin at her breast.

Clearly the rabbit as game here takes second place to the rabbit as a fertility spirit. In a final rite Chakwena and her retinue visit the houses of the village and accept offerings and prayers for success in hunting larger game, from the men, and for children, from the women. There is also a Hopi ceremony, the Mamzrau, in which the rabbit appears as an agent of fertility, but he comes only by suggestion or in the guise of a "Rabbit Mother." The fertility promoted is not that of game, but of crops and women, and there are of course other elements involved as well. On First Mesa girl novices undergo rites in which there is not actual blood, but two coronets are worn by each girl in turn. These are ingeniously made of feathers and cylinders, including two bunches of rabbit fur dyed red.[33]

In the Oraibi or Third Mesa version of another woman's ceremony, there is a priestess called the "Rabbit Mother," though she has no clear relationship to rabbits, other than the name. She is a vegetation fertility spirit who wears a blossom headdress. Sometime before her appearance, squash vines and young, supple cornstalks have been tied to strings. As she comes out these are thrown over her in great number, until she is entirely concealed, except for one hand which holds up a cornstalk bearing an ear of green corn.[34]

The Hopi also use rabbit's blood in various ways to indicate fertility. Hehe'ya is a phallic spirit whose body is painted with marks of rabbit blood. In a different spirit Soyoko Woman, an ogress who cries out in a high falsetto voice, has her hands and arms smeared with rabbit blood. Perhaps this is only because it is easy to come by when one wants blood, but it has already been noted that an ogress may be in part a Keeper or Mother of Game, as in the case of the ogress Atoshle and the Rabbit Huntress. Soyoko appears in the bean ceremony where she forces boys to hunt rats and mice for her. These they offer as surrogates for themselves, while the girls give her cakes. At this time the Phallic Heheya kachinas accompany Soyoko, so they may be fertility spirits as well as bogys.

More importantly rabbit's blood and skin figure in the rites of the Hopi god Masau'u. While as Skeleton Man he is a god of death, like other similar spirits Masau'u is also the owner of crops. When the Hopi emerged from the underworld and first met Masau'u, he was tending a fire which made his plants—corn, squash, beans, and melons—grow to maturity in a single day. At this time he had a bloody mask at his side, and to this day his impersonators wear a mask of rabbit's skin soaked in the blood of these animals. Rabbits can be thought of as a meat "crop" equal in importance for food to corn, squash, and beans. By a slight extension the spirit of cultivated foods is made to include the cottontails and jack rabbits associated with the fields in which they are grown. All are harvested together for human benefit.

Masau'u plays a central role in a preharvest rite which begins with a rabbit hunt in which both jacks and cottontails are brought to the kiva of the god. Stephen describes the following day as he witnessed it in 1891. "This day Masau'u went out to the fields. On his head he has a bloody rabbit skin and rabbit blood over his head, face and body. . . . He has a rabbit club in his right hand and in his left a planting stick and a Middle Mesa tray. He is shoeless and naked save for the shoulder rag."[35] He goes out ostensibly to oversee the harvest, or to see that the men help with the planting, depending upon the season. The men gather greens, *Poliomintha*, a close relative of the bee plant which the Zuñi and Laguna people gathered, which they give to the women, who must return gifts of food in exchange.

The Masau'u impersonator must be exceedingly active as he has to chase the workers about the field and attempt to strike them with a cylindrical club filled with cotton or seeds. "All this running about is good for the crops." When the work is completed the people return to the village and feast on the previously killed rabbits and, if it is harvest time, on the new corn. There is a final rite in the evening called "killing" Masau'u. He appears in the plaza whereupon men rush at him with torches until at last he falls down as if dead and the men roll him off the mesa edge, a sort of "death thou shalt die" episode to allay that side of his nature. Then he gets up and slowly walks back into the plaza where men and women give him meal and prayer-feathers, "for long life, rain, good crops and many children."[36] Thus death is made to serve the purposes of life.

As a final point, the rabbit seems to be the smallest of game animals to possess a soul. The logic to explain rabbit's inclusion with larger game is in part linguistic at Hopi. "Jack rabbit (so'wi) and deer (sowi'inwa) are related closely. They both have the same traits: when the rabbit is coursed and grows tired he doubles back a way and then bounds off at right angles and sits concealed. The deer does the same."[37] The names differ elsewhere, but there is the same close association between rabbits and antelope or water deer; hence they must be treated in the same fashion.

"When the men bring rabbits home the women will greet them happily and will line the rabbits upon the floor against the wall and sprinkle them with the sacred corn meal. After supper the women dress the rabbits and carefully peel the skin off the ear of one animal and place the gall bladder on it. They wrap this with piki bread so that the spirit of the rabbit will carry it home to his ancestors. This is done by throwing the packages into the fire."[38] So treated the rabbits will not be angry. Other small game does not receive such ceremony. When traps are set for rats, mice, and prairie dogs, no prayer-feather is placed next to the trap, "because the Hopi do not believe that the latter possess souls, and so they do not have to be propitiated as do the larger animals."[39]

If the account of the Zuñi hunt in which Cushing took part is recalled, the hunters grasped the dying rabbits and held them to their own mouths so that the last expiring breath of the little animals could be inhaled. It was the breath of life in the larger sense of mana, and the hunters could absorb power from this. It would be wrong, however, to think that all animals smaller than rabbits are without power to dispense. Those that are beasts of prey, however small, even the minute shrew and the small weasel have great supernatural power.

Chapter VII

COYOTE AND KIN

AMONG THE CANIDS wolf is the only Beast God. Fox and coyote are rather pale replicas. Scientifically coyote may be a lesser wolf, but in the Pueblo view he is not at all like his larger brother and is in fact something of a contemptible opposite. While the coyote is often despised, he is far more important than the wolf, in mythology at least. In ritual Wolf has a superior role. The fox which falls between these two has a difficult time establishing a place of his own, since various of his qualities are absorbed by one or the other of the associated canids.

Wolf is the Beast God of the East direction, which brings in the power of these gods for the hunt, for war, and for curing. As a hunter Wolf was thought to be powerful but somewhat inferior to Mountain Lion. "Mountain Lion and Wolf were friends and visited each other regularly. They talked all the time about hunting, how to kill deer and rabbits. Wolf kills them easily, for he can run swiftly. Mountain Lion does not catch so many. He cannot run so fast, he springs on his prey. He sings a song, creeps up on his prey, then springs on them. Wolf sees them, pursues them, and never gives up the chase. They become tired, and then he catches and kills them."[1]

One would expect that Wolf with his direct approach would win the ensuing contest, but that was not the case as the lion would secrete himself ahead and kill the deer when it passed. The Wolf was left "very lean, thirsty, and hungry." Finally they went hunting once more, but again the Wolf killed none. "Mountain Lion, however, killed his deer easily. Now Wolf admitted he was beaten. 'I do not give you any,' said Mountain Lion: 'do not follow me!' He gave Wolf merely the little bones and their marrow and the contents of the stomach. Wolf ate these, for he had killed nothing."

For deer hunting this account is probably correct. While wolves in large packs were most effective against buffalo and also against elk, which can be herded, the same was not true of deer in an often snowless area. The Southwest wolves hunted in pairs or family-size groups in regions where snow seldom piled up and deer had a good chance to escape. Hungry wolves cleaned up the leavings of lion kills, as they will eat the last bone and have no objection to carrion if it is not too far gone. The favorite food of wolves in the West was antelope, and these animals, as well as deer, are very much afraid of wolves. The Hopis put his fear to use in antelope surrounds. When hunters had enclosed a band of antelope in the neighborhood of a corral, they would all cry out in imitation of wolves to frighten the antelope into the mouth of the chute leading to the compound.[2]

Wolf had a place in war as well as hunting, being a pet of the War Twins, joining the lion, wildcat, and bear. A group of animal fetishes is placed around the medicine-water tray of the Hopi Snake altar where they represent the directional animals in a war sequence. The fetishes consist of a conch for the Zenith, stones for the Nadir, Lion for the North, Bear for the West, Wildcat for the South, and Wolf for the East. Each of the animals is represented by both head and paws.[3] Mouth hairs of Wolf are tied into the warrior's bandolier and a wolf painting is on the War chief's kiva wall.[4]

Sometimes Wolf, as one of the Beast Gods, will act as a guardian spirit, an instance of which occurs in the Zuñi version of the White Bison myth. "As he was thinking of his wife, a wolf (*unawiko*) came out of the east, saying, 'U, u, u, u! My father, are you staying here all night?'—'Yes.'—'Have you what I want?'—'What do you want?'—'I want an eagle-feather. Some one gave me an eagle feather long ago, but it is worn out.'— 'Come,' said the young man, 'I will put one on you.'—'Since you have given me the feather, I will guard you all night.'

Early in the morning Wolf said, 'Awake, my father! Get your sacred meal and pray to the Sun. I must be going.' Wolf went away to the east."[5]

As one of the Beast Gods the Wolf has power that may be used in curing, and when the chief of the Great Fire society at Zuñi sets up his altar this beast is included in the sequence of animals addressed.

> *And furthermore, yonder in the east*
> *You who are my father, wolf,*
> *You are life-giving society chief:*
> *Bringing your medicine,*[6]

Unlike the Bear, or the Badger at Hopi, there is nothing special about Wolf's role in curing, that is, the priest does not use wolf paws or leg skins as a part of his curing, nor is Wolf specialized in this respect. At Sia it is said that, "Medicinemen effect their cures only by means of power which they obtain from the animal doctors, especially the bear, badger, eagle, snake, shrew, and wolf."[7] The bones of foxes, mostly the gray, have been found in a number of Pueblo ruins, where it may be supposed that their cased pelts were ornaments for dancers. A single fox bone remain was found at Winona, unspecified fox bones from Nalakihu, gray fox remains at Awatovi and at Paa-ko in New Mexico. A most interesting example came from the ruins of Pueblo Bonito in Chaco Canyon where one room yielded detached skulls of one gray fox and two red foxes.[8] It seems likely that they served as models for the heads on effigy vessels. Some of these vessels with animal heads have survived.

The question of the Fox deity of the Hopis illustrates the difficulty of fixing the position of Fox. Beaglehole several times mentions this deity in his studies of the Second Mesa. When a rabbit hunt is to be held prayer-sticks are made for the Mother of All Animals and one for "Gray Fox deity." In another description of hunting, this time mountain sheep, prayer-sticks were offered. These were to the Mother of Game, to Masau'u,

Sparrow Hawk, Eagle, and "one for Gray Fox ('kwe'wi j); and one for another animal deity (Dzo'hona)."[9]

The last animal deity we know to be directional, even if he is difficult to identify—White thought it might be the swift fox. As for the gray fox, the name is either a mistranslation, or more likely, a recent adaptation, for *Kwe'wuuh* means wolf.[10] No doubt the translator rendered it as gray fox because Fox now fills in for the extinct Wolf Beast God.

Around Hopi clans, the Kokop lineages, or perhaps separate clans, are named after the following canids: Kwe'wuuh, Wolf; Isau'wuh, Coyote; Sikya'taio, yellow fox; Le'taiyo, gray fox; and Zroho'na, mountain coyote.[11] Eggan was of the opinion that group was organized around war. "The Coyote clans are traditionally 'fighters' on Third Mesa; associated with them are the various foxes and the wolf."[12]

Beaglehole's other Fox deity has a different function and seems to be at bottom a Coyote spirit. In *Hopi of the Second Mesa* he refers to a Fox deity who first divided land among the clans and quotes a story of jealousy and witches which ends with, "The Fox ate the dead bodies lying about the village so the people killed him only to learn that the Fox was really the sister of the chief in disguise."[13]

Confusion in canids calls to mind a tale they tell at Acoma. There was an old fox, *mascha*, which is the Keres name for the gray fox, who was carrying water to her young ones. Each time she passed a mourning dove the latter made her laugh, so that she spilled the water—the same story is often told of Coyote. Her young ones die of thirst so she finds a mate again, but despite her advice he is caught in a hide-rope trap. The young trapper found the dead male and said, " 'His hide will do to dance with.' He put the fox on his back, took it home and skinned it. He tanned the hide and fitted it into his girdle. And that is how they came to use fox skins in the girdles at the sacred dances of Acoma."[14]

The use of a fox pelt for dancers, masked or otherwise, is the greatest role of the animal in Pueblo culture; it is used by all groups. The skinning is carefully done, so that head, legs and tail are left attached. The pelt is then attached to the belt, head up, with the tail hanging almost to the ground. For the purpose, the foxes are hunted in the winter when the fur is longest and the hide tough. Before dances pelts are buried for a few days in damp sand to make them soft and flexible.

None of the hunt impersonators of the Río Grande wear these fox tails, but effect instead the plaited sash at the back.[15] Zuñi and Hopi impersonators of the gods do wear fox skins and the Zuñis, like the Acomeans, fit this fact into their mythology. Bunzel points out that it is worn by practically all of the dancing kachinas and many others. "It is considered as a relic of the earliest days of man, for the kachinas were transformed while mankind was still tailed and horned."[16] Fewkes surmised from this explanation that the pelts were left over from the days when the kachinas were animal impersonations, effected by donning an animal skin.

Many animal dancers are not kachinas, and many of the animal kachinas are of minor importance. Hence it seems likely that there existed from the distant past two kinds of impersonations, one of anthropomorphic gods and one of animals. Both strains of this parallel development have from time to time crossed, particularly when the animal in question was also an important god.

The most interesting of the myths accounting for the origin of the use of fox-skin tails by dancers comes from Acoma. The story, called The Windows of the Fox, has a narrative style and unity unusual in Pueblo myths. It begins with a pristine view of nature in which the birds all sang the same songs and the animals were all in one family. The birds dropped seeds all over the earth, the bear and squirrel stored grain and nuts so that there was always food, the gophers dug valleys, and butterflies brought home children who had wandered away.

One day this state of nature vanished. "Lightning flashed and blinded the animals, and when the storm was over, in the middle of the plain, they saw a man standing. He was red like baked clay." This man watched the beasts of prey track a deer, kill, and then eat it; he then did likewise. The man made an altar, then killed an eagle and with its feathers made a prayer-stick. Next he made a corn-ear fetish and soon a woman appeared at his side. "I am White Light Woman," she said, and used her powers to call the animals. While the narrator associates her with the northern lights, in Acoma terms she would be Ko-chinako and associated with the moon.

The animals tried to divine her, but when they came near she called them into her magic circle and killed them. One by one the birds and animals failed in attempts to spy on her secret. "At last Fox went. He saw a dead deer lying on the plain. He waited for a storm, and when all animals were in their dens, Fox crept inside the ribs of the deer. He could look out plainly." From this vantage point Fox sees the White Lightning Woman take strips of fur and feathers of eagles, drawing across them four times a flint arrow-head that she wears about her neck. "The nearest deer felt her power and was drawn down closer and closer until the Man shot him with his arrow."

Since Fox now knew her secret he called all the animals and birds together. "He said, 'When you feel her power, run with all your might in the opposite direction and eat the pollen of all the flowers nearby.' So they spoiled White Light Woman's magic. After that Man had to hunt animals by following their tracks through the woods and across the plains. This is why the ribs of the deer are called 'the windows of the fox.' And for this reason, when we dance, we hang a fox skin at our belts or put it on our war-poles, to mean that we are wiser than the fox because we wear his skin."[17]

Unlike the wolves and more like the red fox of the East, the coyotes learned that they could get along very well with men and succeeded so well that they soon followed livestock into Central America. In the Southwest they followed the flocks of sheep and other livestock into the higher mountains where they also found turkey and other game to their taste. It is not only skill and an omnivorous appetite that have enabled coyotes to adjust and expand; they are also extremely fertile beasts.

In the Southwest the cliffs afford dens in plenty and the young are brought out at about three weeks of age. Thereafter the family runs together, sometimes in groups of more than one generation. Unfortunately, whelping time corresponds seasonally with the nesting of game birds, and the birth of antelope and deer fawns. The mother coyote's milk gives out after about a month and the parents then must bring food to the voracious young.

Coyotes are not too dependent on water. The adults do not go to water often except in hot weather and the young do not need any until they are several months old.[18] When they need water they can smell it out in a dry arroyo and will dig two or three feet down to get it. Food is equally simple as they will eat anything—acorns and pine nuts in season, the fruit of prickly pears or mesquite-beans, grasshoppers and the other insects of spring and summer, rodents, birds up to the size of a crane, the young of game, domestic livestock and poultry, garden truck, and notably any kind of carrion. Since the age or condition of any of these is a matter of no concern, all the world's a paradise to the coyote.

The coyote in turn may be the victim of bears, lions, and wildcats, but caution usually saves him from the first, while a family of coyotes is usually a match for the last. There are too few lions to matter and man has exterminated the wolf which was once an enemy. Coyotes once followed the greater beast at a safe distance and cleaned up the buffalo leavings. Today the coyote has few enemies other than man. He also has few friends.

Coyote's friendship with badger is not a distant relationship such as he once had with wolf. Not every badger has a coyote for a friend, but the union is frequent enough to find a place in scientific literature as well as myths and tales. Young gives several such accounts, one of a badger and a coyote who were several times seen together. "The coyote would go in front of the badger, lay its head on the latter's neck, lick it, jump into the air, and give expressions of unmistakable joy . . . the badger seemed equally pleased."[19]

That may have been an extreme case, but the Indians were in a position to observe and tell many stories of similar friendships, and the Mexicans celebrated the union by calling the badger, *Tlalcoyotl*, earth-coyote, which means that the Aztecs too had noted the association. Both animals pursue small game, but they are also specialized, badger being an excellent digger though slow on his feet and without a good sense of smell. Coyote can only dig shallowly and in soft ground at a slow pace. Each thus can profit from the skills of the other.

Oftentimes a coyote will chase woodrats, ground squirrels, or prairie dogs into holes where he cannot reach them, but badger can dig right in and kill the prey. Nor is the proposition one-sided, for if badger is digging and several of his victims escape, a coyote attending the operation may snap up a fine dinner. This kind of arrangement is so satisfactory that sometimes the two agree to a working arrangement and then one can see, "a badger travelling in apparent high spirits, tail and long front toes turned upward, abrest of two or three coyotes."[20]

The relationship may not always run smoothly. Dobie relates an incident that happened near Cliff, New Mexico. A badger was observed digging furiously after a prairie dog, but he was not making enough progress to satisfy the coyote. The latter, showing no grace at all, ran up and gave the badger a hard nip on the rump, which caused him to interrupt his digging, whirl, and chase the coyote off. This sequence was repeated several times, until the badger had dug himself out of sight; he then turned around and waited. The next time coyote stuck his slender nose in the hole, badger sunk his claws into the nose and held on. Coyote was able to struggle free, but added to his store of wisdom the thought that it is never clever to badger a friend.

In the Zuñi view the relationship between the two animals is most blissful. "Badger Old Man said to Coyote. '*Heh, kihe,* what are you doing?' Coyote said to Badger Old Man, 'I am hunting around.'—'How would it be if we went around together?'—'All right,' said Badger Old Man.—'Whenever a rabbit jumps out, I will run after it. I am a good runner,' said Coyote. 'And whenever a rabbit goes into a hole, you ought to dig down to get him out, you have long claws.' "[21]

In the first chapter of this book the tale of Badger and Coyote was given in which the former revived the dead Coconino maiden. Because Coyote desired the girl, Badger was forced to kill him. Badger as the famous doctor might have paid with his life for this feat, as the Greek Asklepios had before him, but the maiden obligingly died again. One Hopi tale tells of a successful venture between the two animals, but Badger tricks his friend into self-destruction by eating his own fat. In other cases the friendship is allowed to continue peacefully. "Towards evening the Coyote said that he must go. 'Very well,' the Badger replied, whereupon the Coyote left, his friend having wished him a happy journey. After that each one continued to live in his house."[22]

Turning to the status of Coyote in mythology, we must first look at the animal as a big game predator, for in the Pueblo view to be a powerful beast of prey is the important qualification for any animal deity. In Pueblo eyes Coyote is a chaser of rabbits and other small animals and an eater of carrion. Probably this view is correct as a single coyote could master large game so seldom that an occasional killing would have no visible effect on the game supply. There is no doubt that in heavy snow a group of coyotes can, from time to time, kill large game.

In Pueblo opinion Coyote is not only a second-rate hunter, although he may be useful in tiring out rabbits and thus making them easier to catch, but his much vaunted cleverness is more nearly a form of antisocial stupidity which often leads to his own destruction. This attitude is of course an important modification of the trickster-god role that he plays in many other Indian cultures.

First of all, when hunting customs were established, Coyote had an equal chance with the other beasts of prey, but one by one he breaks all of the proscriptions until at last he is utterly damned. When the original Keresan Hunt chief layed down the hunting customs for all the beasts of prey to follow, they were told to fast for four days so that they would be hungry when the hunt began. Wolf and Coyote broke this rule. The turn of these two came jointly and was to be in the east where there was an elk and a rabbit. Wolf tells Coyote that he will take the elk, which he does, eating only half of it.

Coyote next pursues the rabbit, killing it and eating all. When the beasts of prey return they are told that they will always eat game, "But you, Coyote, you will have for your food anything that any time you find and anything that already died by itself. . . . you yourself caused trouble." Then as a final parting curse Coyote is told, "All day you will walk and all night."[23] He is condemned to be an incessant prowler, of no use to the people, forced to eat carrion or whatever else he can find, because he would not follow the rule of hunting only when hungry and eating only a part of what he kills. To a communal culture the violation of these rules is a sin.

Coyote has thus made a muddle of things from the very beginning, but it is not a part of his nature to leave it at that. He must pursue his troubles further and this time into cosmic bungling. As he must prowl he keeps wandering eastward and arrives at the house of the Sun. When he enters Coyote is cheerful. " 'How are things,' said he. 'It is good,' said to him the Sun. Then said to him the Sun, 'Who are you, man?' The wanderer replies that he is Coyote-Youth, and then with the brass that characterizes this beast he proposes, 'Shall I go as the Sun today, this way above westward?'

" 'How is that?' said the Sun." Although perhaps astounded, the Sun lets coyote make the journey that day, providing him with the War Twins as escorts. First, however, he warns him, " 'Please do not go down,' said the Sun to Coyote. 'Please be careful of the people, because if you go down the earth will burn.' " When Coyote arrived at the middle of his journey "Behold," he said, "down there beautiful women are bathing." Coyote begs the Twins to let him go down, but is warned that he will make trouble. "What trouble am I going to make?" he asks in knowing innocence.

Although it is pointed out that he will burn the people, he pays no heed to the Twins' warning. Halfway down, the earth began to burn, so the Twins turned the rainbow, on which the sun disc travels, back up again. After eating they traveled on and went down in the west, knowing that when they arrive back in the east "Mother Sun" will scold them, as she does. The War Twins confess that they have that day burned the people, the animals, and the plants.

"Then Coyote stood up. Then she said to him, 'Enough,' said she to him. 'You are not well-disposed. From now on you will never eat anything nice; only beetles and anything that has died by itself and that is rotten will be your food,' Thus she said to him. 'Thus you will live from now on,' said to him the Sun . . . 'From upstairs on the north side throw him down,' said the Sun."[24]

There are obviously two sections to the above accounts which are linked only because both of them explain why it is that Coyote eats leavings. The first part of the narrative is a myth, explaining the origin of hunting customs, the second part is folktale, or perhaps it should be called an anti-myth. The same event has a place in standard mythology, and it is naturally the War Twins who are sons of the Sun that carry the disc across the sky—they are the real Phaethons, while Coyote's adventure is a parody. The Mother Sun here resembles the Hopi Huruing Wuhti, or Hard Beings Woman, who sometimes has a house both East and West, but is more often thought of as the Sun's wife living in a kiva in the Western ocean, through which the great luminary passes each day. It may be remembered that the mother of Phaethon was the Sea-nymph, Clymene.

Coyote continues his cosmic bungling in the company of the Twins, this time in a Hopi account of placing the stars. He is no deity here but a scapegoat. When the people emerged from the Underworld it was dark, so they made stars and told the War Twins to go place them properly. "Coyote said to himself,

'I will go with the two boys.' They put the seven together, the Pleiades, in a good position, and those six, Orion, they put them together and the biggest one they put toward the east, and another they put on the south side, and another on the west side, and another on the north side. Then they put up the dipper."

It will be noted that the ceremonial circuit which usually goes from north to west, or counterclockwise, is here reversed. "Just when they had put all these up, Coyote said to himself, 'It is a big job!' He said to the boys, 'We shall never finish this work, we shall all die first, why can't we do this?' And he took the stars and threw them in every direction, improperly." The next night the Evening Star came out in its place and by and by the others that had been properly positioned. "Then they saw stars scattered all over the sky. The people said, 'Bad Coyote, you did that?'—'Yes,' he said.—'If you had not gone with them, all the stars would be well placed. But you are bad Coyote; you scattered them all over the sky.' They were very angry. But Coyote said, 'That's all right, It's a lot of work to put them all into good positions, better to scatter them around.' "[25]

At Zuñi, Coyote's cosmic bungling is again related to the sun rather than the planets and stars, but it is of a more important order than in the Keresan tale. Here it is a cause of seasonal change and in particular cold and inclement weather. This role of *kinetikos* or prime mover, which will appear again, is of great interest, for if it had been treated more seriously Coyote could easily have become a deity, by being responsible for setting the universe in motion.

In the most distant past when Coyote hunted only grass-hoppers, he suggested to the eagle that the two work together, but the sun and moon had not been placed in the sky and darkness kept them from having much success. Eagle then suggested that the two should set out to find the sun, so they went to Kachina Village, the home of spirits under a lake where Pau-tiwa, the Chief of the Council of Gods presides. There, when the gods wanted light for dancing it was mysteriously available to them. Eagle and Coyote, "stayed and watched the dance. All the time they were looking for the sun. The kachinas had a square box and when they wanted light they opened it and it was daylight. When they wanted less light they opened another box and there was the moon."

Coyote is an outright thief and makes no bones about it, but Eagle has moral scruples and prefers to think that the two of them will be borrowing the boxes. Eagle flies off to the east, carrying the boxes, while Coyote follows along on the ground. He begins to brood about the fact that he is carrying nothing, while the chief is carrying everything. To his complaint that this is not right the Eagle replies that Coyote cannot do it correctly, but Coyote still insists that if they met someone it would look very bad. So on the fourth and mandatory request Coyote is given the boxes.

By and by he comes to a place where the weeds and flowers grow high enough to conceal him from Eagle. There he cautiously opens one box. "Coyote took the moon out and it slipped away from him and went to the sky. Immediately all the leaves of all the trees dropped off and it was winter." Before Eagle could intervene Coyote had also taken out the sun and it too slipped away and glided far into the sky. " 'What have you done?' scolded the Eagle. 'Now every year we shall suffer from cold weather.' " Coyote is ashamed and realizes that he can no longer be friends with the Eagle. "All the leaves had dropped down off the trees and snow was falling. If Coyote had not done this we should have had summer all the time."[26] Here again is a kind of anti-myth, for in Zuñi origin accounts the sun always existed. Coyote is responsible for the loss of paradise, but his behavior also sets in motion things as they are and, as motion is essential to life, his action is not wholly evil.

The Hopis credit Coyote with responsibility for the succession of human generations, as well as the seasonal journey of the sun which brings the seasons. Coyote had helped with the placing of the stars but these gave little light, so somebody said, "We will make the moon" and they sent for the Twins who made her of a wedding blanket. This was better but still did not give enough light, so when the moon went down they decided to make the sun.

A white fox-skin is produced to make the first daylight, or white dawn, then came a parrot tail to make it yellow. The unexpressed thought here is of a ceremonial dramatization of "making the sun," in which the yellow would be followed by a buckskin disc or a buffalo-hide shield with red hairs around it to represent the parahelion. This disc is spun by a star priest representing the morning star. When the newly made sun came out it merely stood still.

" 'Something is wrong, Why can it not move?' Then they asked one another, 'What can make it go?' At last Coyote said, 'Nothing is wrong with it. All is fixed as it should be. Nothing is wrong, but if somebody should die right now, then it would move.' " At that moment a girl died and the sun moved on to the Zenith but there he stopped again, to move only when the son of a head man died. "It is only by somebody dying every day—morning, noon and evening—that the sun will move every day,' said Coyote. Coyote thinks more than anybody. Smart fellow!"[27]

Coyote takes a further part in the origin of death. At first when people died, in four days they came back again. While this narrative doesn't say so, the Pueblo attitude is that for every birth there must be a death, otherwise there would not be enough food. Of the rebirth at the end of four days, Coyote says: "I don't think that will be right for us. If we die and come back in four days, we won't be afraid to die. I will die and never come back." He then overate and died and after four days did not come back.[28]

Coyote is a death figure, probably for the simple reason that he feeds on dead things and his stench is associated with carrion. A cousin spirit was the Egyptian god Anubis who was a jackal-headed spirit of cemeteries and mummification. Coyote has a special relationship to Masau'u or Skeleton Man, the god of death and fertility. In myth the two are friends of a sort who entertain each other with dances. One time Masau'u decided to show Coyote how he looked in his mask, which the animal had not seen. Masau'u first uttered his cry, a prolonged *hu u u*, beginning on a high note and dropping. Perhaps this cry links the two together.

Then the god appeared wearing his mask. "Over his shoulder, he wore his big sash, and he was besprinkled all over with blood. He stank terribly, just like the dead. Coyote smelled him and came out. Coyote was frightened. He was trembling all over and wanted to jump out." Then Masau'u reveals the fact that beneath this mask he is really Coyote's friend. It is in the nature of Coyote to compete beyond his abilities, so he makes a similar mask and tries to appear as frightening as the god. For this hubris the god takes revenge by making the mask stick to Coyote's face. "Keep it on! You will never again come out of there." No sympathy is felt for the struggling animal. "He was badly hurt and was sick. He kept on trying to break the mask off. ... His neck swelled up, the mask became very tight about his neck. He would never get it off. Thus he died. That is how he killed himself."[29]

Death may be a necessity when viewed broadly, but it is also an evil when seen in particular. Illnesses and accidents that end in death are most often due to witches. In the Pueblo world Coyote is variously First Witch, a pet of witches, or the animal into which witches or their victims are transformed. Among the Apache all of a person after death, except the supernatural breath part, becomes a coyote, and the Navajo likewise believe that the spirit of the dead enters the body of a coyote; hence their taboo on killing this animal, lest in skinning it a ghost be released.[30]

A typical instance of the transformation of witches into coyotes—and other canids—comes from Oraibi. Sorcerers wanted a certain girl so they first captured her breath in a hoop, then shot her in the foot with a poisoned arrow. "The sorcerers upon hearing that the maiden had died, again repaired to their place at Skeleton Gulch and there changed themselves into coyotes, wolves, foxes, etc. whereupon they waited until the maiden had been buried."

In a Hopi-Hano story the origin of witchcraft is attributed to Coyote. A youth hunting rabbits falls through the snow, breaking his leg. Badger in his role as doctor gathers medicines and heals the break, then catches rabbits for him to take home. Being clever, Coyote uses these good deeds to approach and marry the youth's sister.

The girl follows Coyote and he then says, "Now let us do something. Let us both be alike." Her first effort at transformation was a mistake as she became a wolf, but on the second try she was a coyote. "He was a witch coyote and he taught the girl how to turn a person into a coyote or anything else; and how to make a person sick and how to kill a person. He taught the girl to do these things and she learned them."

This state of affairs was bad enough but it became worse. Coyote was killed in a rabbit drive and the girl returned to the village to marry again. Her first child grew rapidly, like a coyote pup. "In twenty days he was strong enough to go out and go around. His mother taught him how to make a person sick and how to kill a person and how to turn himself into any kind of animal. This boy was taught witchcraft. After this there were witches. There were never witches before that, but the girl married a coyote and from that time there have been witches. That is the reason why people are witches now. They have been taught by Coyote."[31]

At Zuñi, Coyote is not directly involved in the myth of the origin of death, but he sometimes acts as a stand-in for First Witch who does have this role. One myth, belonging to the cycle of Kiaklo, the myth-bearing supernatural, makes no mention of witches. It tells that the newly emerged people were migrating toward some mountains, but found their way impeded by a river of turbid red waters. The women, with children on their backs, plunged into the cold waters. This frightened the women and terrified the little ones, who were still in a formative state, and changed them into newts, frogs, toads, turtles, and lizards. "Thus multitudes of them fell into the swift waters." When the new forms sank down and disappeared, "these little ones thus made the way of dying and the path of the dead."[32] The reasoning behind this myth is based upon the fact that the Zuñi afterworld is not underground, but beneath a lake where the dead and the gods live together.

When corn was made it not good, but was hot like pepper. So the War Twins called in the three creatures who are often of evil omen: the owl, the raven, and the coyote. The owl "ate the heart of the grain, leaving the remainder on the cob, so that the corn became soft." Next the raven was called and ate much of the corn. Lastly they called Coyote who "ate of everything in the field." The purpose of calling these birds and Coyote was to effect a transformation in the nature of corn; they softened and sweetened it so that the people could eat.

There are several ideas behind the story. In nature, these birds and coyote regurgitate their food, the mother coyote actually casting up food for her young which is mixed with a whitish viscous fluid somewhat like that found in grain in the "milk" stage. The evil, though, has also remained. "Since that time the fields have had to be watched, for the raven takes the corn in the day and the coyote robs the field at night."[33] The thought is that the birds and animals who take the crops must be the same ones who were responsible for bringing them to edible shape.

In the 1920's Bunzel recorded a long, "Talk Concerning the First Beginning," which repeats much the same story. After the emergence the War Twins realize, because of a continued rumbling in the earth, that someone has been left behind. This time it is not two witches, but "the mischief-maker and the Mexican." The mischief-maker is of course Coyote. Many food crops were of Mexican origin. The two kill a baby, which is later found alive.[34] Coyote the transformer has, in this story, transformed seed into food.

Coyote so far has been a transformer and a trickster. As the

Trickster figure is famous in American Indian mythology, some account is needed of how nearly the Pueblo Coyote fits into a larger picture. Trickster has a number of names, sometimes appearing as just Old Man, but more often he is identified with animals—Hare in the East and Coyote in many parts of the West; Raven is a somewhat similar figure in the Northwest. The form he takes is not important since Trickster is by nature amorphous. He is at once a buffoon and a culture-hero. His tricks transform things, if not always for the better, at least to the state we find today. Because of this, Trickster has a considerable tendency to become a deity. Of his origins Radin says: "I think it safe to assume that it began with an account of a nondescript person obsessed by hunger, by an uncontrollable urge to wander and by sexuality."[35]

On that base is built a more complex figure, that of the culture-hero who is no longer a wandering set of primal urges, but a shaper of the world about man. The culture-hero may bring fire, arrow points, tobacco, edible plants and grains; he may regulate the seasons and to some extent the weather; he frees the world of ogres and cannibals, and he plays some part in the origin of death. The culture-hero is also a trickster. We see in this list many of the elements in Coyote's nature, but it will be noted that the War Twins are parallel and more important tricksters and culture-heroes, which is the reason Coyote's story seems so often to be what I have called an anti-myth. At best Coyote plays second fiddle to the Twins.

Radin concludes from his survey of a great number of tricksters and their myths that they are a recognition, in man's unconscious, of a distant time when the world was not divided into the divine and the nondivine, a time when the only motive force that could be seen at work was the simple combination of hunger, sex, and wanderlust. Trickster is thus a misfit in any ordered scheme of the cosmos and therefore more likely to appear as a clown than a god.

Because the subject of this chapter is Coyote, not Trickster, we will have to be careful to keep the animal rather than the concept in the foreground. If one reads the great number of Pueblo Coyote stories, he will soon note that Coyote is far more often a mere bungler rather than a cosmic bungler, and it is not often that his cosmic doings result in transformations. It is possible to discard the idea of the primal in connection with the Pueblo Coyote, even though wandering and sex are very much a part of his nature, as is hunger. In fact, Pueblo mythology could have gotten along without him altogether, as the Keres Twins were already carrying the sun-disc, at Hopi they were setting out the stars, and at Zuñi First Witch and his wife were making food palatable. Later on we will find the same situation in respect to fire.

Coyote is best seen on the basis of the logic of free association, starting with his natural qualities as an animal. His ceaseless wandering, for example, makes him an excellent messenger and we find that this is one of his roles with the Tewa.[36] His voice naturally associates him with the town crier. As a wanderer he is not only a messenger, but even more often a scout for migrating parties. Scouts are associated with war parties and this role is reinforced by the fact that clowns in real life were also scouts and both clowns and Coyote are buffoons. In part this role came about because their pep and humor held up the spirits of people engaged in difficult and dangerous enterprises, whether in war or in migrations.

As a war spirit Coyote is again marginal. There were the War Twins as always, and among the animals Bear, Lion, and Snake were more central, but Coyote had a place. Among the Hopis, the Coyote clan was designated to come last and to "close the door." In the clan there were two divisions: the Water Coyotes, to inspect any route of migration and to use their special powers for crossing rivers and lakes. Once the people were settled, a member of another Coyote group always acted as guard. This Kaletaka (Guardian) also brought up the rear of ceremonial processions to guard them against evil.[37]

Two natural traits of the animal have given rise to these duties of Coyote clansmen, the one that he always seems to be exploring and the other that he is often seen following along after other animals. The Kaletaka is a kachina who belongs to the Kokop clan, which may also be the Coyote clan. He appears at initiation rites for young warriors. Groups visit each kiva to sing war songs that sound like the "Coyote Dance." The Coyote Dance is in turn a social affair put on by any hunter who kills a coyote during January. The call is similar to that used to announce any dance ceremony, as at Tewa, Coyote is said to call from hill to hill to announce the coming of kachinas.

One item in the war initiation ritual consists in looking back, when passing certain specified points in the village, to see who is following the initiate. If it is his future victim he will be lucky, or if it is Masau'u the god of death, who is also associated with the Coyote clan, his future will be unlucky. In an actual war party the leader would be a war chief, who held the ceremonial office of Kaletaka in the Winter Solstice ceremony. He will be dressed, however, not as the kachina patron of the Coyotes, but as one of the War Twins.

At Zuñi the Coyote clan also has marginal war duties. That clan was given the pottery drum by the War Twins and its members are important in the Scalp Dance. "A young man who is child of the Coyote clan stands with his hands clasping the scalp pole which he gently rocks. In his hair he wears a downy eagle feather, over his shoulders, a large buckskin of which a tail piece is held by a girl of the Coyote clan."[38] The pottery drum that is kept by the Coyote clan is brought into the plaza for a Scalp Dance, placed on a stool, where the drummer embraces it while uttering a prayer that it sound loudly. Around this drum a circle of scalp-takers is formed.

The explanation given by the Zuñis for the role played by the Coyote clansman tells only a part of the story. "It is asserted that at the original ceremonial . . . a son of the drummer, who was at the head of the Coyote clan, held the scalps, and that upon his father's death he took his place as drummer, the father having taught him the songs, and another man of the Coyote clan held the scalps; and since that time the holder of the scalps in this dramatization is either of the Coyote clan or a child of the clan."[39]

The yelp of a coyote is likely to be heard after an engagement, for the scalp-takers leave the dead on the field where they will soon be finished off by these hungry beasts. Likewise the drum cries out to announce that a battle has taken place and a Coyote clansman holds the scalps that are proof of victory in the battle. While Coyote may call out victory, he may also cry out a warning. At Tewa San Juan when a coyote cries out at night, it means that Navajos are near, and at Taos Coyote warns the people of enemies.

Coyote has a marginal role in hunting, with the size of the margin depending on which Pueblo group is telling the story. We have seen at the beginning of Coyote's story that he was disqualified as a Beast God, but that fact does not prevent him from being a hunter of sorts. The rank below a god would be a Hunt Chief, an office which is supernatural in origin, and below that is a successful hunter of big game. The Keres deny Coyote any place at all in this sequence. According to the Sia, Coyote wanted to be a Hunt Chief and when the world was new Coyote was an industrious fellow. Despite this, Coyote's thoughts were even then not good, and the prime requisite for being a chief is to hold good thoughts. He must be honest and selfless, thinking only of the welfare of his group—failing that he will be no vehicle for supernatural power.

Since the other animal's experience with Coyote was limited, Mountain Lion was persuaded that despite initial failures Coyote's thoughts were now good. The first duty of a chief is to purify himself by fasting for eight days before the hunt. On the first night Coyote takes food to shrines, but by the second night he is very hungry. "I have food here and I wish to eat it, for I am hungry and yet I am afraid." After arguing with himself in this fashion he ate the offering.

By the sixth night the lion had grown very thin and without belly, but Coyote stayed fat. On the eighth day Coyote is ordained a Hunt Chief and sent out to kill a deer. "He did not carry arrows, but was to catch him with his hands, and at night the coyote returned worn out. Mountain Lion, who as a supernatural knew all along what had been taking place, points out Coyote's failure and sends one of his own kind to take a deer. When this meat was divided, "he would not give any of the meat to the coyote, because the coyote's thoughts were not good."[40] It is for this reason that coyotes ceaselessly wander about in search of deer and other game but are never successful in killing them.

Not all of the Pueblos agree with this estimate, most notably in the northern mountains where the people of Taos have had experience with Coyote's ability in deep snow. There, for example, to hear the cry of a coyote means that one will take deer. Since Taos also lies near the buffalo country, it is known that coyotes also hunt bison. In the Buffalo chapter it was noted that Coyote by his singing—yelping—led the buffalo into Taos and ever since that time they have had the Buffalo Dance there.

Coyote's singing is a frequent subject in tales, but his music is imperfect, which may in part be attributed to his short memory. Ofter he hears a song, learns it, but then "spills" the song on his way home. In the Taos tale it is Cotton Seed who is singing. After learning the song Coyote happily exclaims, " 'Now, my grandson, I have a new hunting song. Now I can sing when I go hunting.' So he went away singing, repeating the song over and over. As he was going on his way a flock of quails flew away—rr—r. Coyote got scared and forgot the song."[41]

When Coyote asks for the song again and Cotton Seed refuses to repeat, he is eaten. Then Coyote lies down to sleep and hears the song coming from within his own body, so he contrives a stone knife, slits his stomach and Cotton Seed emerges shaking off the blood. Cotton Seed next points the moral of this fable. "Coyote is never firm about what he has done or said and he goes about to scare people, but he does not persist, he always gives up what he is doing. Now he has killed himself . . . he is castaway on the ground."

That is the predictable end of a trickster, but there is one

tale in which Coyote's tricks are actually successful. There seem
to be two reasons for this switch. One that the story is related
to war parties where Coyote does have some value, and the other
that his opponent is Owl. Coyote is a marginal outcast, but Owl
is definitely beyond the pale in utter darkness. Owl, it is said,
was going to war carrying a feather braid, pointed stick, a war
club, and an Apache water jar. He was singing:

> *Yeha ea ea*
> *Yeha yeha yeha*
> *Yeha yeha m! m!*

Coyote meets him saying, "Sometimes we meet when we are
not expecting it and we don't know where we have our beds."
Coyote asks for a song. "Sing me that song! I have no hunting
song." When they part Coyote sticks arrows in himself, draws a
little blood and then lies down as though dead. Owl gathers up
the seeming corpse and puts it in a jar, but as he starts off a loud
whistle comes from within the vessel. "This is what I am most
afraid of," says the Owl. Presumably it is a scalp jar and Owl
thinks that he is being pursued by a scalp ghost. He throws down
his war club and other gear, Coyote climbs out of the jar saying,
"Owl didn't know that I am a wise man." He put the feather in
his hair and went off singing, "Yeha ea ea, etc."[42] Coyote went
home singing and swinging the club and after he got there his
family danced as hard as they could.

At Jemez Coyote always loses out to other animals in tales,
but in religious affairs Coyote men are accorded a definitely
preferential place, which indicates a basic respect.[43] At Zuñi too
respect is shown for his knowledge, if not for his behavior. He
is there the teacher of hunting. The teaching role is based upon
a dance drama, somewhat like Deer Dances, in which a Coyote
kachina appears to teach the people not only the ritual of hunting, but also the ceremonial treatment of dead game. Members
of the Zuñi Hunters' society are called Coyote people and it is
their chief who impersonates this canid.[44]

Coyote's role in hunting, whether rabbits, antelope, or deer, is to tire out the game by chasing them about, not to capture them. The myth behind this Zuñi ritual tells that Coyote wanted to go along with the people. "Do not leave me here. I am a hunter. When your people in Itiwana hunt I give them good luck." He is brought before Pautiwa, Chief of the Council of the Gods, where he looks funny and yellow among the other dancers, but Pautiwa says that since he brings luck he may stay. They danced, sang songs, and made gestures indicating the rain coming down to make the world beautiful. All this running about is good for the crops, seems a central part of his luck-bringing—it sets the clouds traveling.

" 'Now let us dress Coyote.' They sent Coyote just the way he was, but they gave him a red feather because he is a hunter and a member of a society. . . . Then they gave him a blue kilt and they painted him brown all over with white spots, and they gave him dance moccasins and a blue leather belt like society members wear. They gave him a cane too." The figure described is of course not the animal but the kachina spirit who appears in the dance, bending over on his cane as do similar animal impersonators.

"Then Coyote came running after the young deer to show the people how to hunt. He bent down over his cane pretending to smell the deer tracks." Coyotes do have a keen nose, so this kachina finds a little deer hiding behind a clown. A man, not Coyote, then places a noose around the deer's neck, but Coyote pretends to kill and dress the game. All of the acts are instruction by way of mime, so the proper ritual treatment is also shown. The body of the deer is laid out with its head to the east and covered with an embroidered blanket while the people sprinkle meal offerings over it.[45]

In addition to such visual instruction through the dance, the Zuñis also tell stories with similar information. In Cushing's version, which is called The Young Hunter,[46] the ceremonial aspects of the hunt are emphasized, particularly the magic power of singing and the importance of drawing to one's self the last breath of dying game. This youthful hunter had no parents, hence no proper instruction, but a coyote, who was in reality a little old man inside the animal, teaches the youth many things, until a final parting takes place. "Farewell, my child. Be thou happy many days and winters, throughout which thou wilt be a father of thy people, and a keeper and teacher of the medicines of the hunt." To this blessing of the newly instructed Hunt chief, the Coyote-man contributes a less pleasant prophecy, reminding one that at Nambe it is Coyote who will bring news of the end of the world.[47]

"But an evening will come when I or my wandering kind will howl as thou returnest from the chase. Then tell thy people to make thy grave-plumes, and when they are done thou wilt take them and, living, go thy way to the Lake of the Dead."[48] So went the sentence of the first Hunt chief, but now when a hunter returning home late hears a coyote yelping, his thoughts turn naturally toward his own death.

While the Zuñis granted Coyote both teaching and prophetic powers, they were not willing to admit that he was an actual hunter. He appears in another anti-myth, set off against a story that was told about Mountain Lion and his sister. In the proper myth the culture hero marries Lion's sister and goes to live with the Beast Gods at Shipapolima. Coyote is said to have tried the same thing. He was then living as an outsider, literally beneath the Beast Gods. "Whenever he wanted a feast of sinew and gristle, he went below their houses and gnawed at the bones that they had thrown away."

A spotted demon lived on Thunder Mountain where he preyed upon the humans who came to make offerings to the Beast Gods. Coyote overhears these gods offer to give Mountain Lion's sister in marriage to anyone who should kill this monster. For the purpose Coyote uses a trick which is more often played against him. He persuades the monster that his speed is due to breaking his leg. When healed magically he becomes faster. Coyote demonstrates with an old antelope bone; but the demon crushes his own leg and is left helpless.

Coyote has won Mountain Lion's sister, but there are further consequences in that he is now one with the Beast Gods. Long Tail, as the Zuñis call the lion, is contemptuous of his foul-smelling brother-in-law, but the other gods say that Coyote must be taken on a hunt. Coyote only makes a fool of himself, takes wrong directions, falls from a cliff and dies. " 'Good enough for you,' growled the Mountain Lion, as he picked up a great stone and *tuum*! threw it down with all his strength upon the head of Coyote." "That's what happened a great while ago. And for that reason whenever a Coyote sees a bait of meat inside of a stone deadfall he is sure to stick his nose in and get his head mashed for his pains."[49]

That end brings up the fact that Coyote was considered a game animal. In the opinion of some, coyote pups while still in the milk-feeding stage are palatable. The Hopi and the Jemez Indians are said to have eaten adult coyotes in times of scarcity. When the Pueblos took up sheep raising, their flocks were subject to coyote attack, and about the farming plots, particularly where melons were being grown, coyotes were pests that had to be trapped. Coyote fur was sometimes used as part of cere-monial costumes, and the pelts were sold to Americans as the Pueblos had no taboo on killing the animal.

Of all the Pueblo groups the Hopis seem to have made the most of commercial coyote hunting and the result was a curious mixture of ancient ritual and American methods. Steel traps were used but the old rites of placing bits of turquoise and prayer feathers next to the trap still prevailed.

In the old days communal coyote hunting was done by setting fire to the grass and brush, but individual hunters used the stone deadfall. For this a flat stone was propped up with a stick to which the bait was tied.[50] Hopi coyote-takers have a hunt chief, but he is not from any particular clan or kiva. After traps are set and supper finished, offerings are prepared. The chief makes a nakwakwosi, a long wandlike prayer-stick. One has a hik'si, or breath line attached. These are extra strings and feathers. All of these are for coyotes. Offerings are made for Sand Altar Woman, as mother of game, for the Hawk deity, for the Sun and for the Moon—those to the Mother of Game for her children, to the Sun for good weather, and to the Moon for guidance at night. Offerings to the Hawk are for some of his luck and skill.

If a trapped coyote is found still alive, it must be suffocated in the ceremonial fashion by pressing its nose in the sand. Then further nakwakwosi are prepared for the legs and heart of the coyote, which are attached to the body after skinning. At the beginning of a coyote hunt the chief carries on some of the old tradition, in that he is supposed to spend most of his time helping his men, rather than collecting pelts for himself, but after the first day this salute to the past is dropped.[51]

Having seen Coyote as a warrior, as a hunter, and as a victim, we come next to his role as a culture hero. No one has ever disputed the activity and diligence of Coyote; he is forever running about on one kind of business or another. A similar inclination to meddle in the affairs of gods, men, and beasts is characteristic of the culture hero. One of the important benefactions is the gift of fire, and in many Indian cultures Coyote is the bearer of this signal gift. There are one or two instances in which Coyote steals, or at least brings, fire to the Pueblos, but such a natural thing as fire is not withheld by Pueblo gods. Orderly working of the cosmos was from the beginning, and the gods themselves handed down arts of living to the first priests. These priests then handed on seeds, fire, and the ritual manipulations, such as planting or hunting, so necessary for a good life.

Fire was given to the Hopis by Masau'u, who was tending a fire that stimulated his fields when people and god first met. The Zuñis seem to have no myth on the origin of fire, but they have the Little Fire God, Shuliwitsi, who lights fires at the Winter Solstice. Since he is both a deputy to the Sun and a fire lighter on earth, he may be the god who brought this gift. At Keresan Acoma there is a similar figure, "One of the kachina always had fire with him. He was called Shura'sha. . . . so they thought of calling him . . . to bring some of his fire, so that they could have him build a fire in the center of the plaza, from which the people could all light their hearths and in this way always have fire."[52]

The Acomaeans also say that in the very beginning, "they saw a red light drop from the sky" and the Earth Mother told them how to keep this fire going with wood. "Tsichtinako told them this wood would last many years till there was time for trees to grow, and showed them how to build a fire."[53] At Keresan Sia there are two myths, one of which explains the origin of fire in the same orderly way and another which attributes it to Coyote. At Sia it is said, in connection with the organization of the Fire Society, that Thinking Woman, the great creative goddess, "desiring to have fire that their food might be cooked," gave a fire-drill to the original priests. These failed, but Sussistinako herself produced fire, which she handed to the Earth Goddess. The chiefs of the cult societies were called in, "to see the fire and understand it. Then the ho'naaite of the fire society carried some of the fire to the house of the ruler of the Sia."[54]

There is a parallel and contradictory myth from the same pueblo which tells that fire was not given, but stolen by Coyote. "The secret of fire was not brought to this world, and the fire society originated it here in this way. The people grew tired of feeding about on grass, like the deer and other animals, and they consulted how fire might be obtained. It was finally decided by the ti'amoni that a coyote was the best person to steal fire from the world below, and he dispatched a messenger for the coyote." Coyote is very brisk. "It is well, father; I will go." He arrives in the Underworld at night, finding the snake who guards the first door asleep, as was the lion at the second, and the bear at the third door.

After passing the fourth door, guarded by the fire-keeper priest, he comes into the presence of the goddess herself. "Sus'sistinako [was] also soundly sleeping; he hastened to the fire, and, lighting the cedar brand which was attached to his tail, hurried out."[55]

There was a more logical version of this same story in which the fire was "wrapped carefully in his tail by the underground mother," thus making it a gift and Coyote's role that of a messenger.[56] The Tewas of San Juan likewise tell a story which does not speak of getting fire, but of retrieving it. Long ago they always took care of fire, not letting it blow out, but when a certain pueblo was to hold a dance, they found that their fire had gone out. For this reason they wrapped chips and rags to Coyote's tail and sent him to a dance at a neighboring pueblo. He secretly puts his tail near the fire, gets a light, and then with the help of two birds brings the embers across the river to Chamita.[57]

This story is scarcely cosmic, but that Coyote may nonetheless have been the bearer of fire from the goddess to the people is likely, as at Cochiti he brings up the sacred corn-ear fetish which both represents the Mother Goddess and conveys health to the individual who possesses the fetish. During the migrations there were times of troubles, caused either by ignorance or quarreling, and pestilence resulted; at Cochiti it brought on an epidemic. "Then they said, 'Let us send Coyote to Uretsete, that he may fetch from our mother a remedy for our ills.' Coyote said, 'I go very willingly.' He ran hard. On arriving, he recounted to Uretsete the misfortunes of the people. She began to laugh and said, 'What has happened? They have not followed my advice and have behaved badly?' Coyote said, 'I do not know.' "[58] The goddess then sends him back to Cochiti for two men who become the first medicine men and are given a model of the fetish which the Mother herself made. With this they effect cures.

There are a few other positive notes to Coyote's song. At Hopi he transformed the horns of mountain sheep into solid bone, which is useful, although at first disliked, because it is now used in making bows. At Laguna Coyote is something of a weather prophet as they tell that he once planted wheat and wished to know when it was going to rain. Coyote asked the Sun. Sun said, "Tomorrow morning when I come out, when all around my face is a rainbow, then you will know that in four days from there it will rain." On such a day he is told to howl before sundown, and from that the people know when it will rain. "Behold! Keep quiet! Behold, Coyote is howling somewhere; maybe it is going to rain."[59]

Among the Tewas it is said that when the coyotes bark a lot in summer, it is going to rain; in winter their crying brings snow.[60] At Taos he foretells rain by howling during the day, but if Coyote howls at night it indicates that enemies are near. It is in this same pueblo that Coyote is said to be included in the pantheon with Red Bear. They are spoken of as, "our fathers," but the exact meaning of Coyote's inclusion with the other gods here is difficult to determine. Unlike Red Bear he does not seem to have any kind of cult at Taos. He brought the buffalo, as we have seen, but otherwise the tales of Taos treat him harshly. He is a bungler at best and often suicidal.

In most accounts from Taos the ending is something like "They arrived at a big lake where old man Coyote and his family were floating on the lake with their stomachs full of water. Then they said, 'He is always very timid and he scares people about unforeseen things. That is why he put an end to the life of himself and his family forever.' "[61] Perhaps there is some irony here as everyone knows that Coyote is everlasting, and that may be why stories about him are so prevalent and so appealing to wandering peoples.

Chapter VIII

BEARS

FROM THE PUEBLO standpoint there is a polarity in the nature of Bear that accounts for much of his role. Physically he is much like a man, but symbolically he relates to the supernatural and is often a god. When a Cochiti Indian encountered a bear: "He remained hidden in the bushes and held his gun in readiness. Finally, the noise came very near, and he saw a bear which came close to him. The animal was supernatural (mai'mai) and stopped right in front of him. The bear spoke, 'Friend, do not shoot me. I know that if I don't talk to you, you will shoot, for you are holding your gun in readiness. I want to be your friend. Do not shoot me. I am going to help you when you go out hunting deer. . . .' In telling about this adventure he said that the bear was really a person and that he was only wearing a bearskin."[1]

Here the supernatural aspect comes first, then the thought that as one of the Beast Gods, Bear will aid in hunting, and lastly the thought that Bear is really a person. He is in many ways, notably that he stands erect. So killing a bear is like killing a man and one must join the scalp society. Bears, like men, are plantigrade, which is to say they walk on the entire foot, leaving tracks that are very different from other animals. Bears can walk in an erect position and challenge or fight a man while in this commanding posture. Again like humans, the bones of a bear's forearm are separate, thus giving him the ability to rotate his forearm. As a result his skill in handling food, or in digging approximates that of man. When a bear is skinned the exposed musculature also resembles that of a human being.

To these physical resemblances are added similarities of disposition, in that the bear is subject to sudden moods, to joyousness and clowning, or to melancholy and surliness. While a lion always behaves like a lion, a bear is entirely unpredictable. In food habits a black bear would prefer to be a man if he were given a choice. He will strip corn from a field, or eat cooked foods with relish, or he will gather roots and berries and vary these with all variety of game. Bear is himself a game animal, but like man also a predator, and his symbolic role extends well beyond his value as food. Probably no other animal is attended by such widespread ritual attention; bear ceremonialism accompanies the animal wherever he is found.

Farnell thought that Bear was a deity in early Greece and Artemis took his place as a goddess who could take the form of a bear. Perhaps Bear was only an associate of the goddess since a similar arrangement is found in Siberia, where the bear is under the control of the high deity, Numi-torum, or in Finland where Tapio is the god and the bear is said to be nursed by the god's wife, Hongatar.

Bear may also relate to the spirit world without being an associate of a high god. He may be under the tutelage of an abstracted spirit of a region, mountain, or forest. Thus in northeast Siberia, "It is believed that the natural features of their environment and the various species of animals with which they are acquainted all have their respective spiritual 'owners' or 'masters.' Among the Gilyak of the Amur region the bear belongs to the fraternity of the 'owner of the mountain.' "² Bear belongs, among the Pueblos, to the West Mountain where he is the titular god.

In the past the grizzly dominated both beasts and man, for he feared no living thing, until the white man brought traps and firearms. He did not fear these either, but he gradually lost the battle. He is no easy animal to down unless the shot is well placed. There are many accounts from the past century which tell of taking a dozen shots to kill one. How poor then were the odds for an Indian armed only with bow and arrow, perhaps spears, and for a last resort a knife. A single arrow is not very effective even when it penetrates a seemingly vital spot.

Hunters in California cut open a grizzly and found an arrow-head embedded in the animal's lights, where the wound was healed over.

In the far West most of the Indians were content to give this beast all the room that he wanted, but were still never free from his aggressions. In the Pueblo ruins at Winona and Ridge Ruin near Flagstaff, Arizona, the bones of more than one grizzly were found. McGregor points out that these, "must have presented something of a problem to kill."[3] Despite the danger the Pueblos liked to hunt grizzly and other bear. Bailey quotes a game warden at the turn of the century as saying that, "The Pueblo Indians were great bear hunters, even before they had guns."[4] He told of one Indian who wounded a bear that turned upon him and tore his face and chest to shreds before the Indian killed it with a knife. He survived and one may assume that he was treated by a bear curing society and probably also taken into a scalp society.

Of the old species, which would now be races, one called *Ursus perturbans*, or the Mount Taylor grizzly, has a particular interest because of its type locality. It inhabited the mountain for which it was named and the small San Mateo range surrounding the peak. Additionally it was also found in the less wooded Zuñi mountains and, "belonged largely to the half-open country of mountains, plains, and scattered juniper and nut pine forest."[5]

That bears, including the grizzly, were abundant is known from nineteenth century accounts. In 1853, Kennerly made a trip from Albuquerque to Zuñi and reported numbers of bears, among them huge grizzlys, among the bushes on the hillsides. "We found the grizzly bear (*Ursus ferox*) abundant. When impelled by hunger they become very fierce and, descending into the valleys, frighten off the *pastores*, who, in their terror, abandoned their flocks to these huge monsters."[6]

Herders in open country were in quite a different relationship to the grizzly than the hunter, who is seeking game and prepared as well as may be. In a similar position were the people, often completely defenseless women and children, who went out to the mesas in season to gather pine nuts and datils, the fruit of *Yucca baccata*, which is made into a dried conserve. To these gatherers, the grizzly, or other bear, was a menace and their supernatural defender was the Ugly Wild Boy whose tale is told by Cushing.

The Ugly Wild Boy looked much like some of the Hehea kachinas of today, who are runners and helpers of the sacred clowns.[7] His face and body were blue and covered with multi-colored scars, while his hair was filled with red things like peppers. The people had been unable to gather their seeds, nuts, and fruits, because Bear claimed the country around Southwest Mesa. One day the Ugly Boy announced to his grandmother that he was going out to gather these foods. He ascended the path to the top of the wide plateau and had scarcely begun to eat the sweet fruit of the datil when the old bear came rushing out of the nearest thicket.

Ugly Boy immediately struck up a conversation, which is always the best defense against bears, who are themselves great talkers and bargainers. The Ugly Boy claims that these things are no more the bear's than his own and offers to prove the fact. The bear, although still in a rage, talks on until the boy suggests that the right to this plateau could easily be settled by a scaring contest. The bear knowing that he can win agrees.

"Presently the Bear came rushing out of the thicket, snapping the trees and twigs, and throwing them about at such a rate that you would have thought there was a sandstorm raging through the forest.

> *Ku hai yaau!*
> *Ku pekwia nu!*
> *Ha! ha! ha! haaaa!*

he exclaimed, rushing at the boy from the rear. The boy stirred never so much as a leaf, only kept on chomping his datilas."

Ugly Wild Boy then rushed home and asked his grandmother to paint him up as horribly as possible. She blackened one side of his face with soot and painted the other with ashes, so that he looked like a demon, and in his hand she placed an ancient stone axe of magical power. The boy then rushed back to the mesa where Bear was wandering about eating datil fruit.

"The boy suddenly ran toward him, and exclaimed:

Ai yaaaa!
He! he! he! he! he! he! he! took!

and he whacked the side of a hollow piñon tree with his axe. The tree was shivered with a thundering noise, the earth shook, and the Bear jumped as if he had been struck by one of the flying splinters. Then, recovering himself and catching sight of the boy, he exclaimed: 'What a fool I am, to be scared by that little wretch of a boy!' But presently, seeing the boy's face, he was startled again and exclaimed: 'By my eyes, the Death Demon is after me, surely!' . . .

"And again, as the boy came still nearer, once more he struck a tree a tremendous blow, and again the earth thundered and trembled more violently than ever, and the Bear almost lost his senses with fright and thought surely the Corpse Demon was coming this time. When, for the fourth time, the boy struck a tree, close to the Bear, the old fellow was thrown violently to the ground with the heaving of the earth and the bellowing of the sounds that issued forth. Picking himself up as fast as he could, never stopping to see whether it was a boy or a devil, he fled to the eastward as fast as his legs would carry him, and, as he heard the boy following him, he never stopped until he reached the Zuñi Mountains."

The Ugly Boy announces his triumph to the people. Like any good folktale this one has a number of points. Do not be afraid of bears, as you can outtalk them and you do have to go out for the nuts and seeds. It also explains the habitat and range of the bears. "Thus it was in the days of the ancients. And therefore the Zuñi Mountains to this day are filled with bears; but they rarely descend to the mesas in the southwest, being fully convinced from the experience of their ancestor that the Corpse

Demon is near and continues to lie in wait for them. And our people go over the mountains as they will, even women and children, and gather datila fruit, piñon nuts, and grass-seed without hindrance."[8]

The grizzly was a killer, which necessarily doomed him. The black bear is quite a different beast. He does not under ordinary circumstances attack humans and it is only an occasional individual that kills stock. In former times black bears could be found almost anywhere in Pueblo country, but they no longer inhabit the open areas. The statewide estimate for the number of black bears in New Mexico has remained at about 3,000 between 1950 and 1964.

Bears are wandering animals that never cease their search for food, except during the winter sleep. They keep to cover as much as possible and have a keen sense of hearing and smell. Thus they are chance game to hunters of other animals. White hunters use dogs for tracking but the Indian had no such resource. It is of interest then to follow Hibben's account of two bear hunts in which he was aided by Jemez Indians. The country there is broken up by a jumble of volcanic ridges among which are level places where the Gambel's oak grows in stunted profusion, producing a great crop of mast in the fall. Bears like the acorns and the seclusion of this rugged area.

One bear had eluded hunters for three seasons, so they employed a Jemez Indian by the name of Tony Chenana, who was the best tracker in the pueblo. The latter spent a week in the area following the tracks of this particular bear until he knew all of its daily habits—where and when it ate and where it slept. He also discovered that this bear reversed the normal procedure of feeding at night and sleeping by day. It was thus light in the morning and able to fight off and elude the pack of dogs that were sent after him. With all of this precise information the hunters took the bear, despite its cleverness. The incidental information that, "No Jemez Indian will knowingly step in the tracks of a bear, nor even touch the imprint with his hand," occurs in the same account.[9]

At the conclusion of another hunt in the Jemez Mountains a segment of bear-hunting ritual appears. "We turned to see Santiago Chiwiwe. From somewhere out of his tattered clothing he had resurrected some red and yellow paint. Across his cheeks and the bridge of his nose he had smeared a broad band of vermillion. Bears are animals of potent medicine in Jemez pueblo and the giant bear of Bellote was a great spirit indeed."[10]

Bears were hunted as game by most Pueblos except at Isleta where there is a taboo on killing them.[11] Bear is set apart from other game by the fact that he is a game animal who can also kill other game. At Taos the killing of a bear for meat involves no ceremony and the meat is simply eaten at the family table. "Bears are tracked and shot, 'lots of them,' in the autumn when they come down from the mountains for berries. Hunters are always careful to shoot a bear twice to be sure of killing it; for a wounded bear will be quick to get roots or leaves and apply them to the wound and recover."[12]

Even here the idea that Bear is a doctor, in this case a practical rather than supernatural one, is included. South of Taos the Tewa people recognize a dual relationship with the bears. There he is referred to as *tsiwi*, when thought of as a natural creature and *kaye*, when a supernatural character. The Keres Pueblos farther down the Río Grande have elaborate requirements to ritualize the killing and eating of a bear. Cochiti may be taken as an example. There the big game hunts were usually communal and, if directed toward taking deer or antelope, a surround was the method used, and a bear might turn up among other animals. A communal hunt would once have been in the charge of the Shai'yak head, or Mountain Lion Man, who was chief of the Hunt society, but when this society lapsed the role fell to the head of the Shi'kame, a curing society, and the hunts were called by the War Chief. A Mountain Lion Man is nonetheless supposed to accompany the hunt.

Bears, along with eagles and lions, belong to a special class of game, in that one who kills any of these is eligible to join the

Warrior's society, just as though he had killed a man. In addition he enters into a special, lifelong brother relationship with another hunter. At Cochiti the Warrior society has also lapsed but a man who kills a bear still engages in the brother bond. An informant of Lange was easily able to list nine pairs of these brothers.[13]

When a group is hunting, the first man to touch the bear is accounted the killer, whether or not he is the one who shot it; the brother is the second man to touch it. If a hunter has been alone when he downs a bear, he fires a shot and lets out a war whoop when returning to the village. Then the first man to reach him and shake his hand becomes the brother. When the kill is made by a member of a party, the second man is sent to tell the war captain, who in turn announces it to the village. The killer meanwhile builds a fire near the skin and carcass.

The series of rites that follow seem to have more to do with war than the hunt. Villagers, guided by the smoke, make a sneak attack on the dead bear, using weapons both ancient and modern. They approach from behind trees and brush, with war cries. When the dead bear is reached it is either struck or shot by each man. Then amid war songs the whole group takes the parts of the beast back to the village, the killer carrying the skin. Paws and forefeet are given to the first and second medicine man to arrive on the scene, the left paw being the most powerful as Bear is left-handed.

There is a distinction made between the meat and the skin, the meat having no special significance, so the killer may divide it as he chooses. The bones must not be scattered about, and are either thrown in the river or placed in shrines. Skulls are buried under rocks to send the animal home. The skin of the bear is treated with great ceremony, as befits a scalp. When the killer brings it into the pueblo, a singing group follows him in a counterclockwise procession that winds four times about the plaza. Women stop the procession to cast meal on the skin, or it is placed on the ground to be beaten, accompanied by coyote yelps. A feast follows and the killer chooses one of the three medicine societies to care for the skin, which consists of washing it in "shiwanna" suds.[14]

For the Keres of western Acoma, bear hunting took place farther from home. White collected an account of a large scale hunt far to the south of the pueblo, which took place in 1887. The game was to be antelope and deer, but a bear chanced on the scene. One hunter was off by himself on a small hill. "Pretty soon I heard something coming, making cracking noises. It was a bear. He was eating acorns—you could hear him cracking them."

This hunter, who had never seen a bear before, wounded the beast and then with a companion tracked it to a cave where the bear was found dead. "Then we started to skin her. My partner told me not to skin below the bear's elbow. . . . Then my partner took out the bear's stomach. Then he started to take out her heart. He told me to go away. I could not see what he did with the heart and stomach. Those tshaianyi alone know how to do these things; nobody can watch them. . . . We took only the skin and two pieces of ribs back to camp. The medicine man began to cure the [leg skins]. He would fill them with hot sand to dry them out. He stuffed grass in them before we left."[15]

The Acoma hunters ate the meat of this bear, which was said to be just like pork. The skins of the lower legs are of more value as they will be worn by medicine men in curing rituals. Similar "gloves" are worn by the medicine men of other pueblos, including the surviving Towa village of Jemez. There the Flint and Fire societies are collectively known as the Bear group because, "bear calls and leg skins are used in cures in symbolic imitation of their tutelary deity."[16]

Hunters who do not belong to these societies donate leg skins whenever they kill a bear. One Jemez variation on the rites connected with killing a bear is the distribution by the killer of small bits of meat, which are taken by the others in the party and wrapped around the barrels of their rifles. At Jemez the bear killer also becomes a "scalp-taker," but this seems to be only a mark of esteem and does not make him a member of any existing society. He does, however, receive ritual recognition from the Underworld Chiefs who are associated with the Arrow Society. Members of the Hunt societies are thought of as "game wardens" and pay tributes to bears, mountain lions, eagles, and deer, whose spirits they must send home by building little shrines in the mountains. The members of the Flint and Fire societies likewise put the skulls of bears and lions in shrines, after they have painted them with red ochre and decorated them with prayer plumes.[17]

The pueblo of Isleta is Tiwa, as is Taos, but the southern member of this linguistic group has a complete taboo on killing bears. "We don't kill a snake or a bear or an eagle because it might be one of us Indians." Another Isletan said: "Bear is a person, men would not kill one."[18] It is a strong and genuine taboo. Parsons gives the firsthand recollections of an Isletan who accidentally killed a bear and of the rites that were necessary to exorcise the killer.

"I was out hunting for deer. I saw a bush and the leaves were moving. I shot at it. It was a bear." This transgression caused so much fright on the part of the killer that he became sick and his sister asked the town medicine society to work for him. First he was placed in his house where he stayed in isolation for four days. Then the medicine man and his helpers entered and erected an altar in one room and circled the killer's bed singing, while the medicine head sprinkled the patient by shaking water from the tips of feathers. They tell him not to be afraid: "You will see with your eyes that the bear you killed is still alive and will come to you. Do not be afraid."

Next it is explained that his mistake was the result of a plot of someone who wished to kill him and thus not his fault. The medicine head then took a crystal with which he called upon the Corn Mothers for aid, and followed a trail of meal to the door, where he whistled a call to the eagle for power to fly to where the bear had been killed. This spot was twenty-five miles away, but he was to make the journey in three-quarters of an hour. He brought back the bear who knocked on the door with his paws. When the bear followed the pollen road into the house some of the spectators hid their faces in their hands.

"I was trying to make myself strong, but I could not stand it; I was feeling faint. . . . The bear hit the post of the house, and hit the floor, and stopped and growled. He smelt around the altar and acted as if he was going to spring on me, opening his mouth and growling. I was not afraid of him, but I was feeling faint. The closer he came to me, the madder he acted. When he came up to me he struck at me with his paws, and held my head."

While the singing continues the bear swings his head from side to side, until at last he expels something which one of the helpers picks up and washes. The patient is asked to swallow this object and he is then told that it is the other half of his heart which had been lost when he killed the bear. Almost immediately the killer feels strong again. The medicine head then tells the people to thank the god Weide and the Corn Mothers, that the patient was going to live long. The latter smokes and is then pushed toward the bear again. The helpers stroke the bear with feathers while sprinkling meal over him, then the bear rose up, sniffing. "He came up to me, clapping his paws and growling."[19]

This is most unlike the bear rituals of other Pueblo groups, including those for curing where the bear is imitated, but not with the same degree of realism. The Isletan rite is more like the bear shamanism of California where medicine men closely disguised as bears practice curing.

The bears that have appeared in these various accounts of hunting rituals have supernatural powers, but they are not entirely Beast Gods. As a game animal, the bear has the same degree of supernatural power as a dead enemy and differs only in that the skin rather than the scalp is the repository of this power. That is not the end of the matter, however, as there is much more to the story of Bear than his meat. Bear also represents the West direction and the nebulous supernatural chief who rules there and controls all things associated with that cardinal point. In this role Bear has been called the "pet" of that spirit, but the word slights the relationship. The animal associate of each directional spirit represents that spirit's power and conveys it to the people. Bear and Mountain Lion are much the most important of animal-incarnated spirits.

At Zuñi, Bear is not only the associate of the West spirit, but is also closely related to the goddess of developed proportions —the Mother of Game, or Ku'yapalitsa. The latter name is her designation as a deity who appears in myths, but when she comes in person to visit the Zuñi, she is the kachina, Chakwena, who has already appeared in the Rabbit chapter. According to Stevenson, "the Cha'kwena is the deceased Ku'yapalitsa (female warrior) of the Kia'nakwe, who carried her heart in her rattles as she walked to and fro before her army during the engagement with the A'shiwi. She was also keeper of all game."[20]

Chakwena and her counterpart are, like the Greek goddess Artemis, both patronesses of childbirth and mothers of game, a combination of roles we have seen in the Rabbit Hunt with the Gods. Again like Artemis, the various Chakwenas are closely associated with bears, as well as deer. As a mother of game this goddess with the dual names is the subject of petitions from hunters who give her plume offerings. "Men who participate in the hunting of large game give te'likinawe to the Cha'kwena, Ku'yapalitsa having been the original owner of all game, for success in the hunt. The first body of A'shiwanni [rain priests] and such women as wish to become mothers make offerings of te'linawe to ku'yapalitsa."[21]

There is more than one kind of Chakwena kachina at Zuñi, and she also has counterparts in other pueblos who appear with bears in the dances, but the basic myths seem to belong to the Zuñi. At Cochiti the Bear kachina, K'waiye or Ko'hai-o, stands in the middle of the line of Chakwena dancers. "He is their chief," as Dumarest puts it.[22] This same relationship is likewise found at Hopi, where Stephen says of the Cha'chakwainumu, "Ho'nauuh (Bear) is their watchman. He has pieces of sheepskin fastened over his feet to look like bear's feet."[23]

At Zuñi the dress of the Chakwena kachinas varies, some being dressed to represent a bear, or there is a bear as an attendant. In the ceremonies that follow the Shalako, a number of Chakwenas dance and with them may be a man and a small boy who represent bears. "The man representing a bear has his lower legs painted black and spotted white. He wears armlets of uncolored leather. A bearskin covers the body and a portion of the lower limbs and skins of the bear's legs with the claws are drawn over his feet. . . . He carries a wooden hatchet, with goats' wool, significant of a scalp lock. . . . These two remain a short time after the tChakwena leave, running about the room like animals."[24]

The more common associations of this goddess are with fawns and rabbits. When the kachina spends four days lying in as though in childbirth, she wears a fawn skin below her breast and on the ceremonial rabbit hunt the Chakwena kachina prays to her divine counterpart, Ku'yapalitsa, for the increase of rabbits and game. Since in these qualities she so closely resembles the goddess Artemis, a comparison with the latter may cast some light on the nature of both deities.

Artemis is often represented as attended by a stag, but she could also take the form of a hare and she was importantly a bear goddess. The myth in Arcadia is that an attendant nymph, Kallisto, hunted with her. The latter was seduced by Zeus, which caused the jealous Hera to transform her into a bear. Artemis was then incited to shoot the transformed nymph. Artemis too had dual names and was once Artemis Kalliste. A. B. Cook writes that, "Such titles imply that the deity worshipped was originally believed to appear in animal form, and pretends to be the animal in question."[25]

Why this should be done is of course the subject of this chapter. The form taken by the rites of Artemis in primitive regions is made clear in a description of the festival of Laphria at Patrae. In that festival large green logs were placed around the altar with drier wood toward the center. Earth is then piled on the steps to the altar to form a kind of ramp so that live animals may be driven upon the fire. The day before the sacrifice a procession is held in honor of Artemis, in which a maiden acts as a priestess as she rides along in a cart yoked to a deer. On the following day animals and birds of the wild are thrown or driven into the great fire around the altar.

"At this point," say Pausanias who witnessed the ceremony, "I have seen some of the beasts, including a bear, forcing their way outside at the first rush of the flames, some of them actually escaping by their strength. But those who threw them in drag them back again to the pyre."[26]

There are two elements in the nature of this mother of game, as with the Zuñi Ku'yapalitsa. On the one hand she is a goddess of game animals—deer, boar, hare, bear—while at the same time she is a patroness of human motherhood. As a mother of game she governs its increase, which in turn identifies her with all kinds of births.

One aspect of Artemis which has puzzled scholars is clarified by the Ku'yapalitsa myth. Farnell was troubled as to why there should be an opposition between the goddess and the bear, and resorts to an historical explanation. He supposes that an ancient cult of the bear-goddess, Artemis Kalliste, had died out leaving, "but the memory of the bear, a holy and peculiar animal." Then it would become difficult to understand why the once beloved animal was killed in the name of the goddess. "The bear, therefore, was supposed to have incurred the enmity of the goddess, and, to explain the reason, reference was made to the probably later notion of the goddess' chastity."[27]

It is not necessary to seek historical changes to explain the duality of the bear's role, or the ambivalence of his patroness. The goddess is a keeper of game and hence a protectoress of these animals. They are sacred to her. On the other hand, since they are game, the animals must be released by the goddess and killed by hunters. As she supplies game, the goddess also becomes a patroness of hunters. Since the whole situation is ambiguous, the roles of the three parties are interchangeable. Men may imitate the bears, or kill them and, they may also kill the goddess herself.

The Zuñi myth in which this is explained combines both hunting and war themes. In the legendary times of migration, the Zuñis came to a village that blocked their path. Two clowns of the Galaxy fraternity, who had been sent ahead as scouts, find two women washing a buckskin and kill them. This leads to a full-scale war between the Zuñis and these people who are led by Ku'yapalitsa. The goddess wears her heart not in her body, but instead carries it in her rattle and her body is thus impervious to arrows. As the Zuñis can do nothing against her they call on the newly born War Twins for help. These leaders in turn gain the help of the real kachinas from the home of the gods, but four of these supernaturals are captured. As a last resort the Twins ask their Sun father for help and he reveals the secret of the goddess' hidden heart, giving them at the same time two turquoise throwing sticks with which to attack her. The elder Twin throws and misses, then the younger hurls his stick, breaks the rattle and the goddess dies.

"After the A'shiwi [Zuñis] captured the village they opened the gates of the corral in which all game was kept by the tChakwena (keeper of game) and said to the game: 'We have opened for you the doors of the world; now you may roam where you will, about the good grass and springs, and find good places to bear your young; you will no longer be imprisoned within the walls, but have the whole world before you.' Since that time game has roamed over the face of the earth."[28]

Despite the obvious necessity of this battle for the liberation of game, those who were destroyed, the Kia'nakwe, or ghost people must be placated, and a quadrennial ceremony is held for them, ending in the distribution of birds, game, and other food stuffs to the Zuñis. Possibly this myth has been based in part on the destruction of some actual town. The actors in the Zuñi Ki'anakwe are said to speak the Sia language, and Sia often aided the Spaniards in wars against resisting pueblos.

At Hopi the Chakwena kachina is associated with the destruction of Palatkwapi, a semi-mythical city in the far south. For the Hopis, "she is the hostile grandmother. She it is who knows how to slay." In these battles she led the fight against the Navajos, but the Hopi Tewa tell that when they lived on the Río Grande, it was the Utes who attacked them. When they retreated the Chakwena woman denounced the warriors as cowards, "and going among them endeavoured by her taunts to compel them to renew the fight. She seized a bow and slung a quiver of arrows over her shoulders and led them back to the attack, and they routed the Ute with great slaughter."[29]

It will be remembered that the man dressed as a bear in the Zuñi Chakwena dance carried an axe and a tuft of wool indicating a scalp, which brings us to the various associations of Bear with war. As a symbol of power for war, the grizzly was ideal as he dominated other animals and disputed with man the right to hegemony over all the earth. While the emphasis varies from one pueblo to another, the thought of Bear as a warrior is never absent. It is at Taos, however, that this role of Bear reaches its highest development.

In that pueblo Bear has become a true god, of war. Warriors prayed to Red Bear, and while a war party was out the chief of the Bear society remained in his kiva, singing to help the foray. When they returned this same chief was in charge of the scalp dance. This deity does not seem to be identified with natural bears. "Big Red Bear is a spirit, who is prayed to, for power and strength. Formerly they had 'meetings' to pray to Red Bear, asking him to give them courage and bravery, and not to let them be overpowered by their enemies."[30] Taos people placed eagle and woodpecker feathers in the mountains as offerings to Red Bear.

Sometimes there is a link between Sun—Bear—war, as at Santo Domingo a bear imitation takes place in the Winter Solstice ceremony. Sun is of course father of the Little War Twins, whose earthly counterparts are the War Captain and his assistant. At this season the shamans and the War Captains appear in the costume of the Opi or Warrior society, "but with bear-leg skins on their forearms. They come in a procession of two single files and make noises like a bear and dance."[31] The purpose here is not war in the usual sense, but a war on evil spirits who must be exorcised at the solstice. Bear may play a somewhat similar role at Hopi, as "in February, 1951, a kachina impersonator representing a bear visited both kivas and warned the people against excessive drinking."[32]

Such secondary extensions of Bear's war power into regulating village life also appear in tales. At Cochiti a man had been committing some wrong, so "the queen of animals" wished to give him a fright that would set him back on the right course. She asked the animals to do this for her and the grizzly bear offered his services. Being surly tempered he exceeded the command and killed the offender. When the bear in turn is told that he must be punished, he replies, "Well, if anyone is stronger than I am and can punish me, let it be so!" The power of the bear was taken away from him at this point and given to the mountain lion who roped the bear with his long tail, climbed a piñon tree which he split as he went up, and then wedged the unruly bear into the split trunk to dry up.[33]

This and a similar tale in which a grizzly refused to attend a council, leading to his being killed by a lion, indicate that in Cochiti at least the lion was thought to be more powerful than the bear. In theory the mountain lion always takes precedence, as in prayers which are addressed first to the lion of the North, and secondly to the bear of the West. In actual fact this is probably not the case.

Bear finds a place in Hopi war ceremonialism even though there are no bears to be found nearer the Mesas than those in the San Francisco Mountains. Shotokunungwu, the lightning and star god, who is also a great warrior, passed his instructions for the rites to the War Twins. They were to throw a scalp at some Hopi who would thereby become the war chief, whose duty was to make cloud symbols on the floor of his kiva. When the warriors returned the scalps would be thrown on these cloud symbols. "They should then cut out a round piece of bear skin which they should place on the floor in the kiva. . . . The warrior who had brought home the scalp should sit on this bear skin for three days and three nights, and on the morning of the fourth day the warrior should wash his head in the kiva."[34]

There was a circle of meal drawn around the bear skin and if the sitting was an initiation into the War society the line would be drawn very close, but if he were already a member it would be drawn farther out so that he could move a bit during the three days. Before a war party went out the chief rubbed bear leg bones on notched sticks, which was to arouse the anger of the War Twins against the enemy and to arouse fear in them. Members of the war party wore bear-medicine pellets in their bandoliers and wore bear-claw necklaces, as members of the Opi society still do at Keresan San Felipe.

The Hopi Snake ceremony was in part a war rite, as the Snakes were once actual warriors. In the initiation ceremony of this group a bear impersonator takes part, but he does not wear a bear skin. He enters the kiva and passes before the novices with corn stalks and vines in his mouth. "The Bear personator carries the plants and moves them up and down four times in front of the novices' faces that they may grow swiftly and vigorously like the rank vines and corn stalks."[35] While this bear is shaking the corn stalks, the Antelope society members suck from a variety of fetishes, which include a conch shell, a brown stone bear, and a white quartz bear, each about six inches long. It will be remembered that the Antelope members were older men who stayed in the kiva to work and pray for the Snake warriors.

At Zuñi, Bear has war associations, but these are not as important as his role in curing. In former times the O'winahai'ye ceremony included the bear-war theme, although Stevenson calls it a "Thanksgiving festival for crops." It was held after harvest by the Priests of the Bow. Its songs are equally divided between thanksgiving for crops and for respite from Navajo depredations. The ceremony lasted for two days and nights during which there were warrior dances and loud songs to the gods of war asking that they give the Zuñis the lives of their enemies, that there may be rain.

On the first evening the Ant fraternity, which is connected with the Priests of the Bow, performs a dance. The choir of Ants sings to the accompaniment of drum and rattle. "A man and woman of the fraternity begin dancing, and the man appears to grow wilder and wilder as he growls and jumps about as nearly as possible like the bear he represents."[36] The man, who wears only a black breechcloth, dances for half an hour. When the warriors dance next day, members of the Ant society apply bear's grease to the faces and place an arrow point in each dancer's mouth.

Among the Keres, the Tewas, at Jemez, and at Zuñi, Bear is the great doctor. Bear is more importantly a doctor than he is a patron of warriors, but his role in medicine stems more from his warlike nature than from his ability to dig up medicinal roots. The reason for this is the view the Pueblos hold on the origin of disease. As an example we may take the Keres pueblo of San Felipe. There disease is caused almost entirely by witches who shoot objects, such as bits of glass, stones, thorns, or even snakes into the body of their victim, or they may steal a person's heart or a part of it.

Since disease is caused by these objects, the cure consists in removing them, in retrieving the heart, or in the preventive measure of fighting with the witches who do the damage. "But the medicine man could not cure illness nor oppose witches in hand-to-hand fighting without receiving 'power' from certain spirits, and without the aid of their paraphernalia. My informant stated that power was received from bears, mountain lions, and eagles."[37]

The aid of all the beasts of prey is called upon to help in the physical struggle against witches, but it is the bear who is pre-eminent. The medicine man makes a meal painting and lays several leg skins and paws of bears on either side of it, for these bring him the power to cure. Frequently he wears a necklace of bear claws and he may also have a whistle made of bear bone tied about his neck, all to aid him in combats with the disease-causing witches.

That was by no means the whole of Pueblo medical thinking even in times before the advent of the white man's scientific medicine. Among the Hopis, spirits and animals rather than witches, cause and cure disease. Except for the Hopi-Tewas who brought the bear medicine cult with them from the Río Grande, the Hopi doctor is the Badger with his medicinal roots. The Zuñis also make great use of plant medicines and probably the Keres did so too. The Zuñis distinguished between a kind of psychic illness—which is caused by the foreign objects shot into the body by witches, and a physical illness that may be treated by herb medicines.

According to Stevenson, "It is when a theurgist realizes that a person is genuinely ill that he brings his plant medicine into use."[38] In this treatment he uses the medicine which pertains to his particular curing fraternity, and as these are specific for certain kinds of disease, the process can be rationalized by calling in the proper doctor. When the patient does not respond to this treatment it is concluded that the cause of his sickness is not due to some minor enemy, such as ants, but to sorcery. In that case the Beast Gods are invoked to aid the doctor and among these spirits the Bear is pre-eminent.

While the ultimate power to heal is in the hands of spirits, primitive science was also used along with the magical practices. The Zuñis used antiseptics and a narcotic to anesthetize for minor surgery and bone setting, while a great number of herbs, with and without value, were used. The bear medicine of the Zuñis was made from *Senecio multicapitatus*, while that of the Hopis derives from *Aster ericfolia*.

In curing rites Bear is impersonated in front of the patient, although the suggestion of the animal may be slight, such as the bear leg skin gloves, or it may be carried to the point of actually wearing a bear skin and dancing about in imitation of the beast. The purpose of dancing is to make the Beast God appear and assist. "The participants gradually work themselves into a state of mental excitement bordering on hysteria. Finally those who are qualified to impersonate the bear draw over their hands the bear paws that lie on the altar, and in so doing assume the personality of the bear, much as the wearer of a mask becomes a god. They utter the cries of animals and otherwise imitate beasts, especially the bear."[39]

At Zuñi the association between the Bear and the bear shamans is so close that the latter are said to be able to literally turn into bears, just as bears may become people. The two carry on the curing ceremonies jointly, and after death the shamans do not go to the usual Zuñi underworld, but to Shipapolima, the spiritual home of the Beasts of Prey in the Jemez Mountains.

In myth this identity is emphasized by making the founder of a medicine society a half-man, half-bear. The daughter of a priest went at night to draw water from a spring and was surprised by black bear. She is taken to Shipapolima where the bear keeps her in a cave that he seals up during the day when he goes out to hunt. She is homesick, even though the bear becomes a man at night: "He wore lots of beads and earrings and had parrot feathers on his head and yarn around his legs and arms and a bandeau woven of soapweed fibre around his forehead."

This couple produce a child who matures with animallike rapidity and he is soon able to remove the stone from the cave entrance. Mother and child make their escape but are pursued by the bear father. When the latter catches the fugitives the half-human son kills the bear, his father, and returns with his mother to the village. There his physical strength grows apace until it is difficult for him to play with companions and some are even killed when he hits them. For this reason bear-boy must go back to Shipapolima to live, a shift eased by the fact that his father is actually alive—"When you killed me I did not die." Furthermore the son becomes the patron of the Shiwanakwe curing society of Zuñi.

"In Yellow Rocks the people were sick and they called the son of the bear to cure them. He came and growled like a bear and danced and drew sickness from them. He cured those who had called him. After four or five had been initiated (cured) he told them to meet together and pray and dance and cure as he had done. He told them to put bear's leg skins and claws upon their arms and growl with the voice of a bear. So they founded Shiwanakwe and they always cured as the bear' son had done. He went back to Shipapolima and lived with his father."[40]

While only the bear and eagle are imitated in curing ceremonies, the other beasts of prey are invoked and are supposed to be present. The "medicine maker" of the Little Fire fraternity utters this chant as he prepares his brew:

> *Lion of the North, give me power to see disease.*
> *Bear of the West, give me power to see disease.*
> *Badger of the South, give me power to see disease.*
> *White Wolf of the East, give me power to see disease.*
> *Eagle of the Zenith, give me power to see disease.*
> *Shrew of the Earth, give me power to see disease.*
> *Thou, my Sun Father, give me power to see disease.*
> *Thou, my Moon Mother, give me power to see disease.*
> *All ye ancient ones, give me power.*[41]

It is not only by his power for fighting witches that Bear becomes a doctor, as, like Badger, he digs for roots that have curative value. In a Taos tale that centers around a little song sung by Bear, he comes out of his home in the burnt timber and goes to the woods to dig medicine with his cane. When the people see him he dances, repeats the little song, and dabs himself with the medicine he has dug.[42]

All too often bears injure men who are out in the mountains, and who would be better qualified to heal these wounds than the bear himself? At Taos the intermediaries are a group called Bear People who specialize in the cure of bear-inflicted wounds, although they also have such duties as singing to give strength to runners before a race. Once a year, just before the solstice ceremony, the Bear People perform a rite, "so that the bears will be peaceful to the people."

"In the Water People's kiva in the day time, sometimes at

night, dance four men painted black. Each holds a bear head in his hands. Other members of the Bear People sing. They too are painted black. When the song is finished, the dancers raise their bear heads towards the sun four times—moving the head from a position close to the floor up as high as they can reach. Four songs are sung in this manner. Then they lay their heads on the floor. The Bear People's chief gives each dancer a pinch of medicine and two or three turkey feathers. The dancer prays and sprinkles the medicine on the bear's head and puts the feathers in the bear's mouth."[43]

It is the bears of reality that are being placated here, but real bears are close to the supernatural. The Bear men or shamans of the Tewa pueblo of Nambe are described, "as travelling both underground and in the air, great distances in brief periods."[44] The Tewas hold that there are real bears and spirit bears, although these may be modes rather than alternatives. In the Tewa language the word *kaye* is used when one is thinking of the supernatural character of the animal, but if one is thinking simply of the beast, *tsiwi* is used. The spirit animal may have a specific, physical home, as at San Ildefonso, where the *kaye* are said to live on a sacred mesa called Shumak'ere which lies to the south of the village.[45]

The reader will have noticed by this point how little of the bear's role is related to Bear clans, which is the very reverse of the situation with regard to antelope. The associations of bear are almost entirely worked out in relation to various societies for the hunt, war, and curing, which should caution those who habitually speak of animals as clan totems. At Zuñi where the bear plays a considerable role there is a Bear clan, but in the myth of the Shiwanakwe society the bear does not require a member of that clan for any ceremonial role.

All of the Pueblo groups who have clans at all have Bear clans. At Acoma the Bear clan is large but plays no role in ceremonialism. At Zuñi Stevenson found two instances of specific roles for the Bear clan, one being the offering of prayer plumes to the younger War Twin at the Winter Solstice. At the

summer solstice the "god speaker" or Kopekwin was supposed
to have been a member of the Deer clan, but as that group
became extinct a Bear clansman takes part. Parsons adds that
the sand painting for the Sword-Swallowers' society must be
made by a Bear clansman, which follows from the fact that the
members are warriors who wear lion- or bear-paw mittens.[46]

At Hopi the situation is different and the Bear clan has important duties in providing Town chieftancies. There are a number
of reasons why a Bear makes a logical Town chief and some of
these appear in Keresan myth, but they are not put into actual
practice there. For one thing the Town chief, as opposed to the
Outside or War chief, is a "mother" who looks after the welfare
of his people. Bear as the chief supernatural patron of curing
also looks after the welfare of the people. There is also a feeling
that the bear is the chief of animals, even though the mountain
lion may stand first in order, just as the War chief sometimes
stands ahead of the Town chief. Some of these thoughts appear
in the Keresan myth called, "The Chief and the Bear."

The story is told at Laguna, but the setting is long ago in
Santo Domingo which lies at the foot of the Jemez Mountains,
near good bear country. The son of the Chief was hunting deer
to supply meat for the Domingans who were about to husk their
corn crop. Coyote suggested that the bears might do this work
for them, so the Chief's son asks the bear, who agrees. " 'When
you arrive below there at your father's tell him that without
fail we are going to husk corn tonight,' said the bear, 'for your
father is the chief of the town.' "

The Chief had some doubts, so on the following day he went
with his son to the field where they found that all of the corn
was stripped from the stalks, but there was no corn piled up.
" 'Maybe all the bears ate the corn. There is no corn there,' said
the Chief's son. 'Let me tell the people. . . . Let us pursue the
bears.' " Following the tracks the Chief's son caught up with
the bears, shot the leader and one other bear, but did not kill
them. "Then the bear became angry. The bear turned against
him and on his part chased him northward. Then all the men

ran away, but the Chief's son was caught by the bear. It knocked him down and bit his shoulder. The bear also bit the Chief's son's thigh. He was about to kill him. Then the bear said, 'Why did you shoot me? Did we not tell you yesterday that we were going to husk corn that night?' "

The bear takes the Chief's son back to the field and shows him where the bear people had carefully piled the corn underneath the stalks. "Then the bear said, 'Tomorrow night you will die, and when you are dead I shall take you to my house.' " And indeed it was true, the son succumbed to the wounds the bear had inflicted, but not before he had explained to his father's people that the bears had actually husked the corn as they had promised. Then after dark the Bear-Girl came for him. "Then the Bear-Girl entered downward. Then she carried him on her back. Then the Chief's son said, 'Father and mother, I am going for good to the bear's house. I cannot come back. Goodbye.' "[47] With her medicine she cured him but he could not come back to his people.

The myth could very well have served as warrant for placing the Town chieftancy in the hands of the Bear clan, and may have done so for some group at its point of origin, but it does not apply to the Keres. At Hopi, on the other hand, the Bear clan held the Town chieftancy on all three mesas. A Hopi gave Parsons an explanation of the role of Bear clan in the First Mesa solstice ceremony. "Bear clansman picks up from the 'road' the turkey buzzard wing feather and sprinkles ashes on it. Whenever in the song they say: *ma'pedi*, cleanse, *kyenu*, throw, he circles the feather around four times and throws the ashes towards the ladder. In this way anything bad in the kiva he blows away. The Bear clan man is supposed to be bear himself and Bear gets rid of bad things."[48]

Bears, like buzzards, will eat carrion and thus quite literally get rid of bad things. The Hopi Bear clans have a very brief account of their origin and that of related clans. "In the long ago and far away in the west, Bear was very old and died. The Hopi who first came to his body, who first looked upon it, became the first of the Bear clan."[49] It will be noted how closely this origin myth parallels the actual practice at Keresan Cochiti, where a brother relationship is set up with the first man who comes upon the killer of a bear.

Other groups who were to become clans in the same phratry came along and became the Fat-of-the-Eye, Bear's strap, and others, until a Spider spun a web across the empty cavity of the bear's abdomen. Those who saw this became the Spider clan, and lastly a Bluebird arrived, giving rise to that clan name. Among these and other clans the Bear stood first in importance. In the plaza of Walpi on First Mesa there are three *si'papu* symbolic of the points of emergence from the underworld. Of these the one belonging to the Bear clan is the most sacred spot on the mesa.[50]

While the Town chief was drawn from the Bear clan in all other villages, at Walpi this situation was changed by the arrival of the Horn clan. The Flute ceremony in the village seems to be in part a dramatization of the shift of the chieftancy from the Bear-Snake people to the Horns. "Alosaka of the Bear and Snake who always sat on the house tops watching, spied us before we got off the north mesa, and he ran up this mesa, across the Gap and along the far summit, till he came above Sheep spring, and the Horn clan halted and sang."[51] These newly arrived Horns claim that they bring the Flute ceremony which can cause rain. They offer this in exchange for permission to enter. After they set up the Flute altar and sing, the Bear and Snake say, "For a surety your chief shall be our chief."

On Second Mesa it is said that the Raven people once held the Town chieftancy, but the clan became extinct and the Bears succeeded them. According to legend there was a falling out among the Bear people sometime in the nineteenth century, as a result of which a younger brother of the chief, Matcito, founded Old Oraibi. The time sequence is most impossible since Oraibi has been there since the twelfth century while the towns on Second Mesa were not built until the end of the seventeenth.

In theory, but not always in fact, the Town chief of Oraibi

should be of the Bear clan. Why this is no longer the case is a most useful illustration of why the role of animals can never be completely rationalized into either clans or societies. There are logical forces which work to integrate any animal into the scheme of Pueblo life, and at the same time there are social forces at work which vary logical integrations. How this comes about is demonstrated at Old Oraibi.

Lololoma, who became chief of Oraibi in 1880, was of the Bear clan, but after an initial period of anti-Americanism he became convinced of the hopelessness of opposing the whites and his new view led to a split. Behind the Friendly-Hostile issue lay a long dispute between two groups, the Bear and the Spider clans, whose quarrel extends into mythology. The Bears held control of the Soyal, or Winter Solstice ceremony, while the Spiders controlled the warmth-bringing Flute ceremony. The Bears held not only the town chieftancy, but also a bear's share of the suitable farming land. In the migration traditions, when the Spider clan arrived on the scene they asked for admittance on the grounds that they would help the Bear people, and would also contribute their own ceremonies. These were the Flute, Antelope, and Warrior society rites. The ceremonial fusion was a success, but there was no equal division of the farmable land.

In 1906 Oraibi split, and while this seemed to be the result of differing views on what to do about whites, the quarrel was native and illustrates why pueblos break up and form new villages, a process which divides ceremonies as well.[52] In the new dispensation the Hostiles were forced to set up a Soyal ceremony without benefit of the Bear clan and the Town chieftancy in the offshoot villages also passed from the hands of Bear clansmen. Since it is known that such shifts have been at work in Pueblo groups for centuries, one can see why the symbolic roles of animals can never become entirely rigid and logical, why the idea of a clan with its totem cannot be viewed as fixed, and why we may find a myth in one place without a rite, or a rite that has no myth.

Chapter IX

MOUNTAIN LION and
RELATED GODS

It comes alive
It comes alive, alive, alive.
In the north mountain
The lion comes alive
In the north mountain, comes alive.
With this the prey animal
Will have the power to attract deer, antelope;
Will have power to be lucky.[1]

THE MOUNTAIN LION, or puma, is a very secretive animal who is seldom seen by man. He is hence mysterious as well as powerful. All of the powerful animals are called upon for help by the Pueblos, so that we find Mountain Lion sharing with Bear a certain amount of power for curing and war, but his is not so specific for these. The one mysterious power in which Lion surpasses all other beasts of prey is that of the hunt. The bears, though powerful in this respect, are observably not strictly carnivores, while the lion is. Even though the lion is not often seen, anyone who roams through the lower mountains will from time to time discover the kills which the beast has made and covered with sticks and leaves for future use. A lion will kill one deer a week, perhaps less if it is feeding on other mammals as well, or perhaps more if it is a female with young who are out of the den.[2] Since they cannot eat all of a kill, a lion gorges and then fasts for perhaps three days, after which it may return to the same kill or make another.

There are several alternative names for this animal, but in the Rockies, the Southwest, and in California the most frequent is mountain lion. Puma is often used by biologists and it is doubtless a better choice, being the Inca name. Cougar and panther are other regional names. Lion hardly conveys the facts correctly, since the animal is of American origin with no near living relative in the cat family. In Simpson's *Classification* the mountain lion, lynx, domestic cat, and others, are all in the genus, *Felis*, while the African lion, tiger, leopard and jaguar are all in the genus, *Panthera*.[3] The mountain lion prefers rim-rock country and even there sticks to the roughest parts, avoiding easy saddles when he travels cross country. In the Southwest lions now seem to prefer the Transition zone, and their favorite food by far is deer. Most mammals, except for badgers and the rarer carnivores, are eaten as are small birds and turkeys, dead salmon and grasshoppers.[4] In New Mexico and Arizona the lion seems to relish at all times the dangerous little porcupine.

In feeding, the mountain lion makes a wide circuit of trails that crisscross in many places; this may be as little as five miles in diameter, or as much as thirty. It might take the animal two weeks or a month to cross his trail again in his mostly nocturnal rounds in search of food. Two relatively minor points about lions impressed the Indians, they are good eating and the tough hide, which is strong enough to resist the teeth of dogs, made a good and symbolic quiver for arrows. In the Pueblo view, Mountain Lion was a great hunter and also the chief of beasts who controlled all other animals. He was also an animal of great courage, so much so that members of the Cactus War society at Zuñi used "lion medicine."[5] Likewise the head of the San Felipe scalptakers, or Opi, was called "Mountain Lion."

In the mythology of Mountain Lion we find an elaborate set of interrelationships between the animal and various spirits or gods. Since the Pueblos believed that the lion could kill a grizzly bear, he was for them the ruler of all other animals and as such their keeper, which immediately relates him to those deities who are keepers of game. As a link between the animal and mankind, there is Lion Man, a spirit animal or Beast God, in whom all the lion qualities are apotheosized. In essence these were seen as control of game and consequent power for the hunt.

Lion Man, or the lion itself, may act as the patron of a hunter, who carries a stone fetish of the mountain lion to bring the supernatural power of the beast. The Lion who is the spirit of the North direction is closely related to, but not identical with Lion Man, as the directional beast has wider powers, such as curing. There is also a Mountain Lion Girl, in Zuñi mythology, as Gamekeepers of either sex have consorts.

If the deity is a Mother of Game she has a dual role, often reflected in the myths, as both patroness of game and of hunters, two scarcely reconcilable roles. In order to get around this logical inconsistency, the deity may be split into two by the addition of a consort, a husband or brother, who becomes the Spirit of hunters. The Keresan game goddess Kochinako, or Yellow Woman, has as consort Arrow Youth, the friend of Great Star, who is sometimes her brother and sometimes her husband.

There is a myth based upon the promise of the Beast Gods to give their sister in marriage to anyone who could kill a spotted demon. The sister is Mountain Lion Girl and she is named Ku'yapalitsa—presumably it is Lion Man who makes the offer. When this story is told on a simple level, it is Coyote who tricks the demon and marries Lion Girl, but he is in turn tricked by the animal gods, falls off a cliff, and dies.

The same story is told in connection with the life of a gambler. As we go deeper into the elaboration of the Lion god we will find that in all of his forms he is prone to contests. In later times these contests may be with the Christian god or native supernaturals, but as we trace the line back they become contests —gambling games—in which he wins most kinds of animals, or the rays of the sun and rain. In short the gambling is for the purpose of winning control over nature. At Isleta this kind of power is related to the ordinary forms of gambling and Mountain Lion and Bear are patrons of gaming.[6]

Mountain Lion's sister was not married, so Lion told her

that if any man looked in at her door and requested marriage four times, she must marry him, however poor he might be. First a kachina appeared at her house. "He walked right in and called out the girl's name, Ku'yapalitsa. He called her by name and she answered. The man went in and the girl took the man as her husband. He stayed one night and in the morning he went away to the northeast to hunt deer."

Coyote, who had learned what Lion's instructions were, tells them to a gambler who puts the information to good use and marries the Lion Girl. She promises her gambler husband not only stakes, but also her power and that of the other supernaturals, to be used in winning back what he had lost. Naturally that power was overwhelming and the other villagers lost everything and were left so poor that they planned to kill Lion Girl and the gambler.

"Mountain Lion came back from Shipapolima. He got home about sunset. He came in and talked to his sister and brother-in-law and said 'Well, tomorrow the Hopi people will come and kill you and my sister. We have to go to Shipapolima at day break tomorrow.' "[7] Lion then leads his sister, her husband, who is a priest's son, and Coyote to Shipapolima. The latter place is an actual shrine of the Beast Gods in the Jemez Mountains. When the Hopis who had been hired to kill this group arrive and find them gone, they destroy the Zuñi village instead, leading to a legendary period of wars between the two Pueblo groups.

The elements behind this seeming romance are the lion as Beast God and his sister the Mother of Game, in the form of a lioness. Since the two give their power to her husband, the priest's son, it may be assumed that he is the original of the Hunt Chiefs who use their power to control all game animals. The entire group leaves for the home of these deities at daybreak, and we will find that the real stone lions there do face the rising sun, which holds the ultimate power. The myths gathered about Shipapolima concern a greater god, under various names, who is ultimately based upon the Mountain Lion spirit, but who has more complicated elaborations.

Po'shaiyanki is the name of a Zuñi god and Poshaiyanne is a Keresan deity. It seems likely, because of the connection of both with the Keres shrine, that the name is Keresan and was borrowed by the Zuñis to fit a similar deity in their own culture. Mrs. Stevenson notes that the Zuñi gods arrived in two groups, the first of which were called the Great Gods. Four years later, which can be interpreted as four ages later, a second group arrived led by Po'shaiyanki, "who figures as the culture hero of the Zuñis, being their leader. These also followed a northern route to Shipapolima, where they remained. This place is held sacred by the Zuñis as the home of their culture hero and the Beast Gods. The Zuñis believe the entrance to Shipapolima to be on the summit of a mountain about 10 miles from the pueblo of Cochiti, New Mexico. Two crouching lions, or cougars, of massive stone in bas-relief upon the solid formation top guard the sacred spot."[8]

A description of this place follows, but first we need to know a little more about the culture-hero—god, Po'shaiyanki. In Cushing's view this deity was a Sun-Youth, which certainly contains an element of truth. His first appearance was in the Underworld, and the very name Shipapolima is related to Shipapu, the point of emergence from the fourfold Underworld. "Then came among men and the beings, it is said, the wisest of wise men and the foremost, the all-sacred master, Po'shaiyankya, he who appeared in the waters below, even as did the Sun-father in the wastes above. . . . And alone fared he forth dayward, seeking the Sun-father and supplicating him to deliver mankind and the creatures there below."[9]

It is usually the War Twins, who are also sons of the Sun, that lead the people from the Underworld, but in relation to the fraternities this account is correct. An informant told Parsons that Poshaiyanki was a "raw person," meaning supernatural. "He was a man of magic. All the fraternities belong to him.

Some time in the beginning he came out with all the fraternities." He then went to all the different towns, "and he made all the things for them to do in their fraternities."[10] He thus seems to be a magician or patron of magic such as practiced by the societies, and perhaps in particular the magic of medicine and hunt societies.

One specific bit of magic with far-reaching consequences was his transformation of the original medicine men into the Beast Gods. "The Divine Ones, wishing that the world should be well guarded by those keen of sight and scent, visited Shipapolima, home of Po'shaiyanki, Zuñi culture hero, and his followers, and converted the medicine men who came into this world with Po'shaiyanki into Beast Gods. They converted one into the cougar, giving him the north region to preside over," and so on with the Bear, Badger, Wolf, Eagle, and Shrew.[11] I assume that he was the agent or instrument of the magic of the Divine Ones in this change or union of priest and animals. The Divine Ones are the War Twins (although there may be a double set at Zuñi), whose ultimate power of course resides in the Sun, and at the Winter Solstice feather-sticks are offered to Poshaiyanki.

In his travels this god wandered all over the world and in time met Lea, which stands for *rey*, the Spanish king. The king says that they will do tricks to each other, meaning contests. "Tomorrow, when the sun comes out, the sun will shine on one of us first; that is the one who will win." While Poshaiyanki was short, he had parrot tail-feathers on his head and the sun shone on him first. The king admits defeat and says that next they will contest for the animals. "So Lea began. And he called all the animals that belonged to him—sheep, horses, mules, pigs, chickens. So all gathered together. He told Poshaiyanki to try it. 'Now, you try it,'—'All right! I am but an Indian,' he said. So he called all the birds, eagles, hawks, wild turkeys, all kinds of birds, and all flew to them. He called deer, bear, cougar, wolf, and all the other animals. At last all the animals gathered together where they were, and Poshaiyanki had four times more than Lea."[12]

The last contest is but another version of the idea held by all Pueblos, that the animals are won away from their original owner or god in a gambling contest, which is why we have already heard the story of the poor gambler who married Mountain Lion's sister. In Tewa tales all game is owned by Pineto Sendo, or "mean old man." Two youths who are the children of Dark Star, the patron of hunters, are challenged by Pineto Sendo who does not believe they are really of this parentage. He challenges them to a hiding contest. "Now we are going to play at hiding. . . . I bet you all what I have here, deer, buffalo, sheep and turkeys." The contest is one of hiding as a particular kind of animal, which must be guessed by the opponent.

After winning four times the youths defeat the mean old man. "You have beaten me. Now I believe you belong to Dark Star." He then gives them all of the animals they have won. "So Dark Star told Yellow corn girls to take them back [to earth]. They brought them and hung them up by the same string they took them up by, also the goats and deer and buffalo and elk and turkeys and birds of different kinds. Because Yellow corn girl's children won, we have different kinds of animals and birds. That is why we have them everywhere."[13]

While the contests in time come to be with the Spanish king or the Christian god, they were in origin native and have to do with the release of game which has been impounded. Some see in the myths of Keepers of Game a seasonal ritual. The animals are kept in a cavern or hollow hill of winter, from which they are released in spring by a Sun-Youth. With the Pueblos that is only half the story, as the mountain where the game is kept has a broader significance, being a part of the directional system as well as the seasons.[14] The concept here is similar to that mentioned in the Bear chapter for various Siberian tribes, where it is held that the forest and mountains have spirit owners who control the game in their areas.

One of the native contests that Poshaiyanki has is with Shumaekoli, the original of the Zuñi Shuma'kwe society, a medicine group that cures cramps, convulsions, and rheumatism. From the content of the myth they must also be a weather-control society. Poshaiyanki was jealous of Shumaekoli, which would be natural for the chief of the Beast God curers, so he challenged him to a contest. "The first trial between Shumaekoli and Poshaiyanki was for rain. Shumaekoli won. The second trial was with animals, to see how much each had. Shumaekoli gathered together wood rat, deer, jack rabbit, rabbit. Poshaiyanki gathered together bear, sheep, and all the animals except the four Shumaekoli had."[15] Probably that is the origin of the contest with the king of Spain.

As a result of this contest the brother of Poshaiyanki becomes angry, telling him to stop doing those things. He refuses and the brother kills Poshaiyanki. Parsons sees in this death an association with the Jesus myth, which will become more important in the story of the Keresan counterparts, but there may be a native basis as well. Many elements of the Jesus story are integrated into the Keresan god Poshaiyanne, whose name is obviously identical with that of the Zuñi god, and basically the myth is the same if we subtract the Christian overlay.

In Sia mythology Poshaiyanne first appears as a poor youth who is distinguished only by a beautiful turquoise bracelet. A chief is so taken with the beauty of this piece that he challenges the youth to a gambling contest, staking his house in the north—where he is probably the directional chief—and all his possessions against the bracelet. The first game is a sort of Indian Camelot in which stones are moved around a square. Poshaiyanne wins and then appears with more bracelets whose stones represent the colors of the cardinal points. As a final bet the chief stakes all of his people, only to lose them too. When the chief says, "Take them!" his opponent surprisingly refuses. "No," said Poshaiyanne: "I will not, for should I do so I would lose my power over game."[16]

There is no mention of the lion here, but the chief is from the north, the direction with which the lion is associated and further connections will appear later. Before Poshaiyanne began his round of visits to all of the pueblos, the Sia were unable to capture game. When someone was sent out they always returned empty-handed "saying they could see the animals and many tracks but could catch none." This difficulty was explained to the spirit with power over game.

Poshaiyanne then went to a mountain in the north from which he could see the whole world, the deer further north, antelope in the west, mountain sheep in the south, a buffalo on a high peak in the east, rabbits and other small animals all over the earth, and the air filled with all kinds of birds. He then offers to lead the Sia people on a hunt, which is joined by the War Twins who descend to earth for this purpose. First of all Poshaiyanne makes a hunt fire to blind the animals.

"He then made a circle of meal, leaving an opening through which the game and hunters might pass, and when this was done all of the men of the village formed into a group a short distance from Po'shaiyanne, who then played on his flute, and, holding it upward, he played first to the north, then west, then south, and then east. The deer came over the four roads to him and entered the great circle of meal."[17]

After all the animals are within the circle of meal the god closes the entrance and he remains outside while the Indians shoot the deer with their bows and arrows. The fact that he uses a flute to attract the animals indicates that he has been to some extent identified with another son of the Sun, Paiyatemu, the flute-playing Sun-Youth who is patron of clowns and leader of the Corn Maidens. The circle of meal will be recognized as a magical counterpart to the actual corrals of stone or brush into which animals, and in particular antelope, were driven by Pueblo hunters.

Poshaiyanne, like his Zuñi counterpart, is associated with the Chakwena, who will be remembered as the kachina counterpart of the Zuñi Mother of Game, Ku'yapalitsa. In the origin myth from Acoma there is a list of spirits, mostly kachinas, who were created by Iyatiku the Keresan mother goddess. At the end of the list we find, "Sha'koya, who is a great hunter." Parsons indicates in a footnote that these "Tsh'akwiya" who come out at the solstices are to be identified with the Chakwena kachinas of other pueblos.[18] Even without her authority the identity could be guessed from illustrations of the kachina and further material in *Keresan Texts*.

In that work there are at least two accounts that throw light on the relationship of Shakoya to Poshaiyanne. During the legendary time of migrations, the Keresan people had arrived at White House, where they were given knowledge of their ceremonies and became full-fledged Pueblos. The War Twins were there, the shamans were getting their instructions, "and also after some time there arrived Old-Woman Shakoyo's child. And from the northwest region he came. Mountain Lion Man he brought with him . . . 'I am Po'shaiyanne,' thus he said to him. 'Who is your mother?'—'Shakoyo, she is my mother.' "[19]

Poshaiyanne confesses that he does not know who his father is, but he offers the chief his magical power. The chief then asks him what kind of a shaman he is and the reply is, "Shakoyo shaman." He is always accompanied by his Mountain Lion and performs various prodigies, such as making water gush from one wall, or producing an actual bear from the west wall of a kiva. We also find one interesting bit of information about his mother. "At one time the son of the Giantess (Shakoyo) who was called Po'shaiyanne arrived from the north-west. He was accompanied by Mountain-Lion-Man."[20]

His mother then was a giantess, as was the Zuñi Ku'yapalitsa, and we have seen other reasons for believing that female giantesses were Keepers of Game. In this case the hunter-consort is a son rather than husband or brother of the Mother of Game. There is a strange twist to the Poshaiyanne myths at Acoma and Laguna, in that he is not a welcome introduction there. This is the very reverse of the situation at Zuñi and Sia where he teaches successful hunting. There may be three layers to this negative attitude, the first being a conflict between hunting and agriculture.

In one Laguna account the people have lived well, with the

shamanistic societies performing rites according to the rules given them by the twin mothers of mankind. When Poshaiyanne arrives with his lion he announces a new kind of shamanism and contests with the War Twins. The mothers become angry and hide the food plants causing a great famine.[21] In this account the people nonetheless accept his type of shamanism, but elsewhere it is said that he was excluded and killed.

"Years pass away; things are as they should be; plenty of game and plenty of rain for planting, until one day a character came to their village or settlement from Esto-eh Tick-eh (cane breaks) of the north. This man they called Po-shi-ah-ne. He was never born as other people, but came from a parasite. He was a great wizard and juggler and soon obtained a large following. He introduced a new form of medicine and worship. About this time the rains ceased to fall or were insufficient to support vegetation. Po-shi-ah-ne tried very hard with incantations and magic to make rain fall, but failed. Then the people became angry and Po-shi-ah-ne fled in the dark, but he was pursued, captured and put to death."[22] After this event a great famine followed, and the people turned to cannibalism.

It will be remembered that when the Zuñi counterpart, Poshaiyanki, contested with the Shumaekoli, the first round was to see who could bring the rain. Poshaiyanki lost that contest, and even though he won the next by bringing the most animals, he was then put to death by his own brother. The opposition between hunting and rain-agriculture is interesting, because it goes contrary to the fact that slain deer bring rain. Thus we are led to believe that there was some actual opposition of cults that had not been resolved. Further evidence of this comes from Keresan Santa Ana where Chakwena's role has been stretched to include rainmaking. "Tshakwena may be a katsina; at least he lives at Wenima. 'He causes the shiwana to put out forest fires.' He 'takes care' of the vegetation of the earth."[23]

A second reason for the Acoma-Laguna opposition to this group may be that they actually did travel from one place to another and were unwelcome along the way. It is said by

Stephen that the Chakwena people, which is to say a migrating party carrying the Chakwena kachina cult, came from the Río Grande to Hopi, by way of Zuñi.[24] If they also passed through Acoma-Laguna and stayed awhile, they may have interrupted the normal ceremonial pattern, although the Laguna Chakwena kachinas eventually became highly respected for their hunt powers. If the Chakwena was of Keresan origin, we also get a possible explanation for the duality of Ku'yapalitsa-Chakwena at Zuñi, in that a similar warrior-goddess and gamekeeper was at this time added to the one already existing there. The Keresan origin would also explain why the whole Zuñi group, including the Beast Gods, became associated with the shrine of the Stone Lions near Cochiti.

A third possible reason for the opposition to Poshaiyanne at Acoma-Laguna was his eventual identification with the Jesus myth, although this must have been tempered by the fact that he was first identified with Montezuma. A minor sign of this Spanish influence appears in the character of Boshaiyanyi, who is called Santiago. One is a Spanish spirit—in the Pueblo view— and one native, although they dress just alike. The impersonations, which take place on a pueblo's Saint's Day, consist of frame hobbyhorses covered with cloth. The role of this minor supernatural is to produce more horses, and in fact he is said to be, "the father of horses and cattle."[25] The idea is clearly that Boshaiyanyi is the patron of Spanish-derived animals, as Poshaiyanne is patron of native animals.

We have arrived at the name of Montezuma last as it seemed better to fix Poshaiyanne's original role as a patron of game rather than to approach him from the reverse direction as Parsons did. For example: "Montezuma is to be identified with *poshaiyanki*. The greater part of the myth, if not the whole of it, is a Christ myth."[26] If the name is changed from the Zuñi to that of the Keres Poshaiyanne, that statement is not wholly false, for the god did take on Christian features. The virgin birth can be discounted as a number of other Pueblo gods related to the Sun are the result of magical impregnations, but his miracles are Christlike. He could make a bowl he carried with him fill with water. When he, under the alternate name of Montezuma, leaves for Mexico, he says, "I leave you, but another day I will return to you, for this village is mine for all time." Poshaiyanne travels to Mexico where he marries the great chief's daughter, but those who are jealous pierce his heart with a spear. After death he returns to life and wife, but is then thrown into a lake; an eagle drops a feather to him and on this he rises. "And he lived again, and he still lives, and some time he will come to us."[27]

The reason that the name Montezuma is interchangeable with that of Poshaiyanne is that the former is the Indian savior, or at least so the Mexican Indians believed. He would return to save them as Christ was supposed to return for Christians. Actually Montezuma was often used as a false front for the native god when the Pueblos were talking to whites.[28] There are two items in the Montezuma story, among the Pueblos, that are worth noting. To begin with, the name of Montezuma did not appear until after the Pueblo rebellion of 1680. At that time, "Only the Indians from the pueblos around Santa Fe spoke of Montezuma, connecting his name with that of Pose-yemo . . . a historical personage of Tehua folklore."[29]

His first connection is then with the Tewas and their game-spirit, Poseyemu, but at that time it was realized that Montezuma was a separate spirit. The second item appears in 1846 at the time of the Mexican war with the United States. The Mexican government put together a propaganda broadsheet for distribution to Indians. The document, called a "History Of Montezuma," links Poseyemu to him and then goes on to say that Malinche was a daughter of Montezuma, that she married Cortez, and that he gave her New Mexico as a dowry.[30]

Since Poseyemu was in many respects identical to Poshai-yanne, the savior stories were also related to the latter, or at least joined with the possibly native myths of Poshaiyanne's journey to each pueblo. As a native savior Poshaiyanne naturally clashed with the Christian god, which was but a slight extension of the contests he had had with native chiefs, or the ones Poshaiyanki had with the Shumaekoli. At Santo Domingo, God and Poshaiyanki had a contest to see who had the most power. God shot at a tree with a gun and made a small gash in the bark. Poshaiyanne struck it with a bolt of lightning and split the tree in half.

The next contest was more in keeping with his role as patron of game, as it was a contest to see who had the best food. God had a table of good things, but Poshaiyanne spread his venison and corn tortillas on the ground. "God watched Poshaiyanyi eat for a while, then he got down on the ground and ate with him. When god sent soldiers after him the Keresan god got on a duck's back and went to Wenimats, the home of the dead, from where he promised to return one day."[31]

In order to round out the group of similar deities, brief mention must be made of the Tewa deity Poseyemu, even though he is not so closely connected with Mountain Lion as his Zuñi and Keres counterparts. According to Harrington the word *posi* means "moss-green pool" and is associated with a place of ruins and a mineral outflow called Stinking Springs (Joseph's Hot Springs). While he also says that the springs have nothing in common with the god, except the beginning of the name, he quotes from a Santa Clara Indian who said that, "*Posejemu's* grandmother lived and still lives in this pool; that Posejemu comes from the south to visit her one day each year."[32] We know both directly and from myth that he was a patron of animals, the first evidence coming from Bandelier.

"The Ammayo, or shaman of the hunt, opened his heart to me in regard to a deity which belongs to his circle of supernatural protectors, and which at the same time plays a conspicuous part in Pueblo mythology in general. This is the god called Pose-yemo, and also, more properly, Pose-ueve, or the dew of heaven."[33] He then mentions that this Indian was aware that the overlay of the name Montezuma was a recent invention.

In one Tewa story his name is said to mean "dew kick stick," and as kick sticks are used by other Pueblo groups, but not the Tewas, to induce rain, it is probable that he is a moisture controller as well as gamekeeper. In this story a mother and daughter are outcasts; the latter gives birth to Poseyemu who very soon kills woodrats and rabbits. Next he notices that the Tewas have difficulty killing larger game and secretly invents the bow and arrow. Using only arrows made by his grandmother—whose hunter-consort he is—the youthful god becomes a very successful deer hunter. Later he teaches the people how to use these weapons. His other gift to the people was buckskin clothing to cover their previous nakedness.[34]

The Stone Lions of Cochiti join a number of myths with visible reality and bring us back to the more specific meanings of the Mountain Lion. We have already learned that the Zuñi Mountain Lion and his sister, the Mother of Game, Ku'ya-palitsa, lived there, as do all of the Zuñi Beast Gods. The Zuñi Poshaiyanki lived there once, and by inference, although this is never stated, Poshaiyanne did also.

The stone lions are located some twenty miles north of the pueblo of Cochiti, within the boundaries of the Bandelier National Monument, from whose headquarters they can be reached easily. The two lions were cut from bedrock on a piñon-covered open ridge called the Potrero de las Vacas.[35] The original rock was grooved to leave two parallel blocks of stone integral with the mother rock and from these the two Mountain Lions were shaped. The bodies, which are in a crouched position, are about thirty-eight inches long and a little over two feet wide, while the long flat tails that have given this lion his Zuñi name are thirty-two inches long, making the proportions and size fairly realistic.

These two lions face the rising sun, as would be expected from the myths. Enclosing them is a stone wall which is eighteen feet in diameter and in Stevenson's day was four feet high, but is now scarcely standing. On the southeast side is an entrance passage made of two stone walls that were twenty feet long when Prince visited the shrine about the turn of the century—although Stevenson thought they were fourteen feet in length.[36] These walls with the long entrance passage represent a compound such as the one that Poshaiyanne made of meal in the myth in which he taught hunting to the people of Sia, or it may represent an actual stone compound such as the one to the south of Zuñi that is sacred to Ku'yapalitsa and was actually used for impounding animals that were driven into it. Because of its small size it seems hardly probable that this one was used for hunting, but as lions are thought to draw in game it is quite possible that such a ritual once took place there with live deer.

Unfortunately the heads of these lions have been severely battered by vandals, but Prince's Cochiti guide told him that until the mid-1880's the two figures were uninjured. Since that was about the time that big game began to disappear rapidly from the West, perhaps the condition of the lion heads can be taken as a monument to that destructiveness as well. A short distance from this shrine, in the direction of Cochiti, there is a similar one on the summit of the Potrero de los Idolos, where only one lion is left. Dumarest took this figure to be a lizard, but it too is a lion even though less realistically carved.[37] Its body is tubular and very much resembles the mountain lion fetishes used by the Pueblos.

Three miles from this second shrine is a cave called, "the place where the giant is shut up," that feat being accomplished by the War Twins. Both Ku'yapalitsa and the mother of Poshaiyanne were described as giantesses. The shrine of the stone lions was visited by the Zuñi in Stevenson's day, and of course by the Cochiti themselves. Older hunters still visit it before going on a hunt, with the object of sprinkling red ochre on the eyes of the lions, that their own vision may be improved. At the present time this ochre is bought from the Hopis at a dollar per teaspoonful. Bandelier noted the red streaks on the crouching lions and explained its significance.

"The puma was painted red at his toes and in the face. This

is done yet by the hunters, to propitiate the idol, to favor them while hunting. The same was seen at the Potrero de las Vacas. Juan José says that, as the puma is the best hunter of the animal kingdom in the Sierra, they still make these offerings to it, annointing the eyes to secure good eyesight, and the claws and feet for strength and agility."[38]

The deity most directly connected with the shrine of the stone lions is Mountain-Lion-Man. In Keres myths he is the Mountain Lion who was the constant associate of Poshaiyanne. The latter is the son of the giantess Shakoyo, who is to be identified with Chakwena. In Zuñi myth, Mountain Lion is the Beast God, brother of Ku'yapalitsa, who is also Chakwena, so the two are to be closely identified. He is the deified abstraction of the Mountain Lion and the direct patron of the hunt. The Hunt chiefs are his earthly counterparts and take the powers of their office directly from him.

The Keres myths of Mountain-Lion-Man can be divided into two groups, in the first of which he is directly related to the Hunt society. The Shaiyaik, or hunt chief, is Lion Man and the myths tell how the power was transferred from the Lion to the chief. The second group of myths is not so single-minded and various parts of the narrative may be told separately, but the basic elements are clear enough. There is a youth and his sister; sometimes he is called Arrow Youth, the great hunter, but at other times it is the sister who is the huntress. In every case the sister becomes involved in difficulties. Sometimes she is abducted by a storm personification, which may be related to the basic idea that she is the Moon.[39]

In all of the Keresan myths she is Kochinako, or Yellow Woman, who is the Moon Mother of the War Twins, the Sun being their father. The only confusing element in these stories is that Yellow Woman is much more than a spirit of game, as she is also the giver of women's dress—a fact which is transposed when a giantess steals her clothing—the giver of baskets, and

227

importantly the giver of place-names. The latter is a tie between the earth mother and the game mother.

Frequently it is witches rather than a storm chief or kachina who carries off Arrow Youth's sister. In one narrative the hunter comes back and finds his sister dead, with a quill in her breast. After four days, two witches in the form of wolves come and dig up her grave and carry her to a cave where the "Shai-an-ni" who had caused her death removes the quill. Arrow Youth rescues her but, "though she soon recovered her wonted bodily health and her beauty, she was ever afterwards blind during the daytime, but could see at night."[40]

The Shai-an-ni who killed Yellow Woman in this story was one of her suitors. According to White the word "tsh'aia'nyi" means "one who manipulates supernatural power," hence a medicine man.[41] One suspects that it is the chief root of the name Poshaiyanne as well, and while the story is told as though Shai-an-ni were a witch, he is no more an evil sprit than is the storm cloud chief who also carries her away.

The moon is important to both hunting and weather control. Great Star tells Arrow Youth, "Today nothing you will kill. Last night your sister was killed."[42] We do not hear much of night hunting among the Pueblos, but if one is going to rid a field of smaller beasts that feed in the dark, night is the time and only in a relatively good moon can the hunter see to do his work. In weather control the storm chief can lock up the moon, or, what is of even greater concern to the Pueblos, evil spirits can lock up the clouds and no rain will come to earth. We therefore find stories in which Arrow Youth journeys to the sky to release the Shiwanni, or cloud spirits, who are held captive there.[43]

The basis of all these stories is the manipulation of the moon by a medicine man, to achieve the desirable ends of procuring game, or of bringing rain for the crops. Even when they have degenerated into tales of witchcraft, the witches indicate evil forces in the cosmos which the shaman must fight.

Arrow Youth is not a completely rounded being, but basically he is either a great hunter to begin with, or becomes one. Since hunters supplied the skins for clothing, he may be responsible for giving dress to his sister, who in turn hands it on to the people. In a Cochiti tale he is a poor and despised boy—as was the Tewa Poseyemu—who hangs about the village in a woman-ish manner. In an attempt to shame him the people make Arrow Youth hunt chief, without being aware that he has super-natural powers. "The game went straight to where Arrow Boy and the old hunters were standing. Ahead came the turkeys; the deer and the mountain goats hugged the side of the canyon. They had a good day and got much game."[44]

There is a well integrated story from Acoma-Laguna, in which he is already a good hunter and friend of Great Star. After his sister's death he gets no game, but in this moon story she is eventually made to live again, even in the daytime. The story then moves on to baskets, which are to hold corn, and to women's clothing. Her role in this matter has been established previously. "Yellow-Woman who knew how to make baskets and women's dresses,—she carried them on her back." When she becomes tired and stops for a rest, Yellow Woman says, "If anyone knows me, I shall give him knowledge of how to make baskets and also shall I give him knowledge of how to make dresses."[45]

In the story we are following, it is the shaman who gives the dresses to Yellow Woman, who will in turn give them to the populace, just as Tewa Poseyemu invented buckskin clothing, as well as bow and arrows, and handed them on to his people. Arrow Youth and his sister then set out on a journey to Flower Mountain and along the way she gives place-names to points of importance.[46] "There Yellow Woman said, 'Ah,' said she, 'behold, very pretty is up here this stone. It looks like a bear with open mouth.' said she. Then said the people, 'Thank you for your word, Yellow-Woman. This shall be called Open-Mouth-of-Bear,' thus they said."

Then one day Arrow Youth announced that on the morrow he would go out to hunt. He travels to a table mountain and meets Mountain-Lion-Man there. "Then Mountain-Lion-Man sat down. Then he said, 'Arrow Youth, I will tell you something,' said he. 'Today you cannot kill any deer. . . . First you must do something else.' " Then follows an account of hunting ritual, in which he must first cut down a willow or cottonwood to make prayer-sticks. "Also four kinds of beads wrap up, and four kinds of cigarettes and pollen and white earth and red ochre and cornmeal." Arrow Youth gets these offerings and presents them to Lion-Man, who notes that some of them are for other spirits too.

Then Mountain-Lion-Man calls up the game, " 'This morning, I call you here,' said Mountain-Lion-Man. 'Is that so?' said they. 'Arrow Youth came here to get game,' said he. 'It is well,' said they." The youth then drives the game back to the pueblo and into the plaza, where the War Captain who directs hunts is standing. It will be remembered that the Hunt chief does not go with the hunters, but stays home to help with prayers.

The plaza in this story is the equivalent of the magical compound, the stone corral, or the ring of cornmeal, which are under the control and power of Arrow Youth and his sister. "Then spoke Yellow Woman, 'Whatever animal suits yourself, that you will kill.' " First the youth takes game for his sister, then it is the turn of the populace. "Then thereabouts ran the people and each caught four deer." After this the north entrance of the plaza was opened and Arrow Youth chased the animals to the north side of Mt. Taylor. To them he says, "You shall increase in numbers."[47] Earlier, when Arrow Youth had wondered how he might drive the game down to the plaza, Lion Man had given him two crooked canes and these became the staffs of office for hunt chiefs.

The myth of Shaiyaik, or hunt chief, involves the same series of events as those just described, but in this context they are bereft of connections with Yellow Woman. The account is limited to Lion Man and the hunt chief, with the beasts of prey of the six directions acting as his helpers. "Long ago—Eh— Long ago there in the north, Mountain Lion and Weasel and

Wildcat and Wolf and Coyote established the customs. At that time down below, Shaiyaik and Tshai'katse established the customs, for what increases and what is the order of man. First they tried how game should be killed."[48]

There is a contradiction between the spirit-animals and the literal beasts of prey. To the first group belongs Lion Man who gives the customs; he came up with the first to emerge from the Underworld. On the other hand, lions and other prey animals, with the exception of Badger and Weasel who did exist in the Underworld, could not come into being until after their victims were created. Hence, at Acoma, the sisters first bring to life the landscape, then vegetation, small animals, then large game, and finally the beasts of prey. "You will find lion, wolf, wildcat and bear. These are strong beasts; they are going to use as food the same game that you also use. There is now game enough for them."[49]

The Shaiyaik, who is the supernatural hunt chief and head of a long line of human counterparts, directs the first hunt of the beasts of prey. "Go ahead, Muontain-Lion-Man, you will be first. You will go after game. Here in the middle north stand the deer people."[50] The Mountain Lion then knocked down a large deer, killing it and drinking its blood. After each animal has killed his particular kind of victim, Shaiyaik says that they are not to eat the stock of the people, "because only game will be your food.' . . . Thus indeed he who is Shaiyaik established the customs." Said he, " 'after this, when people increase they will know what belongs to you and also you will know it; you will give game to the people.' "[51]

Very few hunters actually belong to the Keresan Hunt societies. In the 1930's at Santa Ana there were only four members, who were recruited much as members of medicine societies are, which is to say by being pledged as a child or by vow. At Cochiti the Hunt society has been extinct since the beginning of this century and its functions taken over by the Shikame, a medicine society, whose head and sole member acts as Lion Man. At Sia the society had, in 1890, only the head and one assistant; in recent times there were but four members, one died, a second did not live at the pueblo, and a third was too old to perform duties. Although the Sia Shaiyaik society has some power to cure, it is thought that this may be limited to illness or accidents that occur during the hunt itself.[52] For the purpose they do not wear bear leg skins, but the leg skins of a lion.

The reason that Hunt societies are allowed to remain small is that their members are not the actual hunters. The purpose is supernatural control of game, and for this end a few old men will suffice. The chief stays at home and hunts with his heart and mind. He must see to it that the hunters place the proper prayer-stick offerings. The night before a Sia hunt, a fire is made at the village edge and the chief sits there. Elsewhere the hunt fire is usually not made until hunters are on the trail, as its purpose is to blind game with its smoke.

The following hunting prayer is sung by those of Acoma, both at the altar and on the trail. It invokes all the beasts of prey, beginning with the lion.

> *On the northern edge*
> *Lion hunt chief has come out.*
> *With glittering paint*
> *With yellow head feather tip waving*
> *He has gone.*
> *Bravely will I go*
> *To get spruce*
> *Acquiring blessings.*[53]

Of the Shaiyaik it is said, "His work will be the power of his songs." The principal physical object used by the Shaiyaik to control game is a stone fetish of the Mountain Lion. A similar fetish is carried by each of the hunters and as soon as the animal is slain this fetish is dipped into the blood of the animal. At Taos these fetishes are said to be made of the concretions sometimes found in the stomach of deer, a custom which is of mixed Indian and Spanish origin, as such stones are called bezoars in

Europe. Among the Tewas the fetish is made of lion bone.[54]

At Zuñi there is a division of labor among fetishes and the Mountain Lion is specific for deer and elk, while a wildcat fetish is used for antelope. Each time such a fetish is dipped in the blood of a slain animal it gains in power. If one is going to hunt one of the beasts of prey, rather than game, he naturally needs something even more powerful and hence uses a serpent fetish.[55]

In addition to the lion fetish, the Mountain Lion is appealed to directly for aid in the hunt. At Sia, "the cougar is appealed to, as he is the great father and master of all game; he draws game to him by simply sitting still, folding his arms, and mentally demanding the presence of the game; likewise when he wishes to send game to any particular people he controls it with his mind and not by spoken words. Although the cougar sends the game it is the sun who gives power to the Sia to capture it."[56] Thus we see that the Mountain Lion's personality has been modified to fit that of the Hunt chief, in that he draws game in without actively hunting. It is for the same reason that the Stone Lions of Cochiti sit inside their stone corral. The actual power of the hunter is derived from the Sun, thus keeping the division between Arrow Youth and his Moon-related sister who rules the affairs of women.

While these two worlds are separate they are also close, as can be seen in the various game animal dances in which a mother of game participates. Along the Río Grande the impersonation of this protogoddess is enacted by a woman, not by a man dressed as a woman. When the animals come out at San Felipe, "They are led by the Shaiyaik headman who carries spruce in his left hand and a small mountain lion in his right. After the head of the hunter's society comes the 'mother of game.' She carries corn meal and spruce in her right hand. In her left she has a small mountain lion, which she keeps close to her abdomen during the dance."[57]

In the Taos Deer dance two Mountain Lions and two Wildcats are impersonated by boys who stand outside the lines of deer, controlling them. Sometimes, as at Isleta, a mantle made from lion skin is worn by the hunt chief. As this animal is either scarce or nonexistent in the Hopi country, these Indians trade with the Supai to get their lion pelts.[58]

Seemingly the mere mention of the lion's name conveys considerable power to the hunter, for at Santa Ana they call each other, "Mokaich" or Mountain Lion.[59] Likewise an imitation of the cry of the beast is used; the Shaiyaik utters a call which his been transcribed as, "Ulululululu, psss." Zuñi hunters also imitate the cry of the lion, which is written as "huhuhu," but I am sure that on an actual hunt they can come up with some more bloodcurdling sound.

The Mountain Lion, as one of the Beast Gods, shares in their collective roles. At Zuñi the Bear does not appear at all in the Hunt society since he is not exclusively a beast of prey, nor is there a medicine order in the Hunt fraternity there.[60] If the proposition is reversed, however, the same does not hold true. While Bear is the great doctor, all of the Beasts of Prey together have curing power. Since the lion is of the North he is always mentioned first in a ceremonial circuit which begins there and proceeds counterclockwise. His position in prayers of medicine cults is thus greater than reality would seem to warrant, but he does have medicine powers both at Zuñi and along the Río Grande. Nonetheless, Bear is distinguished as a curer and Mountain Lion as a hunter.

Since clans have been mentioned in connection with other animals these should be mentioned here, even though they are not greatly significant. Geography and the consequent range of the lion have been the determining factors and symbolism has played a small role. The Río Grande Keres had Lion clans, but the pueblo of Acoma did not. Since lions were not important in the environment there, the Hunt chief in time became an Eagle Man rather than a Lion Man. When the people of Laguna migrated to their present home they brought a Lion clan with them from the north. The Hopis and Zuñis have no such clan, despite the ceremonial importance of the animal.

It would be impossible to separate the ideas of hunting and war, since both activities use the same weapons and similar preparations. Furthermore it is often the War Captains who are the actual leaders of the hunt, when it is communal. Thus the head of the San Felipe scalp-takers is called Mountain Lion and the same chief at Isleta wears the lion pelt. In the Río Grande area, however, the association of lion with war is not as strong as that of Bear and war. At Jemez a man who kills a bear must join the War society, but not if he kills a lion; the only ritual in the latter case is that the skull must be placed in a shrine. A similar situation seems to prevail among the Keres, with the exception noted for San Felipe.

On the Hopi Mesas the role of the Mountain Lion is reversed. They are familiar with the lion as a hunt figure, but place him squarely in the role of warrior. He is pet of the War Twins. On Second Mesa, "Lion is War chief and is always depicted on the Snake altar."[61] The Snakes were once a war society and it is with this group that Mountain Lion is most closely associated. He is depicted on the sand painting before their altar and effigies of him stand beside those of the War Twins. "The mountain lion effigies are the watchers."[62] Impersonators of Lion, Bear, and Wildcat dance before the novices of the Snake society, "so they will have no fear." When the paws of these animals are dipped into the medicine of the Snakes, "It imparts the big strong heart of Bear and Mountain Lion, of the spirit Mountain Lion."[63] Mountain Lion is a familiar of the War Twins, and they, with the god Masau'u and Spider Grandmother, are spirits who confront an enemy.

So far we have followed the paths of animals, as they relate to the supernatural world, from the earthbound Badger to the mountain lion who rules all other beasts from North Mountain. He is a chief in hunting and in war. On the human side there is another advance in complexity as these animal attributes find expression in rituals, ceremony, and myths. Animal spirits relate to individuals, to chiefs, and eventually to gods. Since the process began in a hunting milieu and is based upon the thought that the animals themselves have spiritual power, the quest for the origin of gods might follow the same paths.

The final chapter surveys the inevitable gods, those that had to come into existence from the logic of the Pueblo rites and myths that have been described.

Chapter X

ANIMAL SOULS AND ANIMAL GODS

SOULS, to be operative, must in some way mingle with strictly material forms, and the way in which these two categories are joined is important and variable. To begin with, what is a soul? The Pueblo view does not seem to differ basically from that held by the earlier Greeks. *Psyche* in general meant "life," in a fashion less specific than *bios*, which was a mode of life, or merely a manner of living. For Homer the psyche was the ghost of the departed and it was not until Pindar's time that the word became associated with an immaterial and immortal soul.

For the Pueblos, as for the Greeks, the life principle had two special places of lodgment in material bodies: in the breath and in the blood or heart. These have universal validity, since at the time the breath ceases or the heart stops, life departs. Aristotle mentions the tradition that the word *psyche*, soul, was derived from the process of respiration. The Pueblos quite agree and have many phrases referring to "the breath of life." A line of Homer says, "she gasped out her spirit (psyche)," but for him the spirit more often leaves the body with its blood. That would be expected in a war-oriented culture where life was often seen departing through the blood of a wound.

Blood is less important for the Pueblos as a life principle, but it can be seen in the red "life line" which runs to the heart of deer as they are represented in paintings or on pottery. Blood sacrifice is rare, though weasel blood was smeared on weasel fetishes, and the heart of a slain deer was removed and treated specially.[1] Sometimes the heart is eaten immediately by the hunter to convey the deer's vital quality to the man. The hunting fetish, a repository of supernatural power, was dipped into the heart's blood of the slain animal to reinvigorate the stone image, and in mythology the hearts of monsters are removed to deprive them of supernatural power.

Shifting from the physical seat of the life principle to the question of its continuity, we find that Homer's ghosts had a continuing afterlife as wraiths, but were not immortal. After proper rites they would cease their wanderings and be laid to rest. The Pueblo dead have a wraithlike after-existence as cloud people, but animals of large game size have a physical rebirth. Proper rites will enable a slain deer to be born again in an identical body and to inhabit the same range. What happens to those killed by beasts of prey is never stated.

Small game is not reborn, but when a hunter kills a rabbit, he at once picks up the creature and inhales the last gasps of its breath, which incorporates that life principle and preserves the animal's spirit in new form—by strengthening the hunter.[2] Fox or coyote are given offerings of ground turquoise or shell beads when traps are set, but rats, mice, and prairie dogs get nothing, "because the Hopi do not believe that the latter animals possess souls."[3]

Human souls, with the exception of babes who have lived less than four days in this world, are not reborn in physical form, but they have a continuing Pueblo-like existence as weightless wraiths in villages underground or in lakes. Here they carry on the same ceremonial dances as the living and seem to be much happier than their counterparts in Homer's epic. The form taken by these wraiths is derived directly from the breath-life concept, through a readily understandable visual symbol. On a cold day one's breath can be seen as a little cloud emanating from the mouth, and it is no distance at all from this image to the concept of the dead taking the form of clouds. These spirits in their cloud shapes are able to leave the villages of the dead and pass back over the pueblos of the living, sometimes only for pleasure, but often as rain-bringing cumulus clouds.

In this manifestation, the spirits are unparticularized group-souls; living men having been social creatures, the dead likewise work as a group. The thought also relates closely to the view that "the whole world is one breath," as this group-soul also reaches out to the world of vegetation which is nourished by the rain of the cloud spirits and in turn feeds herbivorous game, upon which both men and beasts of prey feed.

There are limits, however, to the interchangeability of the spirit essence, as palingenesis, or the continued re-entry of souls into differing bodies, is only a minor possibility, not a part of the Pueblo system. One Hopi opined that a person, if he were bad enough while living, might be reborn in the form of a black beetle. But as witches can also transform themselves, becoming coyotes, owls, or other animals, the thought has only negative connotations.

When the idea of the breath-of-life or group-soul is further abstracted, which is to say when it is cut loose from its roots in human or animal bodies, we arrive at an immaterial spirit force which permeates the entire world. This floating breath-of-life or supernatural essence has come to be called mana or orenda in English, but care is needed in applying the term to the Pueblo concept. The Keresan word *ianyi*, which is often taken as a counterpart of mana, is not as immaterial or as nebulous as we are likely to think. The word derives from *hi'anyi*, meaning the "road" over which spirits travel.[4]

Thus the supernatural continuum is likely to be embodied in a something, which travels to or from a place in a form of substance, whether cloud or animal, or even in the boughs cut from a tree, but like a bird it must shortly alight in a specific place. The divine, to choose a more comprehensive term than mana, seems to have two aspects, one of which is simply existence —the life principle which maintains gods and lesser spirits, whatever form they may take. This differs mainly in degree from a similar life principle within man, but in addition to the existential element the divine also has power. Power too is shared, but man possesses very little of it in his own person. Some animals, however, have supernatural power in high degree, especially as they approach to the nature of gods. Divine power does not flow through the universe as readily or as completely as the existential breath-of-life does.

Men may obtain supernatural power to aid them in the hunt, but they get the power from a fetish in which it is housed. The small stone image which is carried by each hunter derives its own power from a larger stone fetish that is kept by the priests of hunting fraternities. The chief officer who places the two images together derives his power, as does the larger fetish, from Mountain Lion Man, a spirit who is the apex of such power as flows through all of the lion kind.

➤If the problem is one of curing, a similar flow of power extends from the medicine man, through the bear as an animal, up to the spirit Bear or Beast God. When this power flows it is not like a river that tumbles freely and easily, but more like the water in a canal which has a system of locks. Each of these gates has to be manipulated by attendants, the priests, who stand in for the animals and deities who do the actual "work."

In examining the relationship between animals and the supernatural we come upon a larger question, in that animal gods must be considered in the broader context of man's belief in a multiplicity of spirits. What objective experience of mankind gave rise to belief in a multitude of gods as opposed to undifferentiated spirits? One theory attributes the origin of gods to fear. Volcanos, hurricanes, and earthquakes are feared, then personified and propitiated. By extension dangerous animals are feared, worshiped, and then deified. Fear does have motivating force—a high emotional charge—but it is hard to prove that ancient hunters were terrified of the game they sought, including mammoths, or by the predators who joined in the chase.

Another theory speaks of divinized animals derived from clan totems and of the rise of shamans from priests to gods. There is a link, as Sir Edward Burnett Tylor pointed out in *Primitive Culture*, between the soul, the elf, and the Great Spirit, but we need a dynamism and a progression that fits known items. Fear of natural phenomena cannot be a base as it accounts for too little. Clan totems are not universal and they seem to be a late construct. What we need to explain in seeking the origin of gods—or at least a few of them—is a theory that is simple and basic.

Religion and its conjunction with spirits and gods began in a hunting and hunting-gathering context.[5] Hence it seems logical to look for the rise of spirits in conjunction with hunting customs. Hunting is not necessarily complex, as small game can be taken without any tools and while gathering other foods. In the New World man seems to have arrived as a specialized big-game hunter. Somewhat later, perhaps 7,000 B.C., the Desert Culture appeared in the Great Basin and Pueblo area. These peoples gathered nuts and berries and datil fruit, wild potatoes and onions, but, "Where opportunity offered . . . the desert culture people killed their bison, antelope or mountain sheep, but often they had to be content with lesser game."[6]

Since hunting has been man's preoccupation for a half million years or more, it is inevitable that whatever developments changed rituals into more complex religions took place in a hunting context. The dynamic force at work is evident: hunting is highly emotional. There is the necessity of providing food for the group, and the chance of getting nothing. Success or failure may depend on a few moments, which is unlike the year-long cycle of horticulture. At the crux of the hunt is a dramatic struggle in which the skill of hunters is balanced against the cunning of game, possibly in a context of danger.

Elements in the hunting contest are innately ritualistic and quickly fall into patterns—hunt fire, type of kill, distribution of parts, and propitiation with songs and chants all the way. Because hunting and hunt ritual contain these powerful emotional charges, they have a driving force capable of transforming simple rites into more complex patterns of behavior. Over these patterns is a gathering of more elaborate mythical structures and religious theory, just as certainly as cumulus clouds gather around a mountain peak.

An expanding pantheon develops alongside the extension of

simple ritual. The details of Pueblo hunting have already been given, but one more instance will provide a starting point for a central group of deities that might be called, "the inevitable gods." Parsons described a Laguna hunt which will serve to begin the argument. "A deer hunter will carry in a buckskin bandolier pouch together with turquoise, coral and *hish* (white shell) the stone image of an animal called *shuhuna* or of a mountain lion. An Arrow point is tied, point forward, to the image and a tiny buckskin bag (ka'pa) of corn pollen fastened around its neck. . . . Somewhere near the hunting ground a shrine (*amuma*, prayer; *ochani*, place) is set up for the image and it is asked to help catch the deer."[7]

Her informant, who was a woman, did not know the rites in connection with the kill, but said the place around it was *tsitya*, sacred. None, for example, might urinate anywhere nearby. The stone image of the lion has been placed in a shrine and supplication made to it or to Lion Man who stands behind. Paul Radin claims that "true gods" are only found where spirits are fashioned into idols, housed in special and sacred structures, and have true theogonic myths attached to them.

It will be remembered that the Lion Man, under the Zuñi name of Poshaiyanki, had in addition to these temporary shrines a permanent house and home in the structure surrounding the Stone Lions of Cochiti, and his theogonic myth is also centered there in Shipapolima. We have then, in this simple instance, all of the qualifications for the development of a deity. That may account for the origin of only a single god, but other animal deities can be derived from analogy. The Bear and the Badger who dig medicine roots, to become supernatural doctors in their animal form, are deified so that they may join the directional pantheon of Beast Gods.

Without leaving the hunting complex we may add another group of inevitable deities who are more advanced in conception than Lion Man. In the male line there is the Hunt-chief supernatural who stands in the shadow of Mountain Lion Man, to whom he looks for power. As this spirit faces toward the human side, he becomes the first in a line of Hunt society chieftains, but in myth he becomes Arrow Youth, an abstract spirit even though based on the archetypal hunter.

There is also a female line in the hunt complex which is centered around the Mother-of-Game. She began simply as a natural animal. One will remember that in the discussion of antelope three such Mothers-of-Game were presented in the order of their increasing complexity. First a human who gave birth to antelope and was then transformed into a doe. The second figure is already a goddess who is the mother of deer and mountain sheep, as well as antelope. She confined the blood that flowed from her during labor and from the drenched sand made both kinds of rabbits. She is called Child-birth Water Woman as she has been associated with fecundity in general.

A related but more complex goddess is Sand Altar Woman whose sphere is extended to include all the moist elements of life. She thus is the mother of all living things, whether in plant or animal form. By these simple steps we have reached an earth goddess who may then take several forms. An earth goddess, such as Spider Grandmother, may be specialized for the care of human affairs including the direction of individual behavior, but she stands aside from horticulture. The Keresan Iyatiku is an agricultural corn mother, but expands her reign to protect health and the general well-being of humankind.

Thinking Woman of the Keres has a spider form like that of the grandmother, but she has spun her web over all of matter and is thus the goddess of creation, not just the moist elements of plant and animal life. A female goddess naturally takes an interest in basketmaking and clothing, as well as childbirth. As an earth goddess she may also be interested in place-names which mark physical earth features of significance. When many of these possible roles are combined in one figure there arises the "Great Mother."

While a goddess is still in the Mother-of-Game stage, certain aspects of hunting shape concepts that gather around her. Hunters are all too well aware that game is often withheld.

Frequent experience of hunting failure gives rise to the Keeper-of-Game figure, who may be identical with the Mother-of-Game, as it is most understandable that a mother would want to protect her offspring. In time the role of keeper is often transferred to a male spirit, who may be a consort or brother. The male Keeper-of-Game is likely to become a Spirit of the year, in so far as the seasons have a role in sending or withholding game. Since a year spirit dies at the end of his period, there may be a consort who is killed by the female deity.

The Pueblos do not follow this possibility but we find in the myths a number of spirits such as Mean Old Man, the North Wind, and ogresses, all of whom are keepers. These are often slain by small heroes or the War Twins to release the game. The logical virtue of a consort is that he may represent the taker of game, or hunt chief, so that the giving, withholding, and taking can be explained.

Another line of supernaturals is just as inevitable in the context of hunting. There are likely to be other groups competing for the same hunting grounds, which leads either to skirmishes on the spot or to prolonged enmity and war. War practices as we have seen, are parallel to those of the hunt as they involve the same skills and weapons. A warrior carries a lion-skin quiver, while at San Felipe a scalp-taker was called "Mountain Lion." Thus a considerable pantheon can develop from the simple rituals of hunting.

I do not mean to be definite for any given culture. Studying the gods is always an approach to mysteries, which is why they are so fascinating—a mystery is never solved. Here I only hope to have shown some of the paths over which the spirits, particularly animal spirits, have traveled in a single culture. Here too is another glimpse of Pueblo religion, which is based on skillfully devised prayers and ceremonial dramas.

Some of these have to do with the hunt, but many simply include the Pueblo gesture of inclusion toward all wildlife. Around the rites and ceremonies their mythology weaves its cloud shapes and mist forms. From these the Pueblo center draws nourishment. For those of us on the outside, the Pueblos have provided a remarkable vision of the place of animals in religion, a concept which has disappeared from our culture as certainly as the great bison herds have vanished from the plains.

BIBLIOGRAPHY

Section I: Works on Mammals and Hunting

Bailey, Vernon. *Mammals of New Mexico*. United States Department of Agriculture, North American Fauna No. 53, Washington, 1931.

Baird, Spencer. *Mammals of the Boundary*. United States and Mexican Boundary Survey, Vol. 2, Part 2. Washington, 1859.

Barnes, Claude. *The Cougar or Mountain Lion*. Salt Lake City, The Ralton Co., 1960.

Beuchner, Helmut. *Life History, Ecology, and Range Use of the Pronghorn Antelope in Trans-Pecos Texas*. Notre Dame, University of Notre Dame, 1950.

————. *The Bighorn Sheep in the United States, Its Past, Present, and Future*. New York Zoological Society Wildlife Monograph No. 4. New York, 1960.

Cahalane, Victor H. *Mammals of North America*. New York, The Macmillan Co., 1961.

Caton, John. *The Antelope and Deer of America*. New York, Forest and Stream Publishing Co., 1877.

Cockrum, E. Lendell. *The Recent Mammals of Arizona, Their Taxonomy and Distribution*. Tucson, University of Arizona Press, 1960.

Dobie, J. Frank. *The Voice of the Coyote*. Boston, Little, Brown and Co., 1949.

Einarsen, Arthur. *The Pronghorn Antelope and Its Management*. Washington, The Wildlife Management Institute, 1948.

Haas, Anabel. *Hunter's Guide to the Deer of New Mexico*. Santa Fe, New Mexico Department of Game and Fish, 1960.

Harris, Arthur. *Ecological Distribution of Some Vertebrates in the*

San Juan Basin, New Mexico. Museum of New Mexico Papers in Anthropology No. 8. Santa Fe, 1963.

———. *Vertebrate Remains and Past Environmental Reconstruction in the Navajo Resevoir District*. Museum of New Mexico Papers in Anthropology No. 11. Santa Fe, 1963.

Henderson, Junius, and John Harrington. *Ethnozoology of the Tewa Indians*. Bureau of American Ethnology, Bulletin 56, Washington, 1914.

Hibben, Frank. *A Preliminary Study of the Mountain Lion*. University of New Mexico Bulletin, Biological Series, Vol. 5, No. 3. Albuquerque, University of New Mexico Press, 1937.

———. *Hunting American Bears*. Albuquerque, University of New Mexico Press, 1950.

———. *Hunting American Lions*. New York, Thomas Y. Crowell Co., 1948.

Knipe, Theodore. *The Status of the Antelope Herds of Northern Arizona*. Phoenix, Arizona Game and Fish Commission, 1944.

Ligon, J. Stokley. *Wildlife of New Mexico*. Santa Fe, New Mexico Department of Game and Fish, 1927.

Mearns, Edgar A. *Mammals of the Mexican Boundary of the United States*. Part I. United States National Museum, Bulletin 56. Washington, 1907.

Merriam, C. Hart. *Results of a Biological Survey of the San Francisco Mountain Region and Desert of the Little Colorado, Arizona*. United States Department of Agriculture, North American Fauna No. 3. Washington, 1890.

Murie, Olaus. *The Elk of North America*. Harrisburg, Stackpole, 1951.

Neal, Ernest. *The Badger*. Baltimore, Penguin Books, 1958.

Nelson, E. W. *The Rabbits of North America*. United States Department of Agriculture, North American Fauna No. 29. Washington, 1909.

O'Conner, Jack. *Hunting in the Southwest*. New York, Knopf, 1945.

Olin, George. *Mammals of the Southwest Mountains and Mesas*. Globe, Southwestern Monuments Association, 1961.

Palmer, T. S. *The Jack Rabbits of the United States*. United States Department of Agriculture, Division of Biological Survey, Bulletin No. 8. Washington, 1897.

Seton, Ernest Thompson. *Lives of the Game Animals*. Boston, Charles T. Branford Co., 1953.

Simpson, George Gaylord. *The Principles of Classification and a Classification of Mammals*. Bulletin of the American Museum of Natural History, Vol. 85. New York, 1945.

White, Leslie. "Notes on the Ethnozoology of the Keresan Pueblo Indians." Papers of the Michigan Academy of Sciences, Arts, and Letters, Vol. 31, pp. 223–43. 1945.

Young, S. P. *The Bobcat of North America*. Harrisburg, Stackpole, 1958.

Young, S. P., and Edward Goldman. *The Puma, Mysterious American Cat*. Washintgon, The American Wildlife Institute, 1946.

———. *The Wolves of North America*. New York, Dover, 1964.

Young, Stanley, and H. H. T. Jackson. *The Clever Coyote*. Harrisburg, Stackpole, 1951.

Section II: Works on Archaeology and History

Bandelier, Adolph. *An Outline of the Documentary History of the Zuñi Tribe*. Journal of American Ethnology and Archaeology, Vol. III. Boston, 1892.

———. *The Southwestern Journals of Adolph F. Bandelier. 1880–1882*. (Edited by Charles H. Lange and Carroll L. Riley). Albuquerque, University of New Mexico Press, 1966.

Bolton, Herbert. *Coronado*. Albuquerque, University of New Mexico Press, 1964.

Clarke, Grahame. *World Prehistory: An Outline*. Cambridge, Cambridge University Press, 1961.

Hibben, Frank. *Excavations of the Riana Ruin and Chama Valley Survey*. University of New Mexico Anthropology Series, Vol. 2, No. 1. Albuquerque, University of New Mexico Press, 1937.

Hodge, F. W. *Spanish Explorers in the Southern United States.* New York, Scribners, 1907.

Judd, Neil. *The Material Culture of Pueblo Bonito.* Smithsonian Miscellaneous Collections, Vol. 124. Washington, The Smithsonian Institution, 1954.

King, Dale. *Nalakihu, Excavations at a Pueblo III Site in Wupatki National Monument, Arizona.* Museum of Northern Arizona, Bulletin 23. Flagstaff, 1949.

Lambert, Marjorie. *Paa-ko, Archaeological Chronicle of an Indian Village in North Central New Mexico.* School of American Research, Monograph 19. Santa Fe, 1954.

Lawrence, Barbara. *Mammals Found at the Awatovi Site.* Papers of the Peabody Museum of American Archaeology and Ethnology, Vol. XXV, No. 3, Part 1. Cambridge, 1951.

Lummis, Charles. *The Land of Poco Tiempo.* Albuquerque, University of New Mexico Press, 1952.

McGregor, John. *Winona and Ridge Ruin.* Museum of Northern Arizona, Bulletin No. 18. Flagstaff, 1941.

Pausanias. *Description of Greece*, Vol. III. Cambridge, Harvard University Press, 1954.

Pepper, George. *Pueblo Bonito.* Anthropological Papers of the American Museum of Natural History, Vol. XXVII. New York, 1920.

Prince, L. Bradford. *The Stone Lions of Cochiti.* Santa Fe, The New Mexican Printing Co., 1903.

Roberts, Frank. *The Village of the Great Kivas on the Zuni Reservation, New Mexico.* Bureau of American Ethnology, Bulletin No. 111. Washington, 1932.

Smith, Watson. *Excavations in Big Hawk Valley.* Museum of Northern Arizona, Bulletin No. 24. Flagstaff, 1952.

———. *Kiva Mural Decorations at Awatovi and Kwaika-a, with a Survey of other Wall Paintings in the Pueblo Southwest.* Papers of the Peabody Museum of American Archaeology and Ethnology, Vol. XXXVII. Cambridge, 1952.

Wormington, H. M. *Prehistoric Indians of the Southwest.* Denver, Denver Museum of Natural History, 1951.

Section III: Works on Anthropology and Mythology

Alexander, H. B. *The World's Rim*. Lincoln, University of Nebraska Press, 1953.

Bandelier, Adolph F. *Final Report of Investigations among the Indians of the Southwestern United States*. Papers of the Archaeological Institute of America, American Series, III, and IV. Cambridge, 1890.

———. "The 'Montezuma' of the Pueblo Indians." *American Anthropologist*, Vol. V, pp. 319ff. New York, 1892.

Beaglehole, Ernest. *Hopi Hunting and Hunting Ritual*. Yale University Publications in Anthropology, No. 4. New Haven, 1936.

———. *Notes on Hopi Economic Life*. Yale University Publications in Anthropology, No. 15. New Haven, 1937.

Beaglehole, Ernest, and Pearl Beaglehole. *Hopi of the Second Mesa*. Memoirs of the American Anthropological Association, No. 44. Menasha, 1935.

Benedict, Ruth. "Eight Stories from Acoma." *Journal of American Folk-Lore*, Vol. XLIII, pp. 59–88. New York, American Folk-Lore Society, 1930.

———. *Tales of the Cochiti Indians*. Bureau of American Ethnology, Bulletin No. 98. Washington, 1931.

———. *Zuñi Mythology*. 2 vols. Columbia University Contributions to Anthropology, Vol. 21. New York, Columbia University Press, 1935.

Boas, Franz. *Keresan Texts*. Publications of the American Ethnological Society, Vol. VIII, Parts I and II. New York, 1928.

Bourke, John. *The Snake Dance of the Moquis of Arizona*. New York, Scribners, 1884.

Bunzel, Ruth L. "Introduction to Zuni Ceremonialism." B.A.E. *Forty-seventh Annual Report*, 1929–30. Washington, 1932.

———. "Zuñi Katcinas." *Ibid.*

———. "Zuñi Origin Myths." *Ibid.*

———. "Zuñi Ritual Poetry." *Ibid.*

———. *Zuñi Texts*. American Ethnological Society Publications, Vol. XV. New York, 1933.

Cazeneuve, Jean. *Les Dieux Dansant a Cibola, Les Shalako des Indiens Zuñis.* Paris, Gallimard, 1957.

Colton, Harold. *Hopi Kachina Dolls.* Albuquerque, University of New Mexico Press, 1949.

Cook, A. B. *Zeus, a Study in Ancient Religion.* Cambridge, Cambridge University Press, 1914–1940.

Cushing, Frank Hamilton. "Outlines of Zuni Creation Myths." B.A.E. *Thirteenth Annual Report,* 1891–92. Washington, 1896.

————. "Origin Myth from Oraibi." *Journal of American Folk-Lore,* Vol. XXXVI. Lancaster and New York, American Folk-Lore Society, 1923.

————. *Zuñi Breadstuff.* Indian Notes and Monographs, Vol. VIII. New York, Museum of the American Indian, Heye Foundation, 1920.

————. *Zuñi Folk Tales.* New York, Putnam's Sons, 1901.

Dockstader, Frederick. *The Kachina and the White Man.* Bloomfield Hills, Cranbrook Institute of Science, 1954.

Dorsey, George A., and H. R. Voth. *The Oraibi Soyal Ceremony.* Field Columbian Museum, Publication 55. Anthropological Series, Vol. III, No. 1. Chicago, 1901.

Dozier, Edward. *The Hopi-Tewa of Arizona.* University of California Publications in American Archaeology and Ethnology, Vol. 44, No. 3. Berkeley, University of California Press, 1954.

Dumarest, Noel. *Notes on Cochiti, New Mexico.* American Anthropological Association Memoirs, Vol. VI, No. 3. Lancaster, 1919.

Eggan, Fred. *Social Organization of the Western Pueblos.* Chicago, University of Chicago Press, 1950.

Ellis, Florence Hawley. *A Reconstruction of the Basic Jemez Pattern of Social Organization, with Comparisons to other Tanoan Social Structures.* University of New Mexico Publications in Anthropology, No. 11. Albuquerque, 1964.

Espinosa, Aurelio. "Pueblo Indan Folk Tales." *Journal of American Folk-Lore,* Vol. XLIX. New York, American Folk-Lore Society, 1936.

Farnell, Lewis Richard. *The Cults of the Greek States.* 5 vols. Oxford, The Clarendon Press, 1898–1909.

Fewkes, Jesse W. "Hopi Kachinas, Drawn by Native Artists." B.A.E. *Twenty-first Annual Report,* 1899–1900. Washington, 1903.

————. "Tusayan Migration Traditions." B.A.E. *Nineteenth Annual Report,* 1897–98. Washington, 1900 [1902].

Fewkes, Jesse W., and A. M. Stephen. "The Naashnaiya: A Tusayan Initiation Ceremony." *Journal of American Folk-Lore,* Vol. V. New York, The American Folk-Lore Society, 1892.

Fontenrose, Joseph. *The Ritual Theory of Myth.* University of California Publications, Folklore Studies, No. 18. Berkeley, University of California Press, 1966.

Frazer, Sir. J. G. *The Golden Bough.* Abridged edition. New York, The Macmillan Co., 1937.

Gunn, John M. *Schat-Chen, History Traditions and Narratives of the Queres Indians of Laguna and Acoma.* Albuquerque, Albright and Anderson, 1917.

Hallowell, A. I. "Bear Ceremonialism in the Northern Hemisphere." *American Anthropologist,* Vol. 28. Menasha, 1926.

Handy, Edward. "Zuni Tales." *Journal of American Folk-Lore,* Vol. XXXI. Lancaster, 1918.

Harrington, John Peabody. "The Ethnogeography of the Tewa Indians." B.A.E. *Twenty-ninth Annual Report,* 1907–1908. Washington, 1916.

Hultkrantz, Ake. *The North American Indian Orpheus Tradition.* Ethnological Museum of Sweden, Monograph Series, No. 2. Stockholm, 1957.

Kirk, Ruth. *Introduction to Zuni Fetishism.* Papers of the School of American Research. Santa Fe, 1943.

Kroeber, A. L. *Zuñi Kin and Clan.* Anthropological Papers of the American Museum of Natural History, Vol. XVIII, Part II. New York, 1917.

Lange, Charles. *Cochiti, a New Mexico Pueblo, Past and Present.* Austin, University of Texas Press, 1959.

Lee, Richard B., and Irven De Vore (editors). *Man the Hunter.* Chicago, Aldine Publishing Co., 1968.

Lummis, Charles. *Pueblo Indian Folk-Stories.* New York, The Century Co., 1920.

Nequatewa, Edmund. *Hopi Customs, Folklore and Ceremonies.* Museum of Northern Arizona Reprint Series, No. 4. Flagstaff, 1954.

―――. *Truth of a Hopi and Other Clan Stories of Shungopovi.* Museum of Northern Arizona, Bulletin No. 8. Flagstaff, 1947.

Newman, Stanley. *Zuñi Dictionary.* Indiana University Research Center in Anthropology, Folklore, and Linguistics. Publication No. 6. Bloomington, 1958.

Parsons, E. C. *A Pueblo Indian Journal,* 1920–21. American Anthropological Association Memoirs, Vol. XXXII. Menasha, 1925.

―――. "Census of the Shi'wanakwe Society of Zuñi." *American Anthropologist,* Vol. XXI, pp. 229–35. Menasha, 1919.

―――. *Hopi and Zuñi Ceremonialism.* American Anthropological Association Memoirs, Vol. XXXIX. Menasha, 1933.

―――. "Isleta, New Mexico." B.A.E. *Forty-seventh Annual Report,* 1929–30. Washington, 1932.

―――. "Nativity Myth at Laguna and Zuñi." *Journal of American Folk-Lore,* Vol. XXXI, pp. 256–63. Lancaster, 1918.

―――. *Notes on Ceremonialism at Laguna.* American Museum of Natural History, Anthropological Series, Vol. XIX, Part IV. New York, 1920.

―――. *Notes on Zuñi.* American Anthropological Association Memoirs, Vol. IV, No. 3, Part I; No. 4, part II. Lancaster, 1917.

―――. "Pueblo-Indian Folk-tales, Probably of Spanish Provenience." *Journal of American Folk-Lore,* Vol. XXXI, pp. 216–56. Lancaster, 1918.

―――. *Pueblo Indian Religion.* 2 vols. Chicago, University of Chicago Press, 1939.

―――. *Taos Pueblo.* General Series in Anthropology, No. 2. Menasha, George Banta Publishing Co., 1936.

————. *Taos Tales.* American Folk-Lore Society Memoirs, Vol. XXXIV. New York, 1940.

————. *Tewa Tales. Ibid.,* Vol. XIX. New York, 1926.

————. "The Origin Myth of Zuñi." *Journal of American Folk-Lore,* Vol. XXXVI. No. 139. Lancaster, American Folk-Lore Society, 1923.

————. *The Scalp Ceremonial of Zuñi.* American Anthropological Association Memoirs, Vol. XXI. Menasha, 1924.

————. *The Social Organization of the Tewa of New Mexico. Ibid.,* Vol. XXXVI. Menasha, 1929.

————. "Zuñi Tales." *Journal of Amercan Folk-Lore,* Vol. XLIII, pp. 1–58. New York, 1930.

Radin, Paul. *The Trickster, a Study in American Indian Mythology.* New York, Philosophical Library, 1956.

Roediger, Virginia. *Ceremonial Costumes of the Pueblo Indians.* Berkeley, University of California Press, 1961.

Sebag, Lucien. *L'invention du monde chez les indiens pueblos.* Paris, François Maspero, 1971.

Stephen, Alexander. *Hopi Journal.* Edited by E. C. Parsons. 2 vols. Columbia University Contributions to Anthropology, Vol. XXIII. New York, Columbia University Press, 1936.

————. "Hopi Tales." *Journal of American Folk-Lore,* Vol. XLII, pp. 1–72. New York, American Folk-Lore Society, 1929.

Stevenson, M. C. "Ethnobotany of the Zuñi Indians." B.A.E. *Thirtieth Annual Report,* 1908–1909. Washington, 1915.

————. "The Sia." B.A.E. *Eleventh Annual Report,* 1889–90. Washington, 1894.

————. "The Zuñi Indians." B.A.E. *Twenty-third Annual Report,* 1901–1902. Washington, 1904.

Stirling, Matthew W. *Origin Myth of Acoma and Other Records.* B.A.E. Bulletin No. 135. Washington, 1942.

Talayesva, Don. *Sun Chief: The Autobiography of a Hopi Indian.* Ed. by L. W. Simmons. New Haven, Yale University Press, 1942.

Titiev, Mischa. *Old Oraibi, a Study of the Hopi Indians of Third*

Mesa. Papers of the Peabody Museum of American Archaeology and Ethnology, Vol. XXII, No. 1. Cambridge, 1944.

Tyler, Hamilton A. *Pueblo Gods and Myths*. Norman, University of Oklahoma Press, 1964.

Voth, H. R. *The Oraibi Marau Ceremony*. Field Museum of Natural History, Publication 156. Anthropological Series, Vol. XI, No. 1. Chicago, 1912.

———. *The Traditions of the Hopi*. Field Columbian Museum, Publication 96. Anthropological Series, Vol. VIII. Chicago, 1905.

Wallis, W. D. "Folk Tales from Shumopovi, Second Mesa." *Journal of American Folk-Lore*, Vol. XLIX, No. 191–92. Lancaster, American Folk-Lore Society, 1936.

Waters, Frank. *Book of the Hopi*. New York, Viking, 1963.

White, Leslie. *New Material from Acoma*. B.A.E. Bulletin, No. 136. Washington, 1943.

———. "The Acoma Indians." B.A.E. *Forty-seventh Annual Report*, 1929–30. Washington, 1932.

———. *The Pueblo of Santa Ana, New Mexico*. American Anthropological Association Memoirs, Vol. LX. Menasha, 1942.

———. *The Pueblo of Santo Domingo, New Mexico. Ibid.*, Vol. XLIII. Menasha, 1935.

———. *The Pueblo of San Felipe. Ibid.*, Vol. XXXVIII. Menasha, 1932.

———. *The Pueblo of Sia, New Mexico*. B.A.E. Bulletin, No. 184. Washington, 1962.

Wyman, Leland C., W. W. Hill, and Iva Osanai. *Navajo Eschatology*. The University of New Mexico Bulletin, No. 377. Anthropological Series, Vol. 4, No. 1. Albuquerque, University of New Mexico Press, 1942.

NOTES

CHAPTER I

1. Don Talayesva, *Sun Chief: The Autobiography of a Hopi Indian*, 54.

2. Junius Henderson and John Harrington, *Ethnozoology of the Tewa Indians*, 24.

3. Matthew W. Stirling, *Origin Myth of Acoma and Other Records*, 2.

4. Stirling, *Origin Myth*, 13.

5. Fred Eggan, *Social Organization of the Western Pueblos*, 278.

6. Frank Hamilton Cushing, *Zuñi Breadstuff*, 31.

7. Ruth L. Bunzel, "Zuñi Katcinas," B.A.E. *Forty-seventh Annual Report* (1929–30), 959.

8. *Ibid.*

9. Herbert Bolton, *Coronado*, 119.

10. Frank Hamilton Cushing, "Outlines of Zuñi Creation Myths," B.A.E. *Thirteenth Annual Report* (1891–92), 387.

11. *Ibid.*, 369.

12. *Ibid.*, 371.

13. *Ibid.*, 394.

14. Bunzel, "Zuñi Katcinas," *loc. cit.*, 934. Also M. C. Stevenson, "The Zuñi Indians," B.A.E. *Twenty-third Annual Report* (1901–1902), 140.

15. Cushing, *Zuñi Breadstuff*, 627–29.

16. *Ibid.*, 328.

17. E. C. Parsons, *Hopi and Zuñi Ceremonialism*, 27.

18. Eggan, *Western Pueblos*, 71–72.

19. H. R. Voth, *The Traditions of the Hopi*, 29.

20. *Ibid.*, 224–27, 228.

21. Alexander Stephen, *Hopi Journal*, 860–61.

22. Ibid., 860 n1.

23. Frederick Dockstader, *The Kachina and the White Man*, 17. Stephen, *Hopi Journal*, 156.

24. Ernest Neal, *The Badger*, 153.

25. For discussion of Poshaiyanne and Shipapolima, see Ch. IX.

26. Stevenson, "The Zuñi Indians," *loc. cit.*, 444ff., Pl. CVIII.

27. *Ibid.*, 455.

28. Eggan, *Western Pueblos*, 243.

29. Ernest Beaglehole, *Hopi Hunting and Hunting Ritual*, 12.

30. Ruth L. Bunzel, "Introduction to Zuñi Ceremonialism," B.A.E. *Forty-seventh Annual Report* (1929–1930), 538.

31. Franz Boas, *Keresan Texts*, 167–69.

32. John M. Gunn, *Schat-Chen, History, Traditions, and Narratives of the Queres Indians of Laguna and Acoma*, 139–40. Boas, *Keresan Texts*, 235.

33. At Acoma the fetish representing the Corn Mother is called, *Honani*, which is the Hopi name for Badger. See Stirling, *Origin Myth*, 31, n80.

34. Florence Hawley Ellis, *A Reconstruction of the Basic Jemez Pattern of Social Organization, with Comparisons to other Tanoan Social Structures*, 10 ff.

35. Ake Hultkrantz, *The North American Indian Orpheus Tradition*, does not discuss any of these three myths, which distorts his account of the tradition among the Pueblos.

36. Victor H. Cahalane, *Mammals of North America*, 226.

37. Hamilton A. Tyler, *Pueblo Gods and Myths*, Ch. II, for accounts of Underworld.

38. Voth, *Traditions of the Hopi*, 114–19.

39. *Ibid.*, 207–209.

40. Boas, *Keresan Texts*, 56–59. Following quote, *ibid.*, 103.

CHAPTER II

1. Charles Lummis, *The Land of Poco Tiempo*, 226.

2. Arthur Einarsen, *The Pronghorn Antelope and Its Management*, 7.

3. Stirling, *Origin Myth*, 24–25. There are variations in detail, but this is a basic pattern for larger game among all Pueblos.

4. Cushing, *Zuñi Breadstuff*, 639.

5. Spencer Baird, *Mammals of the Boundary*, 52.

6. Beaglehole, *Hopi Hunting*, 4ff.

7. *Ibid.*, 6–7

8. Leslie White, *New Material from Acoma*, 336.

9. John Caton, *The Antelope and Deer of America*, 47–48, 60.

10. Stephen, *Hopi Journal*, 279.

11. Stevenson, "The Zuñi Indians," *loc. cit.*, 356.

12. Talayesva, *Sun Chief*, 253.

13. Stirling, *Origin Myth*, 6–10.

14. Beaglehole, *Hopi Hunting*, 4.

15. Stephen, *Hopi Journal*, 1006.

16. *Ibid.*, 1313.

17. Ruth L. Bunzel, *Zuñi Texts*, 150.

18. Boas, *Keresan Texts*, 35–38.

19. Leslie White, "The Acoma Indians." B.A.E. *Forty-seventh Annual Report* (1929–1930), 154–56.

20. *Ibid.*, 142–44.

21. For rutting activity see Einarsen, *Pronghorn Antelope*, 86–88.

22. E. C. Parsons, *Pueblo Religion*, 928 and n.

23. Stephen, *Hopi Journal*, 714.

24. White, "The Acoma Indians," *loc. cit.*, 88–94

25. Stephen, *Hopi Journal*, 718.

26. *Ibid.*, 714.

27. Baird, *Mammals of the Boundary*, 51.

28. Stephen, *Hopi Journal*, 626.

29. *Ibid.*, 605.

30. *Ibid.*, 704.

31. *Ibid.*, 705.

32. *Ibid.*, 24–26 and Pl. I, c.

CHAPTER III

1. Anabel Haas, *Hunter's Guide to the Deer of New Mexico*, 4.

2. Vernon Bailey, *Mammals of New Mexico*, 35.

3. Merriam reports them as abundant in the San Francisco Mountain region: C. Hart Merriam, *Results of a Biological Survey of the San Francisco Mountain Region and Desert of the Little Colorado, Arizona*, 78. See E. Lendell Cockrum, *The Recent Mammals of Arizona, Their Taxonomy and Distribution*, 252. See also bone finds in, Barbara Lawrence, *Mammals Found at the Awatovi Site*.

4. Figures here and at end of the paragraph from personal correspondence with the New Mexico Department of Game and Fish.

5. J. Stokley Ligon, *Wildlife of New Mexico*, 68.

6. Neil Judd, *The Material Culture of Pueblo Bonito*, 64.

7. Frank Roberts, *The Village of the Great Kivas on the Zuñi Reservation, New Mexico*, 135–36.

8. Marjorie Lambert, *Paa-ko, Archaeological Chronicle of an Indian Village in North Central New Mexico*, 145.

9. John McGregor, *Winona and Ridge Ruin*, 256.

10. Watson Smith, *Excavation in Big Hawk Valley*, 181.

11. Lawrence, *Mammals at Awatovi*, 3.

12. Talayesva, *Sun Chief*, 66.

13. Leslie White, *The Pueblo of Santa Ana, New Mexico*, 292ff. Includes following songs.

14. Ruth L. Bunzel, "Zuñi Ritual Poetry," B.A.E., *Forty-seventh Annual Report* (1929–1930), 835.

15. White, *Santa Ana*, 287. Conversely, killing a deer gives a bridegroom the right to sleep with his bride: E. C. Parsons, *Notes on Zuñi* II, 305.

16. E. C. Parsons, "Isleta, New Mexico," B.A.E. *Forty-seventh Annual Report* (1929–1930), 338.

17. Stevenson, "The Zuñi Indians," *loc. cit.*, 440.

18. Ruth Kirk, *Introduction to Zuñi Fetishism*, 28–31.

19. Parsons, "Isleta, New Mexico," *loc. cit.*, 336–37.

20. Stevenson, "The Zuñi Indians," *loc. cit.*, 440. There is a recent doubt about the existence of the god A'wonawil'ona, hence the following evidence may be useful. The name appears once in recent times: E. C. Parsons, "The Origin Myth of Zuñi, *Journal of American Folk-Lore*, Vol. XXXVI (1923), 148, where it is spelled *ulohneillona*. She translates as: "high, world or land having." *Ilona* means the "one who keeps." See Bunzel, "Zuñi Katcinas," *loc. cit.*, 959. From Stanley Newman, *Zuñi Dictionary*, we find that *wilo* = "to be a lightning flash." *wo* = "creature, animal or priest." Hence A'wonawil'ona must have been a sky and lightning god.

21. E. C. Parsons, "Zuñi Tales," *Journal of American Folk-Lore*, Vol. XLIII (1930), 49.

22. Parsons, "Isleta, New Mexico," *loc. cit.*, 337.

23. Parsons, "Zuñi Tales," *loc cit.*, Vol. XLIII (1930), 49.

24. Stevenson, "The Zuñi Indians," *loc. cit.*, 439–40.

25. Parsons, *Pueblo Religion*, 844–47.

26. Virginia Roediger, *Ceremonial Costumes of the Pueblo Indians*, Pls. 25–28.

27. Bunzel, "Zuñi Katcinas," *loc. cit.*, 1041–48. Also following quote. For description of Saiyatasha, *ibid.*, 962.

28. See Charles Lange, *Cochiti, a New Mexico Pueblo, Past and Present*, 470 for this spelling and description.

29. Ruth Benedict, *Tales of the Cochiti Indians*, 11.

30. Noel Dumarest, *Notes on Cochiti, New Mexico*, 178.

31. E. C. Parsons, *Tewa Tales*, 61–70.

32. E. C. Parsons, *Taos Tales*, 40–43.

33. *Ibid.*, 40.

34. Parsons, *Tewa Tales*, 126. Sometimes it does not turn out as well. "At Jemez they had a deer dance. The dancers turned into deer and ran up into the mountains. They never came back any more. For four days they made ceremonies in Jemez to bring them back, but they could not."—Benedict, *Tales of Cochiti*, 17.

35. Parsons, *Tewa Tales*, 267–70.

36. Parsons, *Pueblo Religion*, 206. Ruth Benedict, *Zuñi Mythology* II, 70 n.

37. Benedict, *Zuñi Mythology* I, 76. For the following: *ibid.*, II, 68 ff.

Atoshle also becomes the Morning Star, patron of hunters. Parsons, "Zuñi Tales," *loc. cit.*, Vol. XLIII (1930), 43.

38. Benedict, *Zuñi Mythology* I, 72.

39. For fuller account see Stevenson, "The Zuñi Indians," *loc. cit.*, 227–77. E. C. Parsons, *Notes on Zuñi* I, 183–215. Jean Cazeneuve, *Les Dieux Dansant a Cibola, Les Shalako des Indiens Zuñis.*

40. Parsons, *Notes on Zuñi* I, 195.

41. Stevenson, "The Zuñi Indians," *loc cit.*, 236.

42. *Ibid.*, 260.

43. Parsons, *Notes on Zuñi* I, 201.

44. Bunzel, "Zuñi Katcinas," *loc. cit.*, 846–47. For a criticism of Frazer see Joseph Fontenrose, *The Ritual Theory of Myth.* It is interesting that the one who attacks the 'King' in Diana's grove is called *cervus* = "deer." One of the two "deer" is killed and the other becomes a Keeper of Game spirit through the succeeding year, p. 42.

45. Sir J. G. Frazer, *The Golden Bough*, 390.

46. Stevenson, "The Zuñi Indians," *loc. cit.*, 241–42.

47. Parsons, *Notes on Zuñi* I, 197.

48. Parsons, *Pueblo Religion*, 758.

49. Parsons, *Notes on Zuñi* II, 326.

50. Stevenson, "The Zuñi Indians," *loc. cit.*, 244.

51. Bunzel, "Zuñi Katcinas," *loc. cit.*, 925–27.

CHAPTER IV

1. Adolf F. Bandelier, "An Oultine of the Documentary History of the Zuñi Tribe," *Journal of American Ethnology and Archaeology*, Vol. III (1892), 5.

2. F. W. Hodge, *Spanish Explorers in the Southern United States*, 311.

3. Bailey, *Mammals of New Mexico*, 15.

4. Lange, *Cochiti*, 130.

5. Parsons, *Pueblo Religion*, 22.

6. Parsons, *Taos Tales*, 119–20.

7. Parsons, *Pueblo Religion*, 936 and 467. For dance, 840–42.

8. White, *Santa Ana*, 297.

9. Leslie White, *The Pueblo of San Felipe*, 56–60.

10. White, *Santa Ana*, 301.

11. Leslie White, *The Pueblo of Sia, New Mexico*, 256–59.

12. Lange, *Cochiti*, 328.

13. Stephen, *Hopi Journal*, 130.

14. Alexander Stephen, "Hopi Tales," *Journal of American Folk-Lore*, Vol. XLII (1929), 27.

15. Parsons, *Pueblo Religion*, 828–33.

16. Harold Colton, *Hopi Kachina Dolls*, 41.

17. Jesse W. Fewkes, "Hopi Kachinas, Drawn by Native Artists." B.A.E. *Twenty-first Annual Report* (1899–1900), 31.

18. For references to other versions see: E. C. Parsons, *Taos Tales*, 61 n3. E. C. Parsons, "Pueblo Indian Folk-tales, Probably of Spanish Provenience," *Journal of American Folk-Lore*, Vol. XXXI (1918), 235 n1.

19. White, "The Acoma Indians," *loc. cit.*, 106.

20. Gunn, *Schat-Chen*, 184–89.

21. Boas, *Keresan Texts*, 122–27.

22. *Ibid.*, 71.

23. Parsons, *Tewa Tales*, 85 n3.

24. M. C. Stevenson, "The Sia," B.A.E. *Eleventh Annual Report* (1889–1890), 43.

25. Dumarest, *Notes on Cochiti*, 182.

26. Boas, *Keresan Texts*, 92.

27. *Ibid.*, 64.

28. *Ibid.*, 67–68.

29. *Ibid.*, 103.

CHAPTER V

1. Boas, *Keresan Texts*, 143–44.

2. E. C. Parsons, *The Social Organization of the Tewa of New Mexico*, 198–99.

3. Lange, *Cochiti*, 539, 324.

4. White, *Sia*, 242–44, 256.

5. Boas, *Keresan Texts*, 30.

6. On antelope as wildcat prey see, S. P. Young, *The Bobcat of North America*, 99. Einarsen, *Pronghorn Antelope*, 76.

7. S. P. Young and Edward Goldman, *The Wolves of North America* I, 232–33.

8. Parsons, *Pueblo Religion*, 39, 337.

9. Stephen, *Hopi Journal*, 262.

10. Stirling, *Origin Myth*, 31.

11. Jesse W. Fewkes and A. M. Stephen, "The Naashnaiya: a Tusayan Initiation Ceremony," *Journal of American Folk-Lore*, Vol. V (1892), 201. Next quote *ibid.*, 204.

12. Benedict, *Tales of Cochiti*, 211. Dumarest, *Cochiti*, 219–20.

13. Stevenson, "The Sia," *loc. cit.*, 54.

14. Stephen, "Hopi Tales," *loc. cit.*, Vol. XLII (1929), 14.

15. *Ibid.*, 20.

16. Voth, *Traditions of Hopi*, 83, 87.

17. Hodge, *Spanish Explorers*, 305–306.

18. Helmut Beuchner, *The Bighorn Sheep in the United States, Its Past, Present, and Future*, 14.

19. Frank Hibben, *Excavations of the Riana Ruin and Chama Valley Survey*, 45.

20. Adolf F. Bandelier, *Final Report of Investigations among the Indians of the Southwestern United States*, 141.

21. Hibben, *Riana Ruin*, 29–30.

22. Edgar A. Mearns, *Mammals of the Mexican Boundary of the United States*, 233.

23. Merriam, *Survey*, 78–79.

24. Talayesva, *Sun Chief*, 234–35.

25. Jack O'Conner, *Hunting in the Southwest*, 71–72.

26. Ligon, *Wildlife*, 55.

27. Bailey, *Mammals of New Mexico*, 17.

28. W. D. Wallis, "Folk Tales from Shumopovi, Second Mesa," *Journal of American Folk-Lore*, Vol. XLIX (1936), 43–44.

29. Lange, *Cochiti*, 130.

30. Beaglehole, *Hopi Hunting*, 9–11.

31. Lawrence, *Mammals at Awatovi*, 3.

32. Ernest Beaglehole and Pearl Beaglehole, *Hopi of the Second Mesa*, 19.

33. Stevenson, "The Zuñi Indians," *loc. cit.*, 94.

34. Watson Smith, *Kiva Mural Decorations at Awatovi and Kawaika-a, with a Survey of other Wall Paintings in the Pueblo Southwest*, 57.

35. Stephen, "Hopi Tales," *loc. cit.*, Vol. XLII (1929), 68.

36. Jesse W. Fewkes, "Tusayan Migration Traditions," B.A.E. *Nineteenth Annual Report* (1897–1898), 595–96.

37. Parsons, *Pueblo Religion*, 359.

38. Mischa Titiev, *Old Oraibi, a Study of the Hopi Indians of Third Mesa*, 146.

39. *Ibid.*, 131.

40. Stephen, *Hopi Journal*, 807–17.

41. *Ibid.*, 798.

42. *Ibid.*, 810.

43. Bunzel, "Zuñi Katcinas," *loc. cit.*, 953.

44. Parsons, *Notes on Zuñi* I, 202.

45. Cushing, "Zuni Creation Myths," *loc. cit.*, 427.

46. Stevenson, "The Zuñi Indians," *loc. cit.*, 495.

47. White, "The Acoma Indians," *loc. cit.*, 77.

48. Parsons, *Pueblo Relgion*, 543.

49. Buechner, *Bighorn Sheep*, 53.

50. Lange, *Cochiti*, 468.

51. Fewkes, "Hopi Kachinas, Drawn by Native Artists," *loc. cit.*, 102 and Pl. XL.

52. Colton, *Kachina Dolls*, 41.

53. Cahalane, *Mammals of North America*, 94.

54. Parsons, *Tewa Tales*, 209.

55. Eggan, *Western Pueblos*, 93.

56. Titiev, *Old Oraibi*, 137 n54.

57. Fewkes and Stephen, "The Naashnaiya: A Tusayan Initiation Ceremony," *loc. cit.*, Vol. V (1892), 207.

58. *Ibid.*, 216–17.

CHAPTER VI

1. E. W. Nelson, *The Rabbits of North America*, 24.

2. Bunzel, *Zuñi Texts*, 31.

3. H. M. Wormington, *Prehistoric Indians of the Southwest*, 38.

4. *Ibid.*, 31.

5. Judd, *Pueblo Bonito*, 39.

6. On hares vs. rabbits, see Nelson, *Rabbits*, 13. Cahalane, *Mammals of North America*, 583.

7. Parsons, *Taos Tales*, 100.

8. Bailey, *Mammals of New Mexico*, 47. Ligon, *Wildlife*, 108.

9. Edmund Nequatewa, *Hopi Customs, Folklore and Ceremonies*, 33.

10. Merriam, *Survey*, 76.

11. Sources in order are: McGregor, *Winona*, 256; Smith, *Big Hawk*, 181: Lawrence, *Mammals at Awatovi*, 3; Judd, *Pueblo Bonito*, 246; Arthur Harris, *Vertebrate Remains and Past Environmental Reconstruction in the Navajo Reservoir District*, 29; Hibben, *Riana*, 46.

12. Frank Hamilton Cushing, *Zuñi Folk Tales*, 296.

13. Talayesva, *Sun Chief*, 231.

14. Beaglehole, *Hopi Hunting*, 25. White, *Santa Ana*, 282.

15. Stephen, *Hopi Journal*, 99.

16. *Ibid.*, 100.

17. White, "The Acoma Indians," *loc. cit.*, 102.

18. E. C. Parsons, *A Pueblo Indian Journal*, 1920–21, 120.

19. White, *Santa Ana*, 285.

20. Stevenson, "The Zuñi Indians," *loc. cit.*, 441–43.

21. Cushing, *Zuñi Breadstuff*, 591–96.

22. Beaglehole, *Hopi Hunting*, 15.

23. Parsons, "Isleta, New Mexico," *loc. cit.*, 336.

24. Stephen, *Hopi Journal*, 387.

25. Beaglehole, *Hopi Hunting*, 12.

26. George A. Dorsey and H. R. Voth, *The Oraibi Soyal Ceremony*, 58.

27. Relevant texts are: E. C. Parsons, "Census of the Shi'wanakwe Society of Zuni," *American Anthropologist*, Vol. XXI (1919), 333. Boas, *Keresan Texts*, 292. Gunn, *Schat-Chen*, 87–110. Dumarest, *Notes on Cochiti*, 190. Lange, *Cochiti*, 307.

28. Fewkes, "Hopi Kachinas, Drawn by Native Artists," *loc. cit.*, 113 and Pl. XLIX.

29. White, "The Acoma Indians," *loc. cit.*, 78.

30. Stephen, *Hopi Journal*, 1006.

31. Parsons, *Notes on Zuñi* I, 179.

32. Stevenson, "The Zuñi Indians," *loc. cit.*, 92.

33. Stephen, *Hopi Journal*, 903 and Fig. 469.

34. H. R. Voth, *The Oraibi Marau Ceremony*, 68 and Pl. XXIX.

35. Stephen, *Hopi Journal*, 995. The rag is a woman's dress worn backward. For a lengthy account of this god see Tyler, *Pueblo Gods*, Ch. I.

36. Ernest Beaglehole, *Notes on Hopi Economic Life*, 47.

37. Stephen, *Hopi Journal*, 277.

38. Nequatewa, *Hopi Customs*, 33.

39. Beaglehole, *Hopi Hunting*, 18.

CHAPTER VII

1. Wallis, "Folk Tales from Shumopovi, Second Mesa," *loc. cit.*, Vol. XLIX (1936), 59.

2. Stephen, *Hopi Journal*, 278.

3. *Ibid.*, 699–700.

4. *Ibid.*, 98 and Fig. 64 a.

5. Parsons, "Pueblo-Indian Folk-tales, Probably of Spanish Provenience," *Journal of American Folk-Lore*, Vol. XXXI (1918), 237.

6. Bunzel, "Zuñi Ritual Poetry," *loc. cit.*, 784.

7. White, *Sia*, 114.

8. McGregor, *Winona*, 256. Dale King, *Nalakihu, Excavations at a Pueblo III Site in Wupatki National Monument, Arizona*, 141. Lambert, *Paa-ko*, 145. Judd, *Bonito*, 65. Lawrence, *Mammals at Awatovi*, 5.

9. Beaglehole, *Hopi Hunting*, 9, 12.

10. Stephen, *Hopi Journal*, 1240.

11. *Ibid.*, 1071.

12. Eggan, *Western Pueblos*, 85.

13. Beaglehole, *Hopi of Second Mesa*, 6 n5, and 7.

14. Aurelio Espinosa, "Pueblo Indian Folk Tales," *Journal of American Folk-Lore*, Vol. XLIX (1936), 71–73.

15. Roediger, *Ceremonial Costumes*, 139.

16. Bunzel, "Zuñi Katcinas," *loc. cit.*, 870.

17. Ruth Benedict, "Eight Stories from Acoma," *Journal of American Folk-Lore*, Vol. XLIII (1930), 77–79.

18. Stanley Young and H. H. T. Jackson, *The Clever Coyote*, 85.

19. *Ibid.*, 95.

20. J. Frank Dobie, *The Voice of the Coyote*, 64.

21. Parsons, "Zuñi Tales," *loc. cit.*, Vol. XLIII (1930), 37–42. See also Wallis, "Folk Tales from Shumopovi, Second Mesa," *loc. cit.*, Vol. XLIX (1936), 37ff.

22. For other tales of Coyote-Badger association see, Voth, *Traditions*, 240 ff.

23. Boas, *Keresan Texts*, 29–31.

24. *Ibid.*, 31–32.

25. Parsons, *Pueblo Religion*, 239–40. A different version in Cushing, "Origin Myth from Oraibi," *loc. cit.*, Vol. XXXVI (1923), 166.

26. Benedict, *Zuñi Mythology* I, 16–18.

27. Parsons, *Tewa Tales*, 171.

28. *Ibid.*, 172.

29. Wallis, "Folk Tales from Shumopovi, Second Mesa," *loc. cit.*, Vol. XLIX (1936), 8.

30. Leland C. Wyman, *Navajo Eschatology*, 19ff.

31. Parsons, *Tewa Tales*, 270–75.

32. Cushing, "Zuñi Creation Myths," *loc. cit.*, 404–405.

33. Stevenson, "The Zuñi Indians," *loc. cit.*, 30–31.

34. Ruth L. Bunzel, "Zuñi Origin Myths," B.A.E. *Forty-seventh Annual Report* (1929–1930), 593ff.

35. Paul Radin, *The Trickster, a Study in American Indian Mythology*, 165.

36. Parsons, *Social Organization*, 275.

37. Frank Waters, *Book of the Hopi*, 69–70.

38. Parsons, *Pueblo Religion*, 634. Also, E. C. Parsons, *The Scalp Ceremonial of Zuñi*.

39. Stevenson, "The Zuñi Indians," *loc. cit.*, 604–605.

40. Stevenson, "The Sia," *loc. cit.*, 155.

41. Parsons, *Taos Tales*, 113 and n1, for list of similar tales.

42. *Ibid.*, 112.

43. Ellis, *Jemez Pattern*, 16.

44. Parsons, *Pueblo Religion*, 188 n†.

45. Bunzel, "Zuñi Katcinas," *loc. cit.*, 1045–47.

46. Cushing, *Zuñi Breadstuff*, 395–515.

47. Parsons, *Social Organization*, 276.

48. Cushing, *Zuñi Breadstuff*.
49. Cushing, *Zuñi Folk Tales*, 228.
50. Beaglehole, *Hopi Hunting*, 12, 17–18.
51. Titiev, *Old Oraibi*, 193.
52. Stirling, *Origin Myth*, 69.
53. *Ibid.*, 6.
54. Stevenson, "The Sia," *loc. cit.*, 70.
55. *Ibid.*, 72–73, 146.
56. Parsons, *Pueblo Religion*, 194.
57. Parsons, *Tewa Tales*, 144–45.
58. Dumarest, *Notes on Cochiti*, 215–16.
59. Boas, *Keresan Texts*, 165–66.
60. Parsons, *Social Organization*, 275.
61. Parsons, *Taos Tales*, 126.

CHAPTER VIII

1. Lange, *Cochiti*, 234.
2. A. I. Hallowell, "Bear Ceremonialism in the Northern Hemisphere," *American Anthropologist*, Vol. 28 (1926), 81, 110; earlier quotes, *ibid.*, 89, 99.
3. McGregor, *Winona*, 256.
4. Bailey, *Mammals of New Mexico*, 368.
5. *Ibid.*, 365.
6. *Ibid.*, 364.
7. Bunzel, "Zuñi Katcinas," *loc. cit.*, 1077.
8. Cushing, *Zuñi Folk Tales*, 310–16.
9. Frank Hibben, *Hunting American Bears*, 94 and Ch. VI.
10. *Ibid.*, 59.
11. Parsons, *Pueblo Religion*, 929, 794.
12. Parsons, *Taos Pueblo*, 20.
13. Lange, *Cochiti*, 137.
14. *Ibid.*, 135.
15. White, *New Material*, 336–37.
16. Ellis, *Jemez Pattern*, 28.
17. *Ibid.*, 25, 27, 31.
18. Parsons, "Isleta, New Mexico," *loc. cit.*, 338–39.
19. *Ibid.*, 445–48.
20. Stevenson, "The Zuñi Indians," *loc. cit.*, 89a.
21. *Ibid.*, 93.
22. Dumarest, *Notes on Cochiti*, 182 n6.
23. Stephen, *Hopi Journal*, 117.

24. Stevenson, "The Zuñi Indians," *loc. cit.*, 266. These bears dance with the 'short hair' Chakwena, a hunting group borrowed from Laguna. With the 'long hair' the lead dancers are a man and a woman dressed in a skirt of black bear fur and one of yellow-grey. He carries an axe—Parsons, *Notes on Zuñi* I, 213.

25. A. B. Cook, *Zeus, a Study in Ancient Religion*, I, 444.

26. Pausaniąs, *Description of Greece*, Book VII—ACHAIA, xviii, 11.

27. Lewis Richard Farnell, *The Cults of the Greek States* II, 438.

28. Stevenson, "The Zuñi Indians," *loc. cit.*, 38.

29. Stephen, *Hopi Journal*, 44, 122.

30. E. C. Parsons, *Taos Pueblo*, 109.

31. Parsons, *Pueblo Religion*, 895. Leslie White, *Santo Domingo*, 136.

32. Edward Dozier, *The Hopi-Tewa of Arizona*, 340.

33. Benedict, *Tales of the Cochiti*, 142–44.

34. Voth, *Traditions of the Hopi*, 57.

35. Stephen, *Hopi Journal*, 703.

36. Stevenson, "The Zuñi Indians," *loc. cit.*, 208.

37. White, *San Felipe*, 42–43, 45.

38. M. C. Stevenson, "Ethnobotany of the Zuñi Indians," B.A.E. *Thirtieth Annual Report* (1908–1909), 40.

39. Bunzel, "Zuñi Ceremonialism," *loc. cit.*, 531–32.

40. Benedict, *Zuñi Mythology* II, 32–35.

41. Stevenson, "The Zuñi Indians," *loc. cit.*, 552.

42. Parsons, *Taos Tales*, 91–92.

43. Parsons, *Taos Pueblo*, 86.

44. Parsons, *Social Organization*, 121.

45. *Ibid.*, 251, 273.

46. A. L. Kroeber, *Zuñi Kin and Clan*, 163–64. Parsons, *Pueblo Religion*, 160–61.

47. Boas, *Keresan Texts*, 183–87.

48. Parsons, *Pueblo Indian Journal*, 121, n185.

49. Stephen, *Hopi Journal*, 1088.

50. *Ibid.*, 1076.

51. *Ibid.*, 810

52. For the split, see Titiev, *Old Oraibi*, 69–95.

CHAPTER IX

1. Stirling, *Origin Myth*, 23.

2. Frank Hibben, *A Preliminary Study of the Mountain Lion*, 37.

3. George Gaylord Simpson, *The Principles of Classification and a Classification of Mammals*, 119–20.

4. Claude Barnes, *The Cougar or Mountain Lion*, 72.

5. Stevenson, "The Zuñi Indians," *loc. cit.*, 576.

6. Parsons, *Pueblo Religion*, 794.

7. Benedict, *Zuñi Mythology* I, 160–65. See also 311, 336.

8. Stevenson, "The Zuñi Indians," *loc. cit.*, 407.

9. Cushing, "Outlines of Zuñi Creation Myths," *loc. cit.*, 381.

10. E. C. Parsons, "Nativity Myth at Laguna and Zuñi" *Journal of American Folk-Lore*, Vol. XXI (1918), 262.

11. Stevenson, "The Zuñi Indians," *loc. cit.*, 49.

12. Parsons, "Nativity Myth at Laguna and Zuñi," *loc. cit.*, Vol. XXI (1918), 262–63.

13. Parsons, *Tewa Tales*, 82–85.

14. H. B. Alexander, *The World's Rim*, 151–52.

15. Parsons, "Zuñi Tales," *loc. cit.*, Vol. XLIII (1930), 5.

16. Stevenson, "The Sia," *loc. cit.*, 59–66.

17. *Ibid.*, 64.

18. In Stirling, *Origin Myth*, 15.

19. Boas, *Keresan Texts*, 13–14.

20. *Ibid.*, 223.

21. *Ibid.*, 236.

22. Gunn, *Schat-Chen*, 110.

23. White, *Santa Ana*, 86.

24. Stephen, *Hopi Journal*, 44, 1085–86.

25. White, *Sia*, 279–80. Also, White, *Santa Ana*, 256ff., 66 n141.

26. Dumarest, *Notes on Cochiti*, 228 n4.

27. Stevenson, "The Sia," *loc. cit.*, 66.

28. Parsons recognized this: "Montezuma is still a convenient term if not a 'blind.' " "Pueblo Indian Folk-tales Probably of Spanish Provenience," *loc. cit.*, Vol. XXI (1918), 97 n1.

29. Adolf F. Bandelier, "The 'Montezuma' of the Pueblo Indians," *American Anthropologist*, Vol. V (1892), 322.

30. *Ibid.*, 323.

31. White, *Santo Domingo*, 178–79.

32. John Peabody Harrington, "The Ethnogeography of the Tewa Indians," B.A.E. *Twenty-ninth Annual Report* (1907–1908), 164.

33. Bandelier, *Final Report*, 310.

34. Parsons, *Tewa Tales*, 108–13. For a similar tale, Espinosa, "Pueblo Indian Folk Tales," *loc. cit.*, Vol. XLIX (1936), 97ff, where the mother is Salt Woman disguised as *Salinas*.

35. Both setting and the stone lions are illustrated in Lange, *Cochiti*, Pl. 4, and L. Bradford Prince, *The Stone Lions of Cochiti*, frontispiece.

36. Stevenson, "The Zuñi Indians," *loc. cit.*, 407. Prince, *Stone Lions*. See

also Harrington, "The Ethnogeography of the Tewa Indians," *loc. cit.*, 416ff. The Tewa name for the shrine means, "earth umbilical region where two Mountain Lions crouch."

37. Dumarest, *Notes on Cochiti*, 207.

38. Adolph F. Bandelier, *The Southwestern Journals of Adolph F. Bandelier. 1880–1882*, 176.

39. Charles Lummis, *Pueblo Indian Folk-Stories*, 200 ff.

40. Gunn, *Schat-Chen*, 190–91.

41. White, *Santo Domingo*, 11.

42. Boas, *Keresan Texts*, 56.

43. *Ibid.*, 32. Benedict, *Tales from Cochiti*, 39.

44. Benedict, *Tales from Cochiti*, 44.

45. Boas, *Keresan Texts*, 27.

46. *Ibid.*, 69ff.

47. *Ibid.*, 70–73.

48. *Ibid.*, 28.

49. Stirling, *Origin Myth*, 10.

50. Boas, *Keresan Texts*, 29.

51. *Ibid.*, 31.

52. White, *Sia*, 171 ff.

53. Stirling, *Origin Myth*, 20. White refers to a Lion Society in Acoma— "The Acoma Indians," *loc. cit.*, 101.

54. Parsons, *Social Organization*, 251.

55. Kirk, *Zuñi Fetishism*, 29ff.

56. Stevenson, "The Sia," *loc. cit.*, 118.

57. White, *San Felipe*, 58.

58. John Bourke, *The Snake Dance of the Moquis of Arizona*, 80.

59. White, *Santa Ana*, 287.

60. Stevenson, "The Zuñi Indians," *loc. cit.*, 438.

61. Stephen, *Hopi Journal*, 766.

62. *Ibid.*, 673.

63. Ibid., 651.

CHAPTER X

1. Stirling, *Origin Myth*, 30.

2. Tyler, *Pueblo Gods*, 254.

3. Beaglehole, *Hopi Hunting*, 18.

4. Parsons, *Pueblo Religion*, 489.

5. Richard B. Lee and Irven de Vore, *Man the Hunter*.

6. Grahame Clarke, *World Prehistory: An Outline*, 33.

7. E. C. Parsons, *Notes on Ceremonialism at Laguna*, 127.

INDEX